Wm O'Brien

John Cage

5/13/94

FORTUNE AND FOLLY
THE WEALTH AND POWER OF INSTITUTIONAL INVESTING

FORTUNE AND FOLLY
THE WEALTH AND POWER OF
INSTITUTIONAL INVESTING

William M. O'Barr
John M. Conley

With Economic Analysis by
Carolyn Kay Brancato

IRWIN
Professional Publishing
Burr Ridge, Illinois
New York, New York

Sponsoring editor: Amy Hollands
Project editor: Jean Roberts
Production manager: Ann Cassady
Jacket designer: Sam Concialdi
Designer: Heidi J. Baughman
Compositor: Eastern Composition, Inc.
Typeface: 11/13 Century Schoolbook
Printer: Book Press, Inc.

Library of Congress Cataloging-in-Publication Data

O'Barr, William M.
  Fortune and folly: the wealth and power of institutional
investing / William M. O'Barr, John M. Conley; with economic
analysis by Carolyn Kay Brancato.
    p.   cm.
  ISBN 1-55623-705-7
  1. Pension trusts—United States—Investments. 2. Institutional
investments—United States. I. Conley, John M. II. Brancato,
Carolyn Kay. III. Title.
HD7105.45.U6023   1992
362.6'7254—dc20   92-6936

Printed in the United States of America
2 3 4 5 6 7 8 9 0 BP 9 8 7 6 5 4

For Claire, Emily, Jimmy, Rebecca, Robin, John, and Christina

The research on which this book is based
was funded by
the Institutional Investor Project
Columbia Law School

AUTHORS' NOTE

The research reported in this book is a joint project. We alternate priority of authorship in our publications in order to emphasize our common voice. We have brought different backgrounds and perspectives to the project, and we believe that neither of us would have conceived of, carried out, or reported the research singly in the manner that has emerged from our collaboration. We have worked together throughout and deserve jointly whatever blame or credit our readers accord.

ACKNOWLEDGMENTS

This research was supported by a grant from the Institutional Investor Project in the Center for Law and Economic Studies at Columbia Law School and by additional funding from the Ivey Research Professorship in the School of Law at the University of North Carolina at Chapel Hill. We acknowledge with gratitude the assistance of the pension fund executives and money managers who provided the data for this study of the culture of institutional investing. These individuals and the organizations for which they work are identified in this book only by pseudonyms. We appreciate the contributions of our research assistants, Grady Balentine, Brian Denton, Kenyann Flippin, David Fisher, Melinda Frank, Bill Gentner, Ray Person, and Ingrid van der Spuy, and of Mary Wyer, who helped us to verify and edit quotations. We thank especially Louis Lowenstein and Ira Millstein, respectively Project Director and Chairman of the Institutional Investor Project at Columbia University, and the members of the Board of Advisers of the Project for their conviction that the unorthodox approach of anthropology can illuminate the world of finance. Their assistance in making introductions opened many doors that might otherwise have remained closed to us.

We have benefited from opportunities to discuss our research in progress in a variety of academic contexts. Professor Robert Shiller of Yale University invited us to discuss our research at the National Bureau of Economic Research in Cambridge, Massachusetts, in August 1990. Professor Jeffrey Gordon of Columbia Law School invited us to speak at a conference on corporate governance held at Columbia in May 1991 where we received many helpful comments and suggestions from those in attendance. Professor Bernard Black of Columbia, who participated in that conference, has commented on our work in progress and offered many thoughtful observations on earlier drafts of this book. We have also discussed this research at meetings of the Law and Society Association, the Linguistic Society of America, and the Language, Thought, and Culture Symposium at Duke University.

The management of interview data is an enormous and tedious task. We have benefited from excellent secretarial help at both Duke and the University of North Carolina. We acknowledge with thanks the help of Alice Creighton Garfield, Tira Harris, and Vivian Scales.

Carolyn Brancato wishes to thank the following people for their contributions to her economic analysis: Professor Patrick Gaughan, coauthor of the basic institutional investor data series at Columbia University; Kimberly Ellen Rodgers, her research assistant; Michael deBlois, database manager; Jay Paul Blaustein, senior computer specialist; and Jean Tobin at the New York Stock Exchange.

TABLE OF CONTENTS

INTRODUCTION

There is potential for great mischief in positions like the one I have. One of the fellows, a good friend of mine, we were sitting down and having drinks one night, and he said, "Do you realize that if we decide to dump equities in late October prior to the presidential election, that we would probably influence an election?"

Few people are in a position to tell a story like this. It could be an anecdote from the memoirs of J. P. Morgan, or perhaps an excerpt from the testimony in the Hunt brothers' trial. But it is not. The story's source is much less glamorous, but ultimately far more significant. We heard it from the chief executive of one of America's largest pension funds.

This book examines the wealth of America's pension funds and the economic, political, and social power that flows from their enormous financial holdings. We spent two years investigating nine large and influential American pension funds. Using the methods of field anthropology, in particular its focus on culture, we watched the funds at work and listened as their executives and managers talked at great length and with extraordinary candor about what they do and why they do it. Pension funds are often thought of as cold calculators of financial gain or loss. But we discovered a world where enormously consequential decisions are subject to the same vicissitudes of history, personality, and politics as the decisions that all of us make daily in the most ordinary of contexts.

Anthropologists have long known that to be human means to think in cultural terms, to have myths, and to be shaped by history. Pension funds are no exception. But institutions that control trillions of dollars have a responsibility that goes beyond their own corporate cultures. Their investment decisions profoundly affect the security of their retirees and the country's economic prosperity. To the extent that cultural factors distract those who manage pension funds from the pursuit of sound financial strategies, all of us stand to suffer in one way or another. And so it behooves them—and us—to understand these cultural factors and their influence on America's economic future.

THE MIGRATION OF CAPITAL FROM MAIN STREET TO WALL STREET

In the mythology of American business, the individual investor plays a central role. Depending on the story being told, the character assumes a variety of specific identities: a well-to-do local financier who is the principal owner of the factory on the outskirts of town and provides sage strategic advice to its management, a frugal worker buying a small piece of America to make life better for his children, or a retired couple who have paid off the mortgage and sent the children out into the world and are now dabbling in the stock market.

Despite their differences, all these people belong to Main Street, U.S.A. They are individuals with direct responsibility for their investments. They decide what to buy and when to sell. They tend to invest in what they know and trust, favoring local companies as well as blue-chip national corporations. No leveraged buyouts or junk bonds for these citizen-investors. Significantly, they take a personal interest in the companies in which they invest. They see themselves as owners of companies rather than traders of pieces of paper, and they are in for the long term.

A major theme in this mythology is the partnership between owners and corporate managers. Stable, interested ownership holds management accountable for its actions. The ownership includes enough wealthy, sophisticated stockholders to ensure that management is subject to knowledgeable scrutiny. While looking out for their own financial interests, these stockholders simultaneously protect the interests of their less affluent and less informed co-owners. Management, in turn, can take comfort in the long-term perspective of the owners. Managers can make the capital improvements and do the other things necessary to ensure the future well-being of the company without worrying about transient effects on the price of the stock. Moreover, when new endeavors call for new money, they know where to look.

Today, institutions, not individuals, represent the single most important source of investment capital in America. And pension funds are the most significant of these institutions. Industries hungry for patient capital to finance the research and development and the increased productivity that support the American standard of living must turn increasingly to pension funds and other institutions. Pension funds have also become dominant players in the financial markets. The judgments expressed in their trading patterns can make or break particular stocks, and they often exercise virtual veto power over major financial transactions. Indeed, many of those who run pension funds believe that the funds are so large and so influential that they *are* the markets. Pension funds now own major interests in many of the most important American corporations and are in a position, if they choose, to influence how these companies are governed.

Today's pension funds could not be more different from the Main Street investors of the mythical past. It is true that the ultimate beneficiaries of pension funds are some of the same people who were the heroes of business mythology: workers and retirees, from corporate presidents to minimum-wage laborers. However, although they have a financial interest in the success of their funds' investments, these beneficiaries have little autonomy and no direct influence on the corporations they nominally own. Legal control over a pension fund rests with the corporation or governmental entity that has established it. Decision-making authority is typically delegated to a full-time staff of investment professionals. Thus, the ownership of America's corporations has migrated from Main Street to Wall Street. As a result, the power to buy and sell, the power to hold management accountable, and the responsibility that comes with such power have passed from individual Americans to institutions whose connections with Main Street are attenuated at best.

Since World War II, this shift in control has resulted in a dramatic expansion of the economic influence of institutional investors. An enormous concentration of economic power now rests with a small and extraordinarily stable group of institutions. Although the law has erected numerous barriers to the participation of large institutional shareholders in corporate governance, this elite group may well be in a position to exert a decisive influence on the future direction of American business.

This growing concentration of power in pension funds has given rise to a number of important economic and social questions. Which kinds of industries will pension funds favor with their capital, and with what consequences for individual Americans? Will they be more attentive to long-term economic trends or ephemeral market swings? In what directions will the funds lead the financial markets of the 21st century, and with what consequences? And, most significantly, how will the funds mobilize and deploy their vast resources in the global economic competition that has replaced the Cold War?

One might expect that institutions with such power would have been researched thoroughly and, consequently, would be well understood. In fact, a great deal has been written about the size of the pension funds, the extent of their economic clout, and their historical development, but this material has not been effectively integrated. And virtually nothing is known about the question of greatest practical significance: How do they really work? More specifically, who are the people who wield this power? What are their goals, motives, and concerns? To what extent are they aware of their power, and how do they want to exercise it? How do they and their organizations decide when, where, and how to invest their institutional wealth? How should the political and legal systems respond? And finally, what, if anything, can the individual investor learn from studying the management of almost inconceivably large amounts of money? It is to such questions that this book is addressed.

THE ANTHROPOLOGY OF WALL STREET

The idea for our research originated with the Institutional Investor Project, a research foundation at Columbia University. Aware of the growing influence of pension funds, and concerned about how little is known about them, the directors of the Project decided to fund an investigation that would delve into the inner workings of some large and representative funds. The Project had previously sponsored economic assessments of the recent growth of pension funds and other institutional investors. It expected that a qualitative, behavioral study of how funds are organized and how they make investment decisions would add a new and significant perspective.

Anthropology's bread-and-butter concept is *culture*—the set of shared beliefs and practices that define a society's way of life. Culture provides the mental map that guides individual members of the society through their daily lives. We set out to apply the concept of culture to the study of pension funds. We focused on the details of how the funds are organized, who the people are who run them, how these people conceive of what they do every day, and what factors shape their decisions. In other words, we wanted to investigate within pension funds the same issues we would study if we were researching the culture of an Amazonian village or an island in the South Seas.

Anthropologists have found that the concept of culture is as relevant to contemporary institutions and organizations as it is to traditional societies. For example, anthropologists have successfully investigated the American legal system from a cultural perspective. By studying how the law really works on a day-to-day basis, they have learned a great deal about the goals and motives of people going to court, lay people's conceptions of the law, and the discrepancies between what the law claims to deliver and what it actually delivers. Most importantly, because of their novel perspective, anthropologists have discovered things that legal professionals have never been able to see.

There was no precedent for the application of the cultural perspective to the investment world, but we were strongly encouraged by what had been accomplished in the study of law and other complex institutions. We were confident that our perspective could complement that of the economists, finance experts, and investment professionals who, until now, have had a virtual monopoly on the analysis of financial institutions.

We emphasize the word *complement*. We believe that this book adds an important new layer of detail to the study of investing, but we acknowledge that there remain many questions we cannot answer. Our purpose has not been to address conventional economic concerns, but to develop an entire new set of questions about business and finance. Those who are interested only in numbers may be disappointed. Others may have the experience of van Leeuwenhoek looking through the first microscope at a drop of water and discovering a complex and chaotic world beneath a deceptively uniform surface.

Our study of pension funds began much as any anthropological research project would. We prepared ourselves to go into the field by reading background materials and speaking with economists, businesspeople, and other experts. We studied the native language, which although based on English is barely intelligible to the uninitiated. Before long, we were conversant with terms like *shark repellent, greenmail*, and *cap-weighted*, and we had learned new meanings for such familiar words as *fundamental, value*, and *junk*. Then, to fit better into the native environment, we exchanged our academic tweeds for field clothes—in this case blue suits from Brooks Brothers rather than khakis from an army surplus store—and set out to live with the natives and observe their ways of life.

We chose to study nine large pension funds that seemed to typify the growing power of institutional capital. They include three major state pension funds and six private funds whose sponsors are influential American corporations. We chose these nine funds because the experts we consulted believed that they would differ on such significant variables as investment philosophy, use of outside money managers, and approach to proxy voting and other corporate governance issues.

From the outset, we wondered about the difficulties we would face in getting people to talk with us. The first problem was simply getting in the door. We relied on members of the board of the Institutional Investor Project for initial introductions. At each fund, the board's introduction led to a preliminary conference with the chief executive. From this point, we were on our own.

These preliminary conferences were reminiscent of the anthropological ritual of meeting with the headman in a tribal society. We faced suspicious questions about who we were, why we had come, and what we wanted to do. Once we had established our identities as independent researchers, the chief executives arranged for us to speak with the other members of their funds' decision-making teams. These contacts in turn led to others, and we soon developed our own network of relationships within each fund.

Having solved the problem of getting in the door, we remained concerned about whether people would speak openly. The inhabitants of the business world rarely speak publicly in settings that they do not control. Executives issue written statements or read from prepared remarks, and subordinates usually do not speak to the public at all. We expected these conventions to constrain our ability to gather information, but our experience was remarkably different. Although we offered no tangible rewards, everyone we approached not only agreed to talk with us, but did so at great length and with extraordinary candor.

Once a conversation began, the opportunity to talk about one's work, experiences, and opinions seemed to be reward enough. If nothing else, the chance to talk to us was a diverting break in the daily routine. Many people also seemed pleased that someone was interested in what they did, and enjoyed playing the role of teacher. As each conversation progressed, it became clear that people appreciated the opportunity for reflection and self-evaluation, which are rare commodities in the business world. People talked with little prompting, and we listened. We asked for, and were given in every instance, permission to make tape recordings of the conversations. In turn, we promised anonymity for both the institutions and the individuals.

After the preparatory initial conferences, we spent between one and seven days at each fund. We talked with the chief executive officer and a number of other employees involved in specific areas of the fund's operation, including portfolio managers, analysts, and lawyers. We also met with a number of outside managers employed by some of the funds. Most interviews lasted between one and four hours. All told, we spent more than a year and a half reading background materials, arranging and conducting personal interviews, asking follow-up questions (often by telephone), and poring over hundreds of pages of interview transcripts.

In each interview, we raised general questions about the organizational structure of the fund. Although we had a list of about 20 topics we sought to cover, we introduced them only when the speaker did not do so on his or her own. This technique increased our sensitivity to the interests and concerns of the people we studied. As a result, this book consists in large part of the presentation and analysis of an agenda that was set by the natives themselves. We did not have an outline of a book in mind when we started this research. Rather, we had only the general topic of the management of pension funds. The specific issues that emerged, such as the importance of cultural factors in the economic world, the differences between public and private pension funds, and the salience of corporate governance, were elements of the native worldview. The extensive recordings brought surprising results; in fact, so unexpected were the responses that we felt compelled to quote them at length throughout the book.[1]

THE BIGGER PICTURE

The power of the anthropological method lies in the ability to analyze a particular society or institution in minute detail. But this level of detail is not achieved without cost. Anthropologists sometimes lose sight of the context in which they are working, and treat the societies they study as if they existed in isolation.

Our concern was to make full use of the power of anthropology while minimizing the cost. In particular, we wanted to make sure that the intensity of our focus did not cause us to lose sight of the fact that pension funds are components of a larger economic system. Toward this end, we invited Carolyn Kay Brancato to collaborate with us in producing this book. She is an economist who has spent many years tracking and analyzing pension funds. In Chapter 2 she presents an economic profile of pension funds and other institutional investors. She examines their size, growth, and present and future significance. Throughout the rest of the book, she has written sections that offer an economic perspective on many of the cultural issues that we raise.

WHAT THIS BOOK IS ABOUT

In Chapter 1 we review the history of American pension funds. We discuss the role that they have played in the evolution of American capitalism and comment on the irony of labor's pension assets becoming the country's most important source of capital.

In Chapters 2 and 3 we examine pension funds from, respectively, an economic and an organizational perspective. Chapter 2 brings together a broad range of economic data in order to demonstrate the size and significance of pension funds, to situate them in the context of institutional investment, and to analyze their present and future impact on the economy. In Chapter 3 we describe the various ways in which pension funds are managed and consider the set of decisions that each must make in the course of investing its assets.

In Chapter 4 we begin to examine investment decisions from the perspective of those who make them. We introduce the most important theme in the book: the extent to which cultural rather than economic factors drive decisions in the financial world. We look closely at three aspects of pension fund culture that have a powerful effect on financial decisions: the influence of fund history, the management of personal responsibility, and the maintenance of personal relations.

In Chapters 5 and 6 we look at two other major influences on the investment practices of pension funds. Chapter 5 deals with the ways in which pension fund insiders use the law—or at least their versions of the law—to deflect responsibility away from themselves. In Chapter 6 we explore the differing cultural environments of public and private pension funds and identify the ways in which these differences affect financial decisions.

In Chapter 7 we examine in detail the language of the investment world. We use language as a window on the attitudes and motives of those who direct the investment of pension fund money. We give particular attention to the much-debated question of whether short-term thinking has come to dominate institutional investment.

In Chapter 8 we take up another topic that is making financial headlines: the role of institutional investors in corporate governance. We analyze what the various protagonists have said and done and consider the likelihood of institutional investors becoming a significant factor in the management of American corporations.

In Chapter 9 we take an international perspective on American pension funds, looking at how they influence and are influenced by the global economy. We conclude in Chapter 10 with a critical analysis of how effectively pension funds manage their vast wealth and exercise their growing power, and we offer some suggestions for improving the situation in the years to come.

NOTE

1. In reporting what we learned, we have attempted to stay close to the data we gathered, and in many instances we quote people at length. By staying as close as is reasonably possible to the original spoken word, we hope to give readers some insight into the personalities and thoughts of those whom we interviewed. In every instance the quoted material was taken from the tape recordings we made of our conversations. We made editorial changes only in the following instances: (1) We deleted some fragmentary utterances that carried no meaning, such as "um," "you know," and false starts that occurred when a speaker began and then abandoned a sentence before completing the thought. (2) We made corrections to minor grammatical errors that made the quotations difficult to understand, such as subjects and verbs that did not agree. (3) We edited certain references that would serve to identify the speaker, such as names, dates, and places. (4) In a small number of instances, we substituted a longer phrase that the speaker used elsewhere for a pronoun whose antecedent was unclear, such as replacing "it" with "value investing strategy." In every instance, we are confident that we have retained both the substance and the tone of the speaker's remarks.

CHAPTER 1

THE CAPITAL OF LABOR—
THE EMERGENCE OF
PENSION FUNDS

For millions of workers, the existence of pension funds has altered both the expectation and the reality of retirement. For thousands of corporations, the funds have rearranged the financial landscape. The pension funds, which at some level belong to the workers who are their beneficiaries, have replaced the Vanderbilts, Morgans, and Rockefellers as the most important source of capital. At the same time, they have become the most powerful class of corporate stockholders, with a growing (if still largely unrealized) capacity to influence management decisions.

Pension funds are not the only large pools of capital in the United States. They belong to the larger category of *institutional investor*. This diverse category includes mutual funds, banks, insurance companies, nonprofit endowments, and public and private pension funds. In some respects, these entities have little in common with each other. They do, however, share two important characteristics. First, they are professional investors. Second, they invest for the benefit of others. A mutual fund, for example, sells shares to the public and then directs the investment of the resulting fund. A college endowment invests the contributions of the alumni and other donors to provide income to meet the college's capital needs.

To illustrate how pension funds fit into the institutional investment universe, consider two examples: a state employees retirement fund and a corporate pension fund. In the case of the state fund, individual employees contribute by payroll deduction throughout their working lives, and the state matches their contributions. This money is under the control of a person or entity called a *fiduciary*. The fiduciary may be an individual such as the state treasurer or a board whose members are either elected or appointed. The fiduciary has the legal duty to invest the money for the benefit of the employees. On a practical level, the fiduciary is responsible for investing the contributions so as to ensure that there is enough money on hand to pay retirement benefits as they come due.

The typical corporate pension fund is similarly structured, with the employer (usually called the sponsor) standing in the place of the state. The sponsor and, in some cases, the active employees make ongoing contributions to the fund. It is managed by a fiduciary appointed by the sponsor. The fiduciary is usually a committee of the sponsor's board of directors, but may be a separate corporation that the sponsor sets up to manage the pension investments. Just as in the public sector, the fiduciary must invest the fund's assets in the interests of the beneficiaries in order to provide enough money to pay the retirement benefits.[1]

In both the public and private sectors, the level of pension benefits and the details of administration can be matters for labor-management negotiation. And in both contexts, the plan sponsor has a legal obligation to make good on the promised benefits. In the public sector, however, the last resort is to raise tax money to pay benefits, whereas in the private sector benefits would have to be paid out of the resources of the sponsoring corporation. Thus, both public and private fiduciaries have incentives to invest well and avoid the last resort, but those incentives are somewhat different—in the public case, to avoid the opprobrium of a taxpayer bailout, and in the private case, to avoid a drain on the sponsor's profits.

Although all institutional investors share the common goal of sound investing, pension funds are distinguishable in certain fundamental ways. In addition to their size, pension funds have a stability that other types of institutional investors rarely exhibit. Mutual funds go in and out of fashion, money managers come and go, and even banks and insurance companies are not as permanent as we once believed. But it will be a cold day in hell when, for example, TIAA-CREF or the California Public Employees Retirement System goes out of business.

This stability contributes to another defining characteristic of pension funds, the nature of their economic interests. An institution like a mutual fund may measure success or failure by very narrow criteria—for example, whether a limited number of speculative stocks manage to double in price over the next two years. But because the obligations of pension funds extend over generations, they should be interested not only in the short-term state of the financial markets, but in such long-term indicators of national economic well-being as job growth, productivity gains, increased personal wealth, and global competitiveness. Moreover, unlike smaller institutions with a narrower focus, pension funds are in a unique position to advance their interests by participating in the national economic debate, by making responsible contributions to the governance of the companies whose shares they own, and, most significantly, by the ways in which they choose to allocate their enormous resources. As will become evident in subsequent chapters, though, practice often deviates from theory. Pension funds have had mixed results in determining just what their interests are and deciding how best to advance them.

THE HISTORY OF PENSION FUNDS

The remarkable history of pension funds can best be appreciated in the context of the history of American capitalism. The development of capitalism in this country is often divided into four stages.[2] The first stage was the age of the 19th-century robber baron entrepreneurs who functioned simultaneously as investors, promoters, and managers in building the first great American corporations. The second stage, which began in the early decades of this century, witnessed a division between corporate ownership and corporate control. Corporate ownership came into the hands of largely passive public shareholders, while an emerging class of professional managers took control of business affairs.[3] Although the Depression-inspired legal reforms of the 1930s and 1940s sought to underline the duty that managers owe to their shareholders and to protect public shareholders against insiders trading on superior information, the gap between ownership and management has continued to grow. Indeed, many knowledgeable observers believe that corporate management's lack of accountability is the single greatest problem facing American business today.

The split between ownership and control was exacerbated by developments during capitalism's third stage, which reached maturity during the 1960s. The third stage was characterized by a division in the ownership function between the beneficial or real owners of corporate shares and a new and powerful class of professional portfolio managers (i.e., institutional investors) who buy, sell, and vote those shares on the beneficiaries' behalf. This new division has reduced the accountability of corporate managers even further. Beneficial owners care only about the bottom line of their mutual fund accounts, or whether their pension checks arrive on time; they rarely even know what companies they own, let alone whether they are well managed. The portfolio managers and other financial intermediaries, the argument goes, are equally uninterested in management accountability, but for different reasons: they look at shares of stock as fungible commodities to be bought and sold, not as deeds to pieces of individual companies. The net result is that there is almost no one left to supervise corporate management.

The ongoing fourth stage is a refinement of the third. The class of beneficial owners has been subdivided into those who actively decide to become capitalists by, say, investing in a mutual fund, and those who have this decision made for them by their union negotiators or corporate pension fund managers. These union and corporate officials, the government, and the investment specialists who emerged in the third stage are working continually to expand the class of corporate owners. However, these new capitalists are two steps removed from the public shareholders of the second stage: they lack control over not only the decision *how* to invest, but even the more basic decision *whether* to invest. As a result, according to Harvard Law School Dean Robert C. Clark, American capitalism has been moving in the direction of "increased sharing in benefits and decreased sharing in power."[4]

Pension funds have played distinct but significant roles in all four stages of capitalism. They first emerged as a social and humanitarian response to the laissez-faire depredations of stage one. They declined and then re-emerged in concert with changing economic conditions during stage two. And they have risen to enormous power in stages three and four, functioning simultaneously to create new capitalists and to manage the disposition of their capital.

Pension plans as we now know them—that is, commitments by public or private employers to pay workers during their retirement years—did not appear in North America and Europe until the late 19th century.[5] This should not be surprising, since the phenomenon of retirement itself has been around for only about 100 years. Through the end of the Civil War, and much later in the South and West, most Americans worked in agriculture or the trades that supported it. People made little distinction between their working and personal lives, and they looked to the extended family for support as their productivity declined. All this changed, of course, as industrialization and immigration fueled the growth of cities. For the urban industrial worker, the seamless integration of life and work became a thing of the past. Most significantly, he was no longer a member of a self-sufficient economic unit on which he could fall back when he was unable to work himself.

Despite these social changes, retirement remained largely a moot point during the post–Civil War rush to industrialization. Until pharmaceutical and public health innovations in the late 19th and early 20th centuries revolutionized the treatment and control of infectious diseases, few people had much expectation of life beyond work. For those who escaped disease, work itself was dangerous. As we debate the health hazards of asbestos insulation and video display terminals, it is easy to forget that earlier generations of political and business leaders accepted mine cave-ins, boiler explosions, and sweatshop fires as incidental costs of progress. The net result was that no one thought very much about retirement: some wealthy people managed to drift into a leisurely dotage, while the exceptional working-class individual who managed to survive to what we now call retirement age just kept on working.[6]

Against this background, the first modern pension plan was established in 1875 by American Express Company, then a railroad shipping company. Some of its specific provisions are revealing. First, it was noncontributory, meaning that contributions could be made only by the employer, and not by the workers. Some historians detect a charitable impulse in this, whereas others see a desire to ensure management control. Next, to be eligible for benefits, a worker had to be permanently incapacitated, at least 60 years old, and in the company's employ for at least 20 years. Obviously, these conditions would rarely be met in a business like railroading. The work was often dangerous. Employers hired large numbers of immigrants who had little access to medical care and were likely to move from city to city and job to job a number of times. Finally, the company's management had to approve each pension application on a case-by-case basis. For the fortunate retiree who satisfied all these conditions, the benefit was one-half of average annual pay during the 10 years leading up to retirement, with a maximum annual benefit of $500.

As labor became increasingly organized and assertive at the turn of the century, pensions took a back seat to such issues as humane working conditions, living wages, and reasonable hours. Nonetheless, pension plans on the American Express model spread throughout the railroad industry. According to some estimates, up to 50 percent of railroad workers may have been potentially eligible for some kind of formal or informal benefits by the early years of this century.

A watershed event occurred in 1901, when Carnegie Steel (later U.S. Steel, now USX) established the first pension plan in a major manufacturing company. Between 1901 and 1920, companies in every sector of the economy followed the lead of Carnegie and the railroads. By 1920, pension plans were in place in industries as diverse as rubber, paper, petroleum, and banking. By 1929, 397 industrial companies had pension plans and their employees accounted for 10 percent of the nonagricultural work force.

The plans established during this early period of growth shared many of the features of the original American Express plan. The vast majority were noncontributory, raising the same questions about whether the employers' motives were charitable or manipulative. Although most now permitted retirement without disability, the eligibility requirements remained strict:

the retirement age was set at 65 or 70, and 20 to 25 years of service were required. As a result, while the companies that offered pension benefits in 1929 may have employed 10 percent of the nonagricultural work force, fewer than 10 percent of their employees ultimately qualified for benefits.

A number of labor unions also established pension funds during the same period, for reasons that were both humanitarian and political. Several small unions established old-age and disability plans at the turn of the century: the Patternmakers in 1900, the Granitecutters and Cigarmakers in 1905. The large unions followed their lead, beginning with the Typographical Union in 1906. All of these early plans offered pension benefits only as gratuities. The railroad unions were the first to provide a contractual right to benefits, starting with the Locomotive Engineers in 1912.

Several of the legal and financial aspects of both the corporate and union plans are noteworthy. First and foremost, most were what we would now call *unfunded*. That is, only a few companies, and none of the unions, set aside a trust fund or purchased insurance to pay future benefits. Most simply paid benefits from the company's operating income or the union treasury. If there was no cash on hand, there would be no benefits. At the start of the Depression in 1929, funding was uncertain and plan sponsors were cautious about making commitments. None of the corporate funds and only a few of the unions had made any binding contractual promises to their beneficiaries to continue to maintain their plan. Consequently, the right to receive benefits in the future depended not only on the financial health of the benefactor, but also on the goodwill of its management. Finally, the modern concept of vesting was virtually unknown. Pension rights were an all-or-nothing proposition, and those who stopped working before fulfilling all of the conditions of eligibility were rarely entitled to any partial benefits.

Predictably, the Depression took a heavy toll on the early pension plans. Among the railroads, for example, as business fell off in the early 1930s, company after company reduced pension benefits, and many defaulted on their pension commitments. A partial federal bail-out ensued. The unfunded union plans fared even worse. The collapse of the union plans was a primary impetus to the creation of the federal Social Security system in 1935. Thereafter, union-financed plans declined toward extinction.

World War II exerted a strong if indirect influence on the development of corporate pension plans. Wage and price controls limited the unions' ability to negotiate for pay increases, so they turned their attention to fringe benefits, including pensions. In 1945, John L. Lewis and the United Mine Workers included pension rights among their negotiating demands. After two management refusals, a subsequent strike, and the seizure of the mines by the Department of the Interior, Lewis and the Secretary of the Interior agreed on an employer-financed pension fund in 1946.

Most pension historians have concluded that the pivotal event in the evolution of the modern pension plan was the establishment of the General Motors plan in 1950.[7] Pension rights had been on the table for several years in negotiations between the Big Three automakers and the United Auto Workers. Points of contention included whether the plans would be funded or pay-as-you-go, and the extent of worker participation in plan management. In April 1950, GM chairman Charles Wilson proposed a fully funded plan to be administered by financial professionals employed by management.

Wilson's plan departed from the conventional wisdom in two important respects. First, future liabilities were to be funded by broad-based capital investing. Most existing funded plans had invested exclusively in government and corporate bonds, mortgages, and other debt instruments that paid a fixed, if modest, rate of interest. Wilson thought that this approach was unduly conservative. He also feared that flooding the debt market with pension money would force interest rates down, to the ultimate detriment of the plan and its beneficiaries. He advanced instead the then-radical idea of investing pension money in the stock market. Against the argument that the stock market was too risky for pension funds, he proposed safety in diversity, with the fund putting no more than 5 percent of its assets in any single company.

Second, Wilson rejected the widely accepted practice of investing in the sponsoring company's own stock. He argued that every worker had already made a huge investment in the company—his or her working life—and that to put even more eggs in the same basket would be financially reckless. He also pointed out that over the 30- to 40-year working life of the typical employee, most companies decline or go out of business, with their stock becoming worthless.

The UAW was suspicious of Wilson's proposal. The union leadership raised a question of motive that continues to be debated today: Was Wilson a social visionary, or was his proposal just a thinly disguised stratagem for furthering management control over workers? Moreover, workers were intrigued by the prospect of owning their own company, an idea that Wilson had rejected on financial grounds.

The attractiveness of the proposal quickly overcame these objections, and the fund went into operation in October 1950. The ensuing ripple effect was remarkable. Within one year after the adoption of the GM plan, 8,000 new plans were set up (according to Peter Drucker's *The Unseen Revolution*), more than four times as many as in the preceding 100 years.[8] In addition, Wilson's innovative ideas—that pension fund portfolios should include a diversified list of stocks, and that a fund should not invest in the stock of its sponsor—became the conventional wisdom in the pension investment world.

These new plans operated within an old legal structure. Those who manage money for the benefit of others (e.g., the bank trust officer who oversees a fund established for the benefit of a minor child) are held to what is called a *fiduciary standard*. That is, they are accountable to the beneficiaries, and owe them a duty of the utmost good faith. For hundreds of years, fiduciaries' investment decisions have been circumscribed by the common law's prudent person rule: a fiduciary must invest as an idealized prudent person would in similar circumstances, keeping in mind the objectives of the particular fund. Accordingly, in managing a trust for widows and orphans, a bank officer would be more concerned with preserving principal than maximizing income.

It has never been entirely clear how these rules apply to pension funds. For example, whose money is it? A pension fund is established for the benefit of the workers. But the sponsoring corporation is ultimately responsible for seeing that the pensions are paid, so it, too, has an interest in the fund. Moreover, it can argue with some plausibility that if the fund acts in a way contrary to the interests of the corporation (such as by investing too conservatively and earning too little income, thereby increasing the level of needed corporate contributions), the workers will suffer as well.

Questions have also arisen concerning how the prudent person investment standard should apply to a pension fund fiduciary. For example, how much authority can the fiduciary delegate to outside money managers? Does the fiduciary have to be informed about every individual investment, or only about the general investment strategy? What is the nature of the fiduciary's obligation to diversify a pension fund's portfolio? Is it enough merely to hold both stocks and bonds, or must the fiduciary seek out different kinds of stocks? An alternative interpretation with wide current acceptance is that a fund should diversify by hiring outside managers with different investment styles: for example, one with a fundamental value orientation, another who believes in market timing, and so on.

In 1974, Congress intervened and tried to establish uniform legal standards for private pension funds. The motivation for this intervention can be traced to the closing of the Studebaker factory in South Bend, Indiana, in 1963. The company had been in trouble for years. When the plant closing was announced, with the attendant loss of 5,000 jobs, Studebaker and the UAW entered into negotiations over the pension rights of the dismissed workers. Studebaker had set up the plan in 1950 and had increased benefits every couple of years. However, with the acquiescence of the UAW, Studebaker had not put up sufficient money to fund these benefits. As a result, when the South Bend plant closed, there simply was not enough money in the till to pay the benefits that the dismissed workers believed that they had earned. The settlement reached with the UAW provided full benefits for the most senior workers, but the majority of those dismissed received little or nothing.

In the congressional hearings that ensued, a parade of former Studebaker employees told their tragic personal stories, and a second parade of labor leaders and politicians demanded federal control over pension funds. A few cynics pointed out that the UAW had collaborated in the overpromising and underfunding, suggesting that the union had taken credit for a collective bargaining "victory" that it knew to be meaningless. The personal tragedies got the headlines and the attention of Congress, however, and the momentum for federal intervention was firmly established.

After a series of studies and many legislative false starts, Congress enacted the Employee Retirement Income Security Act of 1974, known as ERISA. Its principal provisions closely reflect the lessons learned in the Studebaker episode. It requires that plans that promise specific retirement benefits (*defined benefit plans*, in contrast to *defined contribution plans*, in which benefits will vary in accordance with how successfully the employer and employee contributions are invested) be fully funded. That is, the employer must set aside money on an ongoing basis to pay for future benefits. How much money must be determined on the basis of sound actuarial assumptions about life expectancies and the rates of occurrence of various disabilities.

ERISA specifies that the pension fund money must be invested "for the sole benefit of the beneficiaries." ERISA adopts and refines the common law's prudent person investment standard, requiring that investments be made with "the care, skill, prudence, and diligence under the circumstances then prevailing that a prudent man acting in a like capacity and familiar with such matters would use in the conduct of an enterprise of a like character and with like aims." As is evident even from these brief excerpts, the language of ERISA did little to resolve the existing questions about whose money it really is and how it should be invested. As we will see in subsequent chapters, differing interpretations of the ERISA standards can lead to radically different investment decisions, with serious implications for the economy as a whole.

A final point is that ERISA applies only to private pension plans. Most public plans continue to be governed by the common law. Some states, however, have enacted ERISA-like statutes to regulate state and local plans. And pension executives in other states usually say that in areas where ERISA has set a higher standard than the common law, the only sensible course of action is to follow the higher standard.

THE SOCIAL SIGNIFICANCE OF PENSION FUNDS

By now it should be evident that pension funds have had a major impact on the social history of 20th-century America. The political irony in the development of pension funds is hard to miss: the capital of workers now fuels Wall Street. In the 19th century, Marx prophesied that the cataclysmic confrontation between labor and capital would lead to labor's control over the instruments of production. This seizure of control would not be immediate, however; a proletarian state would act as intermediary to consolidate the workers' power and then wither away.

Marx had the bad luck to inspire disciples who tried to turn his theory into reality. Recent events in the former Soviet empire are widely seen as discrediting Marx's entire analysis. In the history of the American pension funds, however, one might find evidence that Marx was right, although in ways he never would have expected. The workers, through their pension funds, have gained a tenuous hold on the means of production. The funds might be seen as the analog of Marx's proletarian state, the intermediary through which worker control is achieved.

The analogy is far from precise, of course. Worker control over the means of production may be attenuated to the point of meaninglessness: The funds are directed—and their stock voted—by people who are hired and fired by corporate management. Moreover, these executives see their funds not as ephemeral intermediaries smoothing the path to worker control, but as permanent institutions with independent power.

Nonetheless, the rise of pension funds has been claimed to be both revolutionary and socialistic. As Peter Drucker argues in his 1976 book *The Unseen Revolution*, "If 'socialism' is defined as 'ownership of the means of production by the workers'—and this is both the orthodox and the only rigorous definition—then the United States is the first truly 'Socialist' country."[9] Paradoxically, Drucker goes on to note, this shift toward socialism has proceeded without any perceptible impact on the power dynamics of American institutions: Labor continues to labor, and management continues to manage. The emergence of pension fund socialism is nonetheless revolutionary, he concludes. By merging the most adaptive features of capitalism and socialism, it has rendered the ideological divisions of the 19th century obsolete. Drucker believes that the success of this revolution is due in large part to the fact that it has taken place in the private sector, with the attendant benefits of pluralism and marketplace experimentation.

Others have concluded that the rise of pension funds has been neither socialistic, revolutionary, nor unseen. Drucker's argument seems to depend on a definition of socialism that many would reject. Whereas Drucker stresses only the beneficial ownership of the means of production, others stress that true socialism implies meaningful control as well. In the American corporate context, this means the right to participate in corporate governance by electing directors and voting shares. Pension fund beneficiaries do not have this right, however. Corporate and governmental sponsors retain it for themselves or delegate it to their external money managers.

One critic of Drucker's analysis, William Graebner, contends in his 1980 book, *A History of Retirement*, that what has developed is not pension-fund socialism, but rather pension-fund capitalism. He characterizes the efforts of GM's Wilson and those who followed his lead as seeking "to insure that this growing pool of [pension fund] capital would be responsibly invested—that is, as capitalists like him would invest it."[10] The net result has been that the new class of capitalists created by pension funds are capitalists in name only: They are the beneficial owners of vast sums of money, but have gained none of the power that historically accrues to such wealth. Instead, Graebner concludes, business has successfully subverted the pension funds to prop up a shaky status quo.

Regardless of how one judges the merits of this debate, the point to be kept in mind as we proceed through this book is that the evolution of pension funds since World War II does not represent business as usual. Whether one sees in this development a socialist revolution or a subtle ploy to preserve existing economic arrangements, the funds are new power centers that offer novel opportunities to those who dominate them. As will become apparent in subsequent chapters, this potential is only beginning to be appreciated. A few players of the pension game have started to use the funds as vehicles for advancing various political, economic, and social agendas, but most are bystanders, surprised, often confused, and sometimes embittered by the sudden attention their colleagues are getting.

NOTES

1. The corporate pension funds described in the text are sometimes called *trusteed* funds. Some corporations contract with an insurance company to take over all aspects of the management of their pension fund; these are sometimes called *insured* funds.
2. This analysis originated in an article by Dean Robert C. Clark of Harvard Law School. See Robert C. Clark, "The Four Stages of Capitalism: Reflections on Investment Management Treatises," *Harvard Law Review* 94 (1981), pp. 561–82.
3. This fundamental split between ownership and control was popularized by Adolf Berle and Gardiner Means in their enduring classic, *The Modern Corporation and Private Property* (New York: Macmillan, 1933).
4. Clark, "The Four Stages of Capitalism," p. 568.
5. The historical discussion that follows draws on William Graebner, *A History of Retirement: The Meaning and Function of an American Institution, 1885–1978* (New Haven and London: Yale University Press, 1980); William C. Greenough and Francis P. King, *Pension Funds and Public Policy* (New York: Columbia University Press, 1976); and the introductory chapter of a legal textbook by John H. Langbein and Bruce A. Wolk, *Pension and Employee Benefit Law* (Westbury, N.Y.: Foundation Press, 1990).
6. Credit for establishing 65 as the presumptive retirement age is usually given to Otto von Bismarck, who created a state-sponsored pension program in Germany in 1889.
7. See, for example, Peter Drucker, *The Unseen Revolution: How Pension Fund Socialism Came to America* (New York: Harper & Row, 1976), chap. 1.
8. Ibid., p. 7.
9. Ibid., p. 1.
10. Graebner, *A History of Retirement*, p. 220.

CHAPTER 2

THE WEALTH OF INSTITUTIONAL INVESTORS—AN ECONOMIC PROFILE

Institutional investors control more than $6.5 trillion worth of assets, a number that to most of us seems unreal, utterly unconnected to anything in our own experience. Early in our research, we asked a pension fund executive for help in visualizing $6.5 trillion. He responded by asking us if we had teenage children. When we both nodded in the affirmative, he told us to imagine that we gave each of them a million dollars and told them they were required to spend $1,000 a day. "They'd be back in about three years," he said. Then he told us to imagine giving them a billion dollars each, with the same instructions to spend it at the rate of $1,000 per day. "They wouldn't come back for 3,000 years." Then he upped the ante once more, and told us to imagine giving them a trillion dollars. "They'd be shopping for 3 million years. At the same rate, it would take them more than 20 million years to go through the current assets of American institutional investors."

Throughout most of this book we look at institutional investors from the inside, focusing on the culture of individual organizations. In this chapter, we examine these organizations collectively and attempt to define their place in the American economy. We assemble the best available economic data to document the emergence of institutional investors as an increasingly dominant force in U.S. capital markets. The economic data reveal the dramatic recent growth of institutional investors and the significant but largely unappreciated fact of a potent concentration of economic power in a small and exclusive group of institutions.

WEALTH AND POWER: THE RAW NUMBERS

Institutional investors are diverse. The principal categories within the group include private pension funds, public pension funds (principally state and local retirement funds), investment companies such as mutual funds, life insurance companies, property and casualty insurance companies, non–pension fund money managed by banks (trust funds for wealthy individuals, for example), and foundation and endowment funds. As of 1990, the $6.5 trillion worth of assets controlled by institutional investors represented about one-fifth (20.5 percent) of all the financial assets in the United States.[1]

As Table 2–1 shows, the extent of institutional control of the country's financial assets is impressive and growing rapidly. In 1950, institutions controlled barely one-twelfth of those assets; by 1990, over one-fifth. Another way to look at this growing concentration of economic power is to compare the asset figures

TABLE 2–1
Institutional Ownership of U.S. Financial Assets

	Total Outstanding Assets (in billions)	Total Owned by Institutions (in billions)	Percent Owned by Institutions
1990	$31,801.2	$6,520.4	20.5
1985	21,330.8	3,297.6	15.5
1980	13,110.2	1,769.0	13.5
1975	7,096.5	913.6	12.9
1970	4,639.1	568.9	12.3
1965	3,401.3	391.7	11.5
1960	2,366.9	255.7	10.8
1955	1,798.4	170.1	9.5
1950	1,280.9	107.0	8.4

Sources: Federal Reserve, Columbia Institutional Investor Project, and New York Stock Exchange.

for 1980 and 1990. Over this most recent 10-year period, U.S. financial assets as a whole grew by a little more than 140 percent, while the assets held by institutions grew by nearly 270 percent. Moreover, the trend is accelerating. After growing slowly and steadily in the 1970s, institutional investors' share of the U.S. economy jumped two percentage points between 1980 and 1985, and a full five percentage points between 1985 and 1990.

PENSION FUNDS

Pension funds comprise the single largest group of institutional investors. Since World War II, their growth has been phenomenal. They controlled $2.5 trillion worth of assets in 1990, up

FIGURE 2–1
Growth of Institutional Investors in the 1980s (Total Assets in Trillions of Dollars)

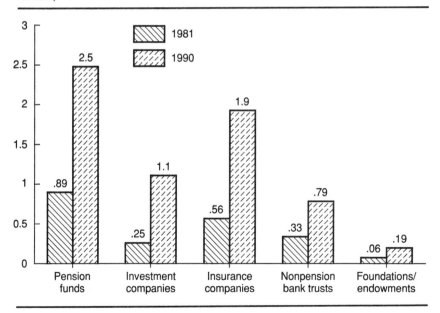

Source: Brancato & Gaughan, Columbia Institutional Investor Project.

from $17.6 billion in 1950 and only $891 billion as recently as 1981. Figure 2–1 (p. 28) shows the holdings of the major categories of institutional investors for the years 1981 and 1990. What is noteworthy is both the absolute magnitude of the pension funds' holdings and the strong rates of growth that all categories of institutional investors have maintained over the last decade. Figure 2–2 shows the shares of total institutional investments held by different types of investors in 1981 and 1990. Although the share controlled by pension funds has declined slightly, principally as a result of the dramatic growth of investment companies, they remain the largest identifiable category. Pension fund assets grew at an average rate of almost 9 percent per year over the period 1986–1990, just under the 11 percent rate for institutional investors generally.

FIGURE 2–2
Proportional Distribution of Total Assets among Types of Institutions: 1981–1990

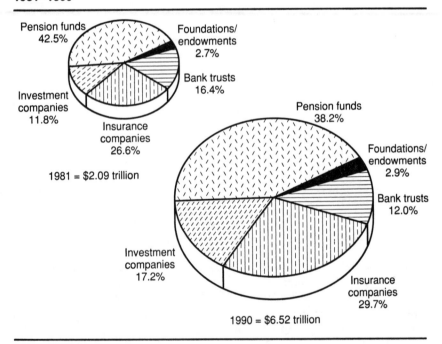

Source: Brancato & Gaughan, Columbia Institutional Investor Project.

Private pension funds still control the majority of pension fund assets, but the public funds are closing the gap rapidly. In 1990, private funds held assets valued at $1.7 trillion. This represents nearly 70 percent of total pension fund assets and just over 26 percent of the assets of all institutional investors. The growth boom in private funds occurred during the 10 or so years after Congress enacted ERISA in 1974 and companies made huge contributions to their pension plans to bring them up to legally mandated funding levels. As funding has caught up, private pension funds have leveled off in recent years, slowing to approximately 7 percent annual growth from 1986 to 1990.

TABLE 2–2
Concentration of Assets of Top 20 Pension Funds: 1984–1990

	As of 9/30/84			As of 9/30/90	
Rank	Fund	Assets (in millions)	Rank	Fund	Assets (in millions)
1	TIAA-CREF	$34,500	1	TIAA-CREF	$83,100
2	NY State	22,800	2	Calif. Pub. Emp.	54,000
3	General Motors	22,799	3	NY State	43,737
4	Calif. Pub Emp.	22,717	4	NY City Retire.	40,763
5	AT&T	21,455	5	AT&T	38,876
6	NY City Employees	21,154	6	General Motors	36,300
7	General Electric	13,338	7	Calif. St. Teachers	30,140
8	NY State Teachers	12,826	8	General Electric	27,108
9	Calif. State Teachers	12,300	9	NY State Teachers	26,689
10	IBM	10,918	10	New Jersey Invest	26,609
11	Texas Teachers	9,753	11	IBM	25,000
12	Ford Motor	9,300	12	Texas Teachers	23,734
13	New Jersey Invest	9,166	13	Ford Motor	20,800
14	Michigan St Employ	8,951	14	Ohio Pub Employ	20,595
15	Wisconsin Invest	8,692	15	Florida St Board	19,268
16	Ohio Public Employ	8,584	16	Wisconsin St Board	18,482
17	Ohio St Teachers	8,507	17	Ohio St Teachers	18,200
18	Du Pont	8,120	18	Du Pont	17,728
19	North Carolina	7,967	19	North Carolina	17,289
20	Exxon	7,388	20	State of Michigan	17,266
	Total	$281,235		Total	$605,684

	Assets (in millions)	Percent Assets Accounted for by Top 20		Assets (in millions)	Percent Assets Accounted for by Top 20
Top 200 funds	$675,136	41.7	Top 200 Funds	$812,400	42.8
Top 1,000 funds	896,100	31.4	Top 1,000 Funds	1,073,000	32.3

Source: Brancato, Columbia Institutional Investor Project. Based on data from *Pensions and Investments*.

In recent years, the strongest growth within the pension
fund sector has been in the public funds. During the first half of
the 1980s, public pension funds grew at the rate of almost 16
percent per year. Even after some slowdown in the late 1980s
their average annual growth rate was almost 13 percent for the
five-year period 1986–1990. As a result of this growth, their
share of institutional assets has increased to the point where
they now account for 11.6 percent of the total holdings of institutional investors.

A significant feature of pension fund growth has been its
uneven distribution. The largest funds have grown fastest, primarily because they have invested more aggressively than their
smaller counterparts and thus have taken fuller advantage of
recent growth in the financial markets. The result has been an
impressive concentration of capital. Table 2–2 (p. 29) illustrates
this trend. It shows the asset growth of the 20 largest pension
funds, both individually and collectively, over the period 1984–
1990. Together, these 20 funds grew approximately 115 percent

FIGURE 2–3
Concentration of Assets in Top 20 Pension Funds

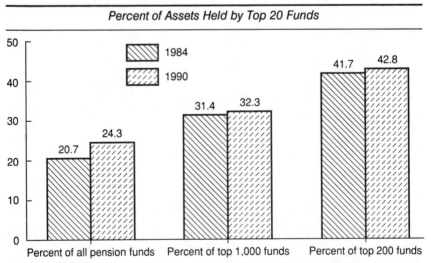

Source: Brancato, Columbia Institutional Investor Project.

in just six years. The largest of them, TIAA-CREF, grew more than 140 percent. All of the public funds that appear on both lists grew at least 100 percent, and many of them by much more. Figure 2–3 makes the same point in a somewhat different way, by showing the growth in the 20 largest funds' share of the total pension fund asset pool.

OTHER INSTITUTIONAL INVESTORS

Other major categories of institutional investors are investment companies, insurance companies, nonpension bank trusts, and foundations and endowments. After pension funds, the largest category is insurance companies, which accounted for nearly 30 percent of all institutional investor assets in 1990 (see Figure 2–2).[2] Life insurers are the principal component of the insurance company category and account for almost 22 percent of total institutional assets. Insurance industry holdings have grown impressively in recent years, at an average annual rate of more than 18 percent during the period 1986–1990. Investment companies comprise the third largest category with just over 17 percent of total institutional assets. Nonpension bank trusts come next, with 12 percent of total institutional holdings, followed by foundations and endowments with about 3 percent.

INSTITUTIONAL INVESTMENT STRATEGIES

Institutional investors are by no means a monolithic group. They have vastly different investment objectives and risk tolerance. Table 2–3 illustrates how the various categories of institutional investors divide their portfolios among equity, bonds, and cash equivalents. The strategies they adopt reflect their individual payout requirements. For example, life insurance companies have highly predictable, long-term payout requirements. To match these requirements, they invest heavily in long-term, fixed-income securities, which yield predictable and dependable returns. The amount of equity in their portfolios tends to be small—under 10 percent in 1990, versus more than 90 percent

TABLE 2–3 Institutional Investor Asset Allocations (Assets in Billions of Dollars)

	Total Assets	Dollar Equity	Percent of Total	Dollar Corporate Bonds	Percent of Total	Other*	Percent of Total
Pension Funds							
1980							
Private trusteed	469.6	223.5	47.6	128.3	27.3	117.8	25.1
Private insured	157.2	16.3	10.4	11.4	7.3	129.6	82.4
State/local	198.1	44.3	22.4	138.6	69.9	15.2	7.7
All pension funds	824.9	284.1	34.4	278.3	33.7	262.6	31.8
1990							
Private trusteed	1,140.4	623.1	54.6	300.3	26.3	216.9	19.0
Private insured	594.6	56.2	9.5	37	6.2	501.4	84.3
State/local	756.3	282.5	37.3	445.3	58.9	28.6	3.8
All pension funds	2,491.3	961.8	38.6	782.6	31.4	746.9	30.0
Mutual Funds							
1980	134.8	41.0	30.4	1.9	1.4	91.9	68.2
1990	1,069.1	245.8	23.0	83.6	7.8	739.7	69.0
Life Insurance							
1980	480	47	9.8	179	37.2	252	52.5
1989	1,299	125	9.6	538	41.4	635	48.8
Property/Casualty							
1980	198	39.7	20.1	146	73.7	12.2	6.2
1989	527	94.8	18.0	404	76.7	5.4	1.0

*Other = Fixed income, cash, market funds, and government securities.

Source: Brancato & Gaughan, Columbia Institutional Investor Project.

in bonds and other fixed-income instruments. Property and casualty companies, by comparison, have a less predictable and more immediate payout horizon. Because of their payout demands, property and casualty companies tend to invest more aggressively and to allocate more of their portfolios to equities.

Table 2–3 also reflects differences in the investment philosophies of public and private pension funds. Historically, public pension funds have had a strong commitment to bonds and other conservative fixed-income investments, and an equally strong aversion to equity. As recently as 1980, public funds invested more than three-quarters of their portfolios in fixed-income instruments. The public funds' aversion to equity was influenced both by state laws restricting their investment discretion and by a pervasive belief that it was imprudent for public trustees to do more than dabble in the stock market. Over the last decade or so, however, state legislators and regulators have given public fund trustees a freer rein, and they have taken advantage of it to adopt a more aggressive investment posture. As a result, by 1990 equities comprised almost 38 percent of public fund portfolios, and bonds had declined to 59 percent.

EQUITY HOLDINGS OF INSTITUTIONAL INVESTORS

Although the trend has been most dramatic among public pension funds, institutional investors as a whole have greatly increased their equity holdings in recent years. As Table 2–4 indicates, during the 1980s institutional investors overall increased their ownership share of the U.S. equity market from 38 percent to just over 53 percent—for the first time, a majority position. The value of those holdings in 1990 was over $1.9 trillion.

Pension funds have been responsible for much of the institutionalization of equity ownership. Pension funds now own well over one-quarter (28.2 percent) of all outstanding U.S. equity. Private funds account for almost 20 percent of this total and public funds about 8 percent. This ratio continues to change as public funds reorder their investment priorities in the direction of greater participation in the stock market. Among the other categories of institutional investors, nonpension bank trusts

TABLE 2–4
Institutional Investment in Equities (In Billions of Dollars)

	1981		1986		1990	
	Equity Holdings	Percent of Total Equity Market	Equity Holdings	Percent of Total Equity Market	Equity Holdings	Percent of Total Equity Market
Pension funds						
Private	239.1	15.5	493.4	16.7	679.3	19.9
State/local	47.1	3.0	150.2	5.1	282.5	8.3
All pension funds	285.2	18.5	643.6	21.8	961.8	28.2
Mutual funds	38.6	2.5	200.6	6.8	245.8	7.2
Insurance companies						
Life insurance	47.7	3.1	60.0	2.0	140.8	4.1
Property/casualty	39.6	2.6	81.0	2.8	94.9	2.8
All insurance funds	87.3	5.7	141.0	4.8	235.7	6.9
Bank trusts	155.2	10.1	298.7	10.1	431.7	9.2
Foundations/endowments	18.5	1.2	37.9	1.3	61.7	1.8
Total all institutions	584.8	38.0	1,321.8	44.8	1,936.7	53.3

Source: Brancato & Gaughan, Columbia Institutional Investor Project.

hold just over 9 percent of outstanding equity, insurance companies and mutual funds about 7 percent each, and foundations and endowments less than 2 percent.

As Tables 2–5 and 2–6 indicate, institutional investors are especially prominent as stockholders in America's largest corporations. Institutions own more than half the stock of the 50 largest companies and almost 60 percent of the second 50. In many flagship companies like IBM, General Electric, Johnson & Johnson, and Mobil, institutions own more than half of the outstanding stock.

Certain industries are particularly dominated by institutions, as shown in Table 2–7. The paper industry leads all others, with over 62 percent of its outstanding stock owned by institutional investors. Transportation is almost as high, with an average of 61 percent of outstanding stock held by institutions. Even in the utilities and telecommunications industries, which have the lowest level of institutional ownership, the figures are still substantial—about 39 percent for utilities and 38 percent for telecommunications.

Impressive as these trends in overall institutional ownership may be, they mask another development of even greater significance: the potential for a few very large institutions—the biggest American pension funds—to influence the governance of major corporations. Figure 2–3 demonstrates the enormous

TABLE 2–5
Institutional Investor Ownership in U.S. Corporations: 1990

Companies Ranked by Stock Market Value	Percent Outstanding Stock
Top 1–50 companies	50.1
Top 51–100 companies	59.2
Top 101–250 companies	54.7
Top 251–500 companies	51.1
Top 501–750 companies	47.5
Top 751–1,000 companies	44.6

Source: Brancato, Columbia Institutional Investor Project. Based on *Business Week*'s Database on Top 1,000 Corporations Ranked by Stock Market Value.

TABLE 2–6
Institutional Ownership of Top 50 Companies

Company	1990 Rank	Percent Institutional Holdings
IBM	1	51%
Exxon	2	38
Philip Morris	3	65
General Electric	4	52
Merck	5	56
Wal-Mart Stores	6	31
Bristol-Myers-Squibb	7	61
AT&T	8	24
Coca-Cola	9	55
Procter & Gamble	10	46
Johnson & Johnson	11	59
Amoco	12	46
Chevron	13	43
Mobil	14	51
Pepsico	15	60
Du Pont	16	40
Bellsouth	17	27
General Motors	18	41
Eli Lilly	19	73
GTE	20	56
Atlantic Richfield	21	56
Waste Management	22	54
Abbot Laboratories	23	52
Minnesota Min. & Mfg.	24	65
American Int'l. Group	25	50
Bell Atlantic	26	32
American Home Prod.	27	63
Pfizer	28	72
Ameritech	29	29
Boeing	30	55
Pacific Telesis Group	31	37
Texaco	32	66
Walt Disney	33	42
Southwestern Bell	34	41
Ford Motor	35	53
Schlumberger	36	49
NYNEX	37	39
US West	38	44
Eastman Kodak	39	51
Dow Chemical	40	55
Anheuser-Busch	41	54
American Express	42	63
McDonald's	43	54
Hewlett-Packard	44	47
Microsoft	45	28

TABLE 2–6 *(concluded)*

Company	1990 Rank	Percent Institutional Holdings
Schering-Plough	46	65
Sears, Roebuck	47	59
Fed. Nat'l Mortgage Assoc.	48	96
Marion Merrell Dow	49	11
Warner-Lambert	50	65
Average Institutional Holdings		50%

Source: Brancato, Columbia Institutional Investor Project. Based on *Business Week*'s Database on Top 1,000 Corporations Ranked by Stock Market Value.

TABLE 2–7

Institutional Investor Holdings in U.S. Corporations: Average Percent Holdings by Industry Groupings—1990

Industry Group	
Aerospace	55.6%
Automotive	52.2
Banks	43.6
Chemicals	54.7
Conglomerate	53.5
Consumer	51.1
Container	40.6
Electrical	58.8
Food	41.5
Fuel	51.6
Health care	54.5
Housing	45.9
Leisure	52.0
Manufacturing	57.7
Metals	50.1
Nonbank finance	54.2
Office equipment	55.3
Paper	62.2
Publishing/TV	40.2
Retailing	53.5
Services	47.1
Telecommunications	37.5
Transportation	61.1
Utilities	39.2
Average—all corporations in top 1,000 group	50.6%

Source: Brancato, Columbia Institutional Investor Project. Based on *Business Week*'s Database on Top 1,000 Corporations Ranked by Stock Market Value.

TABLE 2–8
Holdings of Stock of 10 Largest Corporations by Top 20 Funds

Top 10 Corporations	Percent of Total Value Stock Held as of 12/31/89
1 IBM	9.1
2 Exxon	7.4
3 General Electric	8.5
4 AT&T	6.1
5 Philip Morris	9.0
6 General Motors	10.6
7 Merck	5.7
8 Ford Motor	8.3
9 Du Pont	4.8
10 Amoco	7.9
Average	7.7

Source: Brancato, Columbia Institutional Investor Project. Based on data from Spectrum CDA Database.

concentration of wealth in the 20 largest pension funds. The near-identity of the 1984 and 1990 top-20 lists in Table 2–2 evidences the impressive stability of this group. Table 2–8 examines the same concentration from the perspective of America's largest corporations. By themselves, the top 20 pension funds control almost 8 percent of the outstanding stock of the country's 10 largest corporations.[3]

FUTURE TRENDS

All of these figures point in the direction of more institutional wealth and more institutional power. There is no sign of any diminution in the growth of institutional asset holdings, either in absolute or proportional terms. On the contrary, there is every indication that by the year 2000 the holdings of institutional investors will move into double digits in trillions of dollars and these institutional investors will control one-quarter of total U.S. assets. The institutional dominance of the equity market is also likely to grow at least at its present rate. The single most important factor in this growth may be the newly felt freedom of public fund trustees to invest major portions of their portfolios in common stocks. By conservative estimate, more than two-thirds of the total U.S. equity market could be in the hands of institutional investors by the millennium.

As the wealth and power of institutions continue to increase, the largest and most stable of them, the huge private and public pension funds, will play an increasingly dominant role. The 20 largest pension funds alone seem destined to hold double-digit stakes in many of America's most important companies. If they have the will, they will have the wherewithal to demand that corporate managements hear them out on the critical issues of philosophy and strategy that will determine the fate of American business in the 21st century.

NOTES

1. The Federal Reserve defines financial assets to include cash, demand deposits, money market fund deposits, corporate equities, bonds, government securities, mortgages, open market paper, life insurance and pension fund reserves, and miscellaneous assets.
2. The holdings of insurance companies may be understated. Many pension funds, particularly defined contribution plans, invest in guaranteed investment contracts offered by insurance companies. Although the control of GIC investments is actually in the hands of the insurance companies, they are treated as pension fund assets.
3. For a more detailed discussion of the concentration phenomenon, see Carolyn K. Brancato, *Institutional Investor Concentration of Power: A Study of Institutional Holdings and Voting Authority in U.S. Publicly Held Corporations* (New York: Columbia Institutional Investor Project, 1991).

CHAPTER 3

WHO'S IN CHARGE?— HOW PENSION FUNDS MANAGE MONEY

The diversity of management structures and investment techniques among multibillion-dollar pension funds is staggering. Some funds manage their money actively, believing that they can outperform the market. Other funds adopt a passive approach, tying their investments to indexes that track segments of the market. Indexed funds forgo the opportunity to beat the market, but also avoid the risk of underperforming it. Many funds, both active and passive, manage their assets internally, assigning particular investment areas to particular employees. Others hire outside managers with varied investment philosophies, entrusting to them sums of money that often exceed a billion dollars.

Despite this sometimes overwhelming variation, a number of unifying themes repeatedly emerge. In arriving at an investment strategy, all funds—in fact, all institutional investors— must confront the same set of basic questions about the philosophy of investment and management. Although individual funds answer these questions in radically different ways, in arriving at their answers they are motivated by cultural factors that remain remarkably constant from fund to fund.

In this chapter we describe the range of management structures and investment options available to a pension fund. Developing an overall investment strategy requires that a fund make a number of fundamental decisions. No fund that we studied actually works through each of the fundamental decisions explicitly and systematically. More often, a fund focuses on a single decision; the outcome of that decision then limits further options and determines some of the other choices that must be made. And in some cases, even this initial, driving decision is more the product of historical or political happenstance than of conscious choice. Nonetheless, these fundamental decisions shape the complex realities of pension fund management.

Toward this end, we do three things in this chapter. First, we identify the four fundamental decisions that determine a pension fund's structure. Second, we describe how these decisions are made and analyze the consequences of different outcomes. Third, we present five case studies of fund management structures, each reflecting a different combination of decisions.

THE FOUR FUNDAMENTAL DECISIONS

Every fund—in fact, every institutional investor—must make four critical decisions in structuring its investment portfolio (see Table 3–1). The *asset allocation* decision determines the distribution of the portfolio among such broad categories as stocks, bonds, and real estate. One of the few universally valid generalizations we can make about pension funds is that every fund in fact makes this decision first, and does so in a careful, systematic way. The three remaining decisions pertain to the way that a fund invests that portion of the portfolio that it allocates to equities.

In theory, the management of fixed-income and other investments requires a parallel, equally complex set of decisions. But equity investing dominated our discussions with fund officials. Equity is the largest single segment of the portfolio of each

TABLE 3–1
Four Fundamental Decisions in Managing Pension Funds

1. Asset allocation
2. Active versus passive investment strategies
3. Inside versus outside management
4. Consistent versus cafeteria philosophy

of the funds we studied, and it yields the greatest variety of management structures and investment strategies. By contrast, most funds manage their fixed-income assets internally, using relatively similar approaches. When we asked about investment strategies generally, fund executives invariably put their primary emphasis on equities. They claimed to spend most of their time on equity problems, and characterized their fixed-income strategies as mechanical and uninteresting. They stressed that the defining characteristic of an individual fund is its approach to equity investing. Moreover, equity ownership is accompanied by the rights and responsibilities of corporate governance. It is thus the source of pension funds' growing potential to influence the direction of American business. Consequently, our analysis will focus on equity investment.

A second fundamental decision facing every fund is the choice between *active* and *passive* equity management. *Active* describes a fund's investment decision making, but not necessarily its trading pattern. The term implies only that a fund consciously selects one or more strategies that it believes will enable it to outperform the market. Thus, a fund is active even if it chooses to invest in fundamentally sound companies and then hold their stock indefinitely. By contrast, the defining feature of passive investing is the belief that one cannot beat the market, and should therefore build a portfolio which samples the entire market or replicates some significant segment of it. This process of sampling or replication is called *indexing*.

A fund that manages some or all of its assets actively must make a third decision: whether to do so *internally* or *externally*. (Since indexing is inexpensive and relatively straightforward, large pension funds usually do passive management internally.) Internal management involves hiring and supervising investment professionals, traders, and support personnel. With external management, all of these services are provided by the investment firms that the fund hires—for a substantial fee, of course.[1] Moreover, structuring and maintaining relationships with external managers can be complicated. Funds often find it difficult to establish criteria for evaluating performance, and terminating managers is usually costly in every sense of the word.

All funds that engage in active management must then make a fourth decision: between *consistent* and *cafeteria* investment approaches. With a consistent approach, a fund settles on a single investment philosophy—for example, buying stock in fundamentally sound companies and holding it for the long term, or predicting economic trends and investing in promising market sectors. The fund then implements that philosophy itself or hires managers who are committed to doing so.

The cafeteria approach is just what the name implies.[2] The fund does a little of this and a little of that, often carrying out more than half a dozen investment strategies simultaneously. Because of the obvious logistical problems that are involved, most funds that take the cafeteria approach use outside managers. The reasons for adopting the cafeteria approach are complex, involving conceptions of personal responsibility and legal duty. Its financial soundness is also hotly debated.

Except for the asset allocation decision, different funds do not make these fundamental decisions in any consistent order. Moreover, the decisions are frequently made by default. For example, a fund might be attracted to a particular outside manager. The decision to hire him and one or two others that he recommends may result in an active, outside, philosophically consistent strategy, even though the only conscious decision the fund made was to express a preference for a single individual.

ASSET ALLOCATION

Most pension fund executives agree that the asset allocation decision is the most important decision they make. As contributions accumulate in a fund, its managers must decide how to allocate them among such broad investment categories as equities, fixed-income securities (corporate and Treasury bonds, for example), real estate, leveraged buyout partnerships, and cash. As the chief executive of a large private fund explained:

> The most critical thing of all is the asset mix decision. All other decisions are likely to be overwhelmed by the basic decision of whether you're in or out of the stock market, or the balance that

you've got between bonds, real estate, international, domestic, and so on, at any given point in time.

Although the details differ somewhat, the general principles of allocating assets are the same at all large funds. The highest level of the fund's management makes an overall asset decision at least yearly. This decision may be the responsibility of the fund's fiduciary (for example, a public fund's board of trustees or a committee of the corporation's board of directors in the case of a private fund) or a committee appointed for that purpose by the fiduciary. The decision will be preceded by extensive research and discussion by the fund's professional investment staff and will typically follow the professional staff's recommendation. A committee or working group of investment professionals will reassess the decision throughout the year and may fine-tune the asset mix periodically.

Asset allocation is influenced by the demographic profile of the sponsoring employer's work force. If the employer has an aging work force, the fund can anticipate many retirements in the near term. To ensure that it will have enough cash on hand to pay the benefits as they become due, the fund is likely to tip its asset mix in the direction of shorter-term, fixed-income investments. Conversely, a fund whose sponsor has a young work force will have more freedom to invest in equities, where the return is less predictable and a longer-term perspective is necessary.

A related process called *portfolio rebalancing* goes on throughout the year. Assume that a billion-dollar fund allocates 50 percent of its assets to equities, and thus invests $500 million in the stock market. Assume further that it invests well, and that the equity portion of its portfolio appreciates in value faster than any other. After six months, the fund finds that equities now comprise 60 percent of the total portfolio. It then has two choices. It can ratify these investment results by formally changing its asset allocation decision. Alternatively, it can rebalance the portfolio by selling off equities until this category is once again 50 percent of the portfolio, reinvesting the proceeds in other categories. Although it may seem counterintuitive to transfer capital from more successful to less successful invest-

BOX 3–1   Asset Structure of Pension Funds

- During the past 40 years, pension funds have dramatically shifted their asset allocation toward equities and away from bonds.
- In 1950, pension funds held 6 percent of their assets in equities and 56 percent in bonds.
- By 1990, however, pension funds had increased their equity base substantially, with 38 percent of their assets in equities and only 32 percent in bonds.
- In 1990, pension funds held 28.2 percent of the outstanding equity in the United States, up from only 0.8 percent in 1950.
- In 1990, pension funds held 13.9 percent of outstanding bonds in the United States, up from 3.2 percent in 1950.

Total Pension Fund Assets

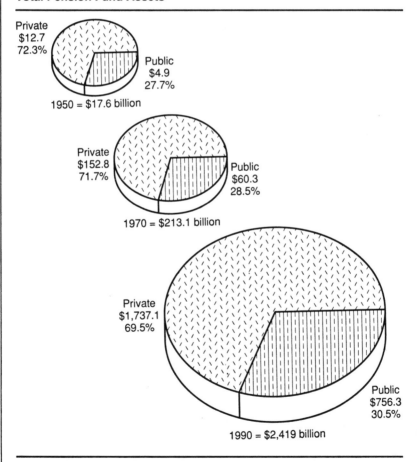

Private
$12.7
72.3%

Public
$4.9
27.7%

1950 = $17.6 billion

Private
$152.8
71.7%

Public
$60.3
28.5%

1970 = $213.1 billion

Private
$1,737.1
69.5%

Public
$756.3
30.5%

1990 = $2,419 billion

Source: Brancato & Gaughan, Columbia Institutional Investor Project. Based on EBRI data.

ments, the latter choice is at least as common as the former. Outside money managers are particularly aggrieved by this course of action, complaining that their reward for doing well is to have money taken away from them.

The asset mixes that result from these processes are remarkably similar across large funds. Typically, 45–55 percent of a fund is allocated to equities.[3] Most large funds are beginning to devote a portion of their equity portfolios to international stocks, usually 5–15 percent of the equity component. Fixed-income securities account for 35–45 percent of the typical fund. These fixed-income investments tend to be traditional and conservative, emphasizing high-quality bonds and government securities. Large pension funds have generally shied away from junk bonds and other high-risk, high-yield debt instruments. Nonetheless, some funds now invest up to 10 percent of their portfolios in areas that fund managers characterize as nontraditional, such as real estate and mergers and acquisitions.[4] They do so by participating in partnerships organized by specialists in the relevant areas. Even with this outside help, nontraditional investments are labor-intensive, and fund executives complain that the resources required to oversee them are grossly disproportionate to the dollars invested. Finally, the portion of the portfolio held as cash or highly liquid cash equivalents varies considerably from fund to fund and from day to day. For example, a fund that employs several outside equity managers may find its cash position changing constantly as the managers make independent judgments about moving in and out of the market. There is a broad consensus, however, that leaving any significant portion of the portfolio in cash for an extended period entails unacceptable opportunity costs.

Why do funds show such broad agreement in how they allocate assets? One possible answer is that everyone agrees that these percentages in fact yield the best results. If so, however, asset allocation would represent the only substantive point in the entire institutional investment universe on which there is virtual unanimity. It seems more likely that each fund is glancing around at its competitors, making sure that it is not departing from the mainstream on this most critical of decisions. Although pension fund executives know surprisingly little about

BOX 3–2
Nontraditional Investments

- In 1990, 43.7 percent of the total assets of the top 200 pension funds were internally managed, up slightly from 42.6 percent in 1989 and 41.7 percent in 1985.
- Investment in real estate by the top 200 pension funds grew from 2.9 percent of total assets in 1985 to 3.9 percent in 1990. By 1990, these pension funds had committed $55.1 billion to real estate equities.
- Pension fund investment in international assets more than doubled over the second half of the decade, jumping from 1.4 percent of total assets for the top 200 funds in 1985 to 3.6 percent in 1990.
- Levels of investment in other alternative investment vehicles, such as venture capital, oil and gas, private placements, and LBOs, remained relatively stable over the last half of the decade. The total amount dedicated to these categories continues to represent a very small portion of the total assets of the top 200. While none of these investments comprises more than 2.0 percent of their total assets, when pension funds enter these relatively small markets, the size of their investments can represent a significant portion of the market itself.

Selected Investment Strategies of the Largest 200 Pension Funds (in billions)

	1990 Assets	Percent of Total Assets
Internally managed	$ 618.8	43.7%
Equity index funds	164.9	11.6
Internally managed	47.7	3.4
Bond index funds	67.0	4.7
Internally managed	25.5	1.8
Real estate equity	55.1	3.9
Mortgages	43.4	3.1
Mortgage-backed securities	65.8	4.6
GICs/BICs	39.6	2.8
International	51.1	3.6
Equity	39.7	2.8
Fixed income	10.5	0.7
Other	0.9	*

BOX 3–2 *(continued)*

	1990 Assets	*Percent of Total Assets*
Venture capital	5.0	0.3
Dedicated/immunized bonds	26.8	1.9
Oil and gas	0.9	*
LBOs	6.5	0.5
Private placements	21.7	1.5
Noninvestment-grade bonds	2.7	0.2
Contributions paid	40.2	2.8
Benefits paid	44.0	3.1

Data is as of September 30, 1990.
*Less than $100 million.

Source: Brancato, Columbia Institutional Investor Project. Based on data from *Pensions and Investments*.

the operational aspects of other funds, comparative information about asset mix is readily available from specialized publications to which most large funds subscribe and from the small group of elite consultants that many of them employ.

ACTIVE VERSUS PASSIVE INVESTMENT STRATEGIES

Once a portion of the fund's assets has been allocated to the stock market, it must be invested. In structuring its equity portfolio, a fund must decide between active and passive investment strategies. All active strategies exercise judgment in an effort to outperform the market. At one extreme, judgment can be exercised on a minute-by-minute basis as the fund trades constantly, attempting to anticipate minor market fluctuations. But active decision making can also lead to an inactive trading posture if the fund decides to make long-term investments in fundamentally sound companies. Other commonly adopted options include hunting for bargains among underpriced stocks; looking for *franchises* (companies with natural monopolies such as television stations, newspapers in one-paper towns, or the photographer who has the Christmas concession in a major department store chain); investing in sectors of the market (e.g., small-capitalization growth stocks) that seem promising during a given period; and attempting to identify industries with unusual near-term promise (for example, before the Persian Gulf War began, some investors foresaw the destruction of Kuwait's oil fields and the opportunities for companies that could repair them). Again, the point is not that all of these investment styles require active trading, but rather that they require active judgment about the best ways to invest.

By contrast, passive management seeks to tap the overall rate of growth in the economy, as reflected in the performance of the market. Rather than exercising judgment in an effort to beat the market, the investor renounces judgment and becomes a passenger who rides the market. This is usually accomplished by indexing equity investments. This involves creating and maintaining a portfolio of stocks that represent the market as a whole or some specific component of it. A number of commercial services compile and publish different kinds of indexes. The best-known domestic indexes are the Standard & Poor's 500, which is dominated by large corporations, and the various Wilshire indexes, which are more representative of the broader market. One can find an index that purports to represent almost any segment of the market, whether domestic or international. When the market (or the relevant segment) rises or falls, the index follows.

Many governmental and some private pension funds invest more than 50 percent of their total assets by indexing. A pension fund can invest in a professionally managed index fund, create a portfolio that tracks an established index and manage it on its own, or even design its own index. Once the fund chooses the set of equities and decides on the relative weightings of particular stocks, indexing operates without much need for intervention.

The few decisions that need to be made—such as selling a stock that has been dropped from the S&P 500 and buying another to replace it—are formulaic.

The starting point for any decision to manage actively has to be a belief in one's ability to beat the market. Sometimes this is little more than a belief. Funds that pursue active management, either internally or externally, expect their money managers to add value to the fund. They expect the managers collectively to outperform the market as a whole, and they expect individual managers to beat some benchmark that is based on the average performance of those using similar strategies. In practice, the expectation that active managers can do better than average does not mean that they have to do much better or even do better all the time. Fund executives typically say that a few basis points (that is, a few hundredths of a percent of the total value of the portfolio) annually will suffice, and achieving this three out of five years will usually do.

A passive style is based on different assumptions about successful investing. The primary assumption is that because the stock market is an efficient pricing mechanism, it is difficult if not impossible to outperform it over the long run. Advocates of passive investing contend that short-term fluctuations in the market are seen as so unpredictable that attempting to anticipate them is unacceptably risky. Proponents of indexing also argue that even long-term active strategies do not outperform the market by a sufficient margin to justify their costs.

Two affirmative beliefs underlie indexing. The first is that the market is such an efficient pricing mechanism that looking for bargains is a waste of time and money. The market price of a stock almost always reflects its true value. The second belief is that equities may be expected to do well in the future because their value has increased steadily over previous decades.[5] Indexing is thus an act of faith in the general, long-term well-being of the American and global economies.

Fund executives rarely explain their choice between active and passive strategies in absolute terms. They talk instead about why their choice is better than the alternatives. Thus, one hears not so much about what is right with one choice as about what is wrong with the other. Indeed, it is in the context of such comparisons that they often give their most candid and critical assessments of their own approaches.

For example, the chief executive officer of a large private pension fund gave this description of his fund's decision to forgo indexing in favor of an active investment strategy:

> It doesn't make any sense to think that you couldn't do any better than the market as a whole. But nevertheless, we have indexed with a small amount of money. From the early 80s on, we kept addressing this question of whether to invest actively or passively. We became convinced that, even though our outside managers had not turned in a good performance, it was possible to create a group that could. And so, we basically went on the premise that we would be able to gradually restructure the stable of outside managers and get it into an aggregate group that would be able to do better than an index fund. And we still believe that, although the case is not an overwhelming one. I mean, it's not a powerful case.

At the other end of the spectrum, those who index argue that indexing keeps costs low and makes performance predictable. However, this assessment of cost and risk is relative to what might happen if the equity portfolio were more actively managed. In the words of an investment officer at a large public fund:

> The rationale behind it is to have the core of the equity essentially replicate the performance of the overall U.S. market. . . . The cost of managing the index is extremely low, particularly since we're doing it internally, as compared to active management. [Our decision to index] was based on historical data that seemed to indicate that there were very few active managers that over time had records that exceeded the broad market indexes.

The ease of operating an index reinforces its appeal. Active decision making requires extensive research, and someone must take responsibility for choices that do not work out. Indexing reduces the whole investment process to a formula. Buy and sell decisions are largely mechanical.

BOX 3–3
Indexed Equity Investments

Top 20 Funds with Defined-benefit Assets in Indexed Equities and Bonds (As of September 30, 1990)

Fund	Total Assets	Rank of Fund by Total Assets Held	Total Indexed Assets	Indexed Equities	Percent of Total Indexed Assets	Indexed Bonds	Percent of Total Indexed Assets
New York City	40,763	4	22,146	0	0.0%	22,146.0	100.0%
California State Teachers	30,140	7	20,005	9,175	45.9	10,830.0	54.1
New York State & Local	43,737	3	13,914	13,914	100.0	0.0	0.0
California Employees	54,000	2	13,800	13,800	100.0	0.0	0.0
New York State Teachers	26,689	9	13,019	13,019	100.0	0.0	0.0
AT&T	38,876	5	11,475	7,639	66.6	3,863.0	33.7
Florida State Board	19,268	15	8,472	5,868	69.3	2,604.0	30.7
Minnesota State Board	12,098	28	7,623	2,188	28.7	5,435.0	71.3
NYNEX	14,383	22	4,638	3,372	72.7	1,266.0	27.3
Pennsylvania School	17,268	21	3,748	1,239	33.1	2,509.0	66.9
General Electric	27,108	8	3,641	3,641	100.0	0.0	0.0
Teamsters, Central States	9,398	39	3,401	959	28.2	2,442.0	71.8
Ford Motor	20,800	13	3,300	3,000	91.0	300.0	9.0
Du Pont	17,728	18	3,246	3,246	100.0	0.0	0.0
Washington State Board	12,839	26	3,116	2,439	78.3	677.0	21.7
Maryland State	10,761	32	2,995	2,485	83.0	510.0	17.0
Virginia Retirement	10,687	33	2,869	2,869	100.0	0.0	0.0
Pennsylvania Employees	9,485	38	2,625	2,008	76.5	617.0	23.5
Southwestern Bell	8,303	46	2,382	2,382	100.0	0.0	0.0
Teamsters, Western	9,292	40	2,122	1,372	64.7	750.0	35.3
					Average % 71.9%		*Average %* 28.1%
					Percent of Dollar Total		*Percent of Dollar Total*
Totals	433,623		148,537	94,615	63.7%	53,949	36.3%

- As of September 30, 1990, the top 15 pension funds had invested a total of $143.6 billion in equities, or 41.3 percent of their total assets. Of this, $89.0 billion was invested in indexed equities. Indexed equities therefore accounted for a dollar weighted average of 62.0 percent of all equities in these funds and 25.6 percent of their total assets.

- Over the past two years, the 15 pension funds with the largest investments in indexed equities have nearly doubled indexed equity holdings—these rose from $75.9 billion as of September 30, 1988, to $143.6 billion as of September 30, 1990. As a percent of these funds' total equities, indexed equities rose from 56.3 percent in 1988 to 62.0 percent in 1990.

Source: Brancato, Columbia Institutional Investor Project. Based on data from *Pensions and Investments*.

INSIDE VERSUS OUTSIDE MANAGEMENT

A fund that manages its equity portfolio actively must decide whether to do so internally or externally. Internal management means that employees of the fund decide what stocks to buy, how long to hold them, and when and under what circumstances to sell. In addition, internal personnel must do much of the research on which those decisions will be based. Fund employees must also either execute trades or communicate with the brokers who will.

For many funds, the inside-outside choice is no choice at all because the outcome is dictated by circumstances unrelated to investment preferences. A certain critical mass of personnel and equipment is required to operate an in-house equity department, no matter how modest its objectives. Someone who knows what he or she is doing must be in charge, assisted by one or more analysts, traders, and support people. (*More* is the preferred option here, since those with a fiduciary responsibility for other people's money are uncomfortable doing anything on a bare-bones basis.) A small fund ($1 billion in assets is often cited as a cut-off point) may find the cost of this critical mass to be grossly disproportionate to the anticipated income. The kind of people that a prudent fiduciary would hire to manage pension fund equities are likely to be on Wall Street earning very large incomes. Despite the fact that pension funds are awash in money, they sometimes find it impossible to hire such people. A private corporation may not be willing to let its fund break out of its established executive compensation structure, and a public fund may be bound by civil service restrictions.[6] In these instances, the only answer may be to go to outside management without regard to any other considerations.

Inside management also requires a workable chain of command. Because of their fiduciary status, pension fund executives are extremely cautious about delegating major decisions to individual subordinates. Thus, the tendency is to set up layers of committees to review investment decisions. The problem, of course, is that such bureaucracies can stifle initiative and drive away the very sort of entrepreneurial people that inside management requires.

For many pension executives, these burdens are prohibitive. They take a cursory look at the difficulties of inside management and reject it out of hand. They sometimes take additional comfort in the belief that reliance on outside managers will help them and their employers avoid responsibility for investment decisions that turn out bad.

Those who favor internal management cite two advantages. First, they avoid the fees that outside managers charge—fees that, in the view of many, are rarely justified by performance. Second, internal management can have educational benefits. Some of the funds that use both internal and external management are convinced that their internal experience makes them better able to evaluate the performance of their outside managers.

What is particularly interesting about these divergent views is the certainty with which they are held. To many who use external managers, inside management looks like a practical impossibility. Conversely, many who have tried and abandoned outside management cannot imagine why others readily pay so much money for so little performance.

INVESTMENT PHILOSOPHIES

Any fund that manages equities actively, whether internally or externally, must also choose an investment philosophy. There are two basic philosophical orientations. Some funds select one or two investment styles and pursue them consistently. Others hold to a cafeteria philosophy, identifying a wide range of investment styles and doing a little of each. The choice between these two philosophies is sometimes made consciously, as when a fund decides to pursue fundamental value investing, and sometimes by default, as when a fund is attracted to an individual manager who happens to use a particular approach.

For most funds, there is a practical correlation between the choice of philosophy and the inside-outside decision. For example, it is extraordinarily burdensome to implement a cafeteria approach internally, so much so that only the largest funds even think about trying it. The converse point is that most funds that make a commitment to internal management end up pursuing a consistent philosophy, usually fundamental value investing. (No fund would want to put all of its equity eggs into a single basket that was highly speculative, like market timing.)

Proponents of the cafeteria philosophy emphasize the value of diversification. Their argument partakes of both law and economics. On the legal side, they point out that the law requires fiduciaries to be prudent, and diversification is a time-honored way to exhibit prudence. Thus, they conclude, the more diversification, the better job they are doing of meeting their legal obligations. Their economic point is that by employing a wide range of styles that are adapted to different market conditions, a fund will be positioned to take advantage of whatever moves the market makes.

Proponents of consistency vigorously dispute both of these contentions. They acknowledge that diversification is part of a fiduciary's obligation. But they argue that this means only that a fund should own a number of different stocks. They view the economic argument as patently silly. In their view, the cafeteria approach is a recipe for mediocrity. While they admit that a fund with multiple styles is likely to have at least one that is working at any given time, they contend that it is also almost certain to have a number that are not. In most instances, the functional and dysfunctional styles will cancel each other out, leaving the portfolio with indifferent results. An external money manager gave this blunt assessment of multistyle investing:

> It does not make any sense to me, but I know that's what they do. . . . They want to cover their asses. . . . It almost ensures mediocrity.

FIVE CASE STUDIES

To illustrate the practical implications of these fundamental decisions, we next examine in detail five of the funds that we studied. Each approached the decisions in a different way, and arrived at a different combination of outcomes. These five cases are representative of the range of decision-making styles we observed. Their diverse experiences demonstrate the relationship between the four fundamental decisions and a fund's investment behavior.

Case 1: IndustrialCo

IndustrialCo is a manufacturing company whose pension fund has assets of approximately $10 billion. The fund is managed by a staff of about 10 investment professionals assisted by traders and other support personnel. Earlier in its history, the fund developed a strong commitment both to internal management and to a consistent philosophy of buying and holding stocks in a limited number of fundamentally sound companies. The fund's executives and employees do not have a clear sense of when or how these commitments were made, but both are now seen as essential elements of the fund's identity. They also have important consequences for the fund's day-to-day operations.

The present staff is uncertain whether the commitment to inside management or to the buy-value-and-hold strategy came first. One interpretation is that the fund first made the decision to manage its assets itself and then addressed the question of how to do it. In answering that question, the decision makers were probably influenced not only by the attractiveness of the value-investing philosophy, but also by the realization that it would be difficult to implement any other philosophy with their limited internal resources. An alternative interpretation of the fund's history is that the decision makers were originally drawn to the buy-value-and-hold philosophy. They then noted that it would be possible to implement it internally and eliminate the need to deal with external managers and pay their fees. Regardless of the order in which the decisions were made, it is clear that one influenced the other. Moreover, in light of the fund's dual commitment, the choice of an active investment strategy has always been taken for granted, and indexing has never been seriously considered.

Although the people at IndustrialCo are not sure about the origins of their investment philosophy, they have no doubt that it works very well. They take great pride in their ability to manage money successfully and efficiently. The chief executive of the fund described his organization as follows:

> We've had a large amount of money for a long period of time managed entirely in-house. There have been very, very few mistakes. We've certainly not invested in a whole lot of companies that have gone belly-up. We have very high quality standards, because we have a small staff, and we don't have time to work out a problem. So we're very conscious not to get into problems in the first place. We do it very cost effectively, and that's with the small staff that we have, 15 people plus secretaries. And about $10 billion under management. That's a very, very cost efficient way of doing things.

The fund's structure and philosophy have a significant impact on the daily lives of its employees. For example, the fund's equity professionals must function as both asset managers and investment analysts. Because the fund invests in a relatively small number of stocks and has low portfolio turnover, each equity professional can focus on a few areas of specialization such as pharmaceuticals, transportation, or entertainment. He watches the stocks that the fund owns in his areas and reports on their performance to his colleagues. In addition, he investigates other stocks to determine whether one or another of them might be a better investment.

Specialization produces expertise, but in time it can also cause stagnation. The chief executive of the fund recognizes this and encourages the equity specialists to trade areas of responsibility from time to time. An added benefit of this policy is that each of the specialists has some residual knowledge of areas in which he is not currently working and can therefore offer informed advice and criticism to his colleagues. The chief executive described the objectives of the policy as follows:

> If someone is just dying to do chemical stocks and no one else is, we try to benefit from that enthusiasm. We'll also try to take into account any expertise. If we hire a new person who has expertise in an industry, it's more natural to assign it to him. On the other hand, we try to avoid having people get stale and bored, which can happen if they cover something too long. So, occasionally we'll change them just to stay fresh.

The policy is apparently successful. The chief executive's statement of goals is echoed in an equity specialist's description of the benefits as he perceives them:

> I have the beverage and tobacco industry, Coke, Pepsi, and Philip Morris, and I have the movie and entertainment industry. Our only investment there, right now, is Disney. About every year or two, there is a change here of some sort or another. Somebody leaves, somebody quits, somebody retires, we hire somebody new, and that always shuffles the deck of cards a little bit. And I've always tried to change one industry at least every two years, if not more, just to stay fresh.

The intimate atmosphere and the buy-value-and-hold investment philosophy lead individual equity specialists to focus intensely on the question of how strongly they believe in a prospective investment. According to one, the ultimate test is whether he is willing to put his beliefs on the line in front of an audience of astute colleagues who will judge him according to the success of his picks:

For me personally, before I'll buy a name, the mental screen is: Am I willing to stick my neck out with this company and this management for at least the next five years? And, if I'm not willing to do that, then I tend to stay away from it. . . . I wouldn't want to have to turn around two years later and recommend that we sell it because things are not going at all like we had hoped. So, it's a pretty tough screen.

The research that leads to a recommendation to buy a new company tends to be lengthy, careful, and methodical. Another equity specialist described it in great detail:

I will hear an idea and it will flicker my interest for it, but it will have to grow on me. I have to get very comfortable with it before I can really go in and say, "Now this is a good investment for the fund." And a lot of the ideas that I'm currently recommending are things which I've sat with for maybe five or six months, and I've listened to other people talk about them. I've done my own thinking about them. I've met with management in person during that period to get a much better feel for what they are doing and try to improve my knowledge base. So, it's not really like some of the funds that you've probably encountered, where they're very trading-oriented and where you go to a lunch downtown with a company appearing, and you come back and say, "I like this company. I think it's cheap. Let's buy it, and put some in this afternoon." We don't operate quite that way. I will say, however, once we do own a name or we know a name, even though we don't own it, if an opportunity presents itself, in terms of the stock market inefficiency, and the stock we like sells off 15 percent for no terribly important reason, or one that we certainly can't figure out, it's very easy for us in our kind of operation here, to go in and say, "I like the stock. I've done my homework on it. We already own some, but we don't own it as much as we would like. I think we should add to it, and take advantage of this drop." So, initial deals, I find that at least personally, take time to really nurture, but once the work is done, there is a lot that can be done with that knowledge base.

Perhaps the most significant consequence of the fund's structure and philosophy is a consensual, collegial approach to decision making. Because the buy-value-and-hold philosophy requires relatively few buy or sell decisions, there is time to consult and share information. And because there are only a few employees and they know each other's work well, there is a willingness to do so. The net result is that decisions are ratified informally. The regular, formal meetings that are at the core of the decision-making process in most other funds are viewed as a curiosity. According to the chief executive, even the minimal concession to the formality of monthly staff meetings has been tried only in the recent past as "something of an experiment."

Case 2: MediaCorp

MediaCorp, a media company, established a defined benefit pension fund only in the 1970s. The fund currently has assets of less than a billion dollars, making it the smallest fund we studied. It has delegated the management of its equity assets to two external managers. These managers have been in place since the fund was set up in its present form. (There was originally a third manager, but he was terminated a couple of years ago for reasons explained below.) A high-ranking executive of the sponsoring corporation manages the fund's relations with the external managers. He works alone with only clerical support and reports to the sponsor's board of directors.

As at IndustrialCo, the MediaCorp fund made a fundamental commitment that has determined how it manages its equity assets. Here, however, the commitment was to individual money managers rather than to a particular investment philosophy. The fund puts all of its equities in the hands of two well-known, highly successful managers who have a long record of producing better-than-average returns. The two managers were recommended by influential members of the board of the sponsoring corporation who were personally acquainted with them. The managers are individuals whose style and outlook match the corporation's self-image—energetic, quietly aggressive, anxious to be ahead of the competition, and willing to take a few risks to get there, but at the same time maintaining a reputation for reliability and solid profitability.

MediaCorp's essentially personal decision to hire these particular managers determined the outcome of the other structural choices. Apparently, the fund and sponsoring corporation never considered the possibility of inside management, probably because they believed the fund was too small. In addition, the initial decision to hire these managers mooted the active-passive question.

MediaCorp's outside managers pursue a value-investing strategy, so their hiring committed the fund to a consistent investment philosophy. This commitment was not accidental, of course, since the managers' philosophy is part of their appeal to the corporation's executives and board members. In fact, the fund terminated the third original manager a couple of years ago when he abandoned his philosophy and made a drastic shift to market timing. However, the fund seems never to have made any comparative analysis of various philosophies. Rather, the people who set up the fund gravitated toward these particular value investors as self-evident and indisputable choices. It may be significant that the fund's chief (and only) executive described one of his managers simply as "a good guy."

When the fund hired these managers, it did so with the intention of establishing long-term relationships. At least in part because of the strength of these relationships, the managers are not subjected to the kind of formal, short-term monitoring and review that goes on at many other funds. The managers see this as an expression of confidence that gives them discretion to do what is necessary to succeed in the long run. The result of this working relationship is a strong bond, both personal and professional, between the managers and the principals of the fund and the sponsoring corporation. One of the managers reflected on this relationship:

> MediaCorp, when they gave us money, the CEO of the pension fund told us that we could expect to be with him for 10 years. He said, "Probably the most we'll do is want to see you once a year, maybe for lunch, just to see how things are coming along." And I think that we had lunch the second year. We haven't had lunch on the subject since. That has given me my feeling that I can invest for the long term and not worry about whether I might underperform in particular years.

MediaCorp's confidence and patience should not be mistaken for inattention, however. It might surprise the outside managers to learn that the chief executive of the fund examines every trade ticket. His objective is not to second-guess buy-sell decisions, but to make sure that the managers are still doing business in the same way—that they are still the same people he hired. When the third manager was fired, it was because the trading tickets revealed a Jekyll/Hyde metamorphosis from value investor to high-turnover market timer.

Because MediaCorp's management team is small and its philosophy consistent, its decision-making processes are simple and direct. The fund's head is in constant informal contact with the corporate board, and even a decision as dramatic as firing one of only three external managers can be made without recourse to cumbersome committees. Once the head of the fund determined after months of study that a change was in order, his recommendation was ratified almost immediately. As he explained:

> We're small. You have to realize we're very small. There are really only three, four, or five people who are involved in a decision like this. It's very easy to say, "I see a change here, and we ought to think about changing." We're in touch and we talk to each other.

As at IndustrialCo, MediaCorp's investment approach is now a deeply ingrained part of its corporate culture. Those who are responsible for carrying out the strategy are thoroughly convinced that it has served them well and see no reason to think about alternatives. Indeed, this very certainty has become one of the fund's defining characteristics:

> We have a philosophy, we've stayed with the philosophy, it's been successful, and we want to continue to stay with the philosophy.

Case 3: ChemCo

ChemCo, another manufacturing company, has a pension fund with assets in excess of $5 billion. The fund is run by three employees of the financial department of the sponsoring corporation. The chief executive of the pension fund reports to the corporate board, which makes or approves all major fund decisions. This individual is assisted by two other people to whom he has delegated specific areas of responsibility. One supervises the fixed-income and equity portions of the fund's portfolio, and the other is responsible for international investments, real estate, and venture capital. The fund has hired 20 external investment firms whose diverse styles attempt to capture the benefits of different investment strategies. Managing the outside managers and reporting on their activities to the corporate board occupies much of the time of the fund's three executives.

The structure of ChemCo's fund is largely determined by its commitment to a cafeteria investment philosophy. The fund's initial attraction to the cafeteria approach seems to have preempted any consideration of the comparative benefits of active and passive management. The inside-outside choice is also a moot point, because this fund sees itself as lacking the resources and expertise to pursue diverse strategies internally.

In explaining the kinds of managers he has hired, the chief executive of the fund gave some idea of how complicated the cafeteria approach can be:

> There's the growth type manager versus the value type manager. There's the large cap type manager and there's the small cap type manager. And you can pick the pockets of all those. You can get guys who may want to concentrate in sectors, such as the technology guys. Technology guys are going to act very much like growth stock managers, because the technology area has been a growth type area. They're not exactly the same. And one manager can come in and say that I'm a value tech guy. And he can give you statistics to make a case for that. Now, whether that sector will do any good, who knows? Then there are the sector rotators. The guys that don't profess to be an expert or to concentrate all the time in one area, but they're more market timers. They'll try and anticipate where the economy is going and which sectors should benefit from that, or if they think the economy is going south, which sectors are going to be hurt the least. Even when the rest of the world is bearish, the investment community will still stay in the market because, quite frankly, nobody can call it. When you're at the bottom, and it moves up, if you're not in there, you missed most of the play. So we have all of those styles.

A consequence of this mélange of investment strategies is that it is hard to determine how well individual managers are doing. The fund's executives evaluate their external managers on two primary criteria: whether they add value to the fund and whether they continue to pursue the particular investment strategy they promised when they were hired.

Fund executives usually define adding value as beating a market benchmark over some specified period of time, say three to five years. The problem is identifying the relevant benchmark. There is general agreement that it is not fair to compare a manager with a particular style (investing in small capitalization growth stocks, for example) to the market as a whole. The rationale is that an entire class of stocks can do poorly for several years at a time. As a result, a manager who invests in that class will underperform the market, even though he has been executing his chosen style skillfully. The solution, as fund executives see it, is to measure managers primarily against other managers with the same style. ChemCo's chief pension executive explained it this way:

> Well, you evaluate them against the index long term. The short term, you evaluate them against their niche in the marketplace. The small cap stocks have not on the average beat the market for the last five years. It's not necessarily realistic to expect your manager to beat the market. You expect him to beat his peers. You want him to add value over his peers, so that he's saved enough of the assets when his day in the sun comes. Assuming that you believe that over the long term, small cap stocks will beat large cap stocks. There's a great case to be made for that. That hasn't been the case in the 80s, but it has been the case in the stock market since the major crash of the 1929–30 era. But it's in spurts. So you have a little bit exposed to a small cap manager and if his performance comes up to the historical statistical expectations, he'll be there and he'll capture that. And as long as he can perform as well as his peers in that area, in the aggregate, he should be able to add value over the index stock. If each of them in their specific areas adds value, even if in fact in the aggregate you have an index, we still preserve the opportunity to be better than the index.

Critics of ChemCo's diversity-for-diversity's-sake approach —including, ironically, some outside money managers who benefit from it—argue that it begs the question of whether certain styles will ever have their day in the sun. Surprisingly, ChemCo's pension chief commented that he had never had occasion to give up on any of the styles he used. In every instance, he looked beyond poor performance in the belief that its day would come eventually. The critics also point out that the multistyle approach has a "my vote cancels yours" effect. That is, in any given year the successful strategies are likely to be offset by the unsuccessful ones, with the fund's overall performance converging on mediocrity. Critics claim that in the long term it is far better to live with the ups and downs of one or two carefully selected strategies.

With respect to the second criterion, ChemCo's chief pension executive views adherence to the promised strategy as a binding obligation on the part of the managers. In some instances, consistency proves even more important than profitability. Managers whose strategies fail to produce profits for several years may be forgiven if they stick to the approach for which they were hired, whereas managers who "change their stripes" (as fund executives often put it) may be fired even if they are making money. According to the chief pension executive at ChemCo, the source of greatest concern is systematic change in a money management firm—"changing the personnel in the firm and changing investment direction, starting to do things differently than the basis on which you've hired them."

Case 4: ProductCo

ProductCo has the most complex structure of any of the funds we studied. Its sponsor is a large manufacturing company, and it has assets well in excess of $10 billion. The management of the fund is characterized by constant, often frenetic activity. The most critical investment decision in its recent history was one that it made about 10 years ago to take a much more active approach to equity investment. Until then, its portfolio had featured indexing and value investing. At that point, indexing was rejected because, in the words of the current chief executive, "it doesn't make any sense in thinking that you couldn't do any better than the market as a whole." The buy-value-and-hold philosophy was discarded as "50 years behind the times." The present approach is to implement almost every conceivable strategy to some extent.

A single fundamental decision underlies this complex structure. In arriving at its present structure, ProductCo focused almost exclusively on the choice between active and passive strategies. Its executives not only decided on an active approach, but committed themselves to it with near-fanaticism. As in a child's candy-store fantasy, the next step was to lay every possible active option on the table and take some of each. Once they made the commitment to activity, their answer to every other question became yes.

An excerpt from the chief executive's description of the portion of the portfolio that is managed externally conveys a sense of just how complex ProductCo's approach is:

> In equities we've got U.S. large capitalization equities, and we use a benchmark of the Wilshire 1000. Then we've got small stocks, which is the Wilshire 2000, which is the 3000 minus the 1000 biggest. And then, we've got international equities that are separate categories. There are some subclasses within there. We've broken it down within U.S. large cap equities, we break that down into different manager styles. We've got maybe 15 equity managers, and we've got some growth stock managers, and some defensive managers, some stock rotators, and so on. So, within small stocks we've got probably several different approaches to small stocks. We use some passive approaches, index bonds, and some other actively managed approaches. In international investments, we've got some specialty managers like one that focuses on Canadian securities, and one that focuses on Far East, Japan mainly, and some others. And then we've got several that can move their funds any place outside the U.S. And we've got one that has sort of a global charge; they could move the funds in equities any place in U.S. or foreign securities.

Aside from a general preference for investing in large companies, the approach taken by ProductCo's internal managers is also highly variable, adding further complexity to the overall picture. Moreover, there is little time for the sort of exhaustive research typical of IndustrialCo:

> The style of the group of people that we have managing equities on our own staff is pretty much to buy large stocks. They tend to rotate between different market sectors depending upon which industries they think are going to be favored in the next six months.

So they don't have that much attachment to the individual companies. They will decide, "Well, it looks like the next six months it's good for oil companies," and they will buy some oil company stocks. They will be unlikely to get into any close dialogue with those companies. We do not do internal research. We rely upon previous research to help us.

To an even greater degree than at ChemCo, it is difficult to evaluate how well so complex a strategy is working. As Product-Co's chief executive explained, the fund cannot hold all of its managers to the same standard, but must compare each to the performance of the particular market sector in which he operates. The overall efficacy of the strategy remains in doubt:

> As time has passed we've changed our method of dealing with the managers we chose and called it the normal portfolio approach so that they don't all have the same benchmark. Each one has a customized benchmark, so a growth stock manager is running against a growth stock index that is approximate to his normal investment style, rather than the market as a whole. And, we're still operating on the following basis: By taking all of the domestic equities and placing them with a number of managers of different investment styles that we carefully select, we will produce a result over a market cycle or a period of time that will exceed the S&P 500 index fund by more than enough to pay the extra fees—to make up for the extra risk that you have in such an approach. Now, as I say, the case is not an overwhelming one, but we're still working on it.

Carrying out this strategy requires a very large staff. Its members tend to be highly specialized, and narrowly focused on their specific assignments. In addition to the previously noted lack of time for research, there is little time or incentive for learning about what other people do.

Decision making is extremely formal, and there are multiple layers of supervision. There is a network of committees with overlapping membership, and some decisions must be approved by several individuals and/or committees. In response to a question about how much discretionary authority he has, one of the in-house money managers said:

> Well, I don't have any. No, I should take that back. I have discretion to say no. To say yes requires that we go through the commit-

tees. Up to $10 million gets approved by one level, between 10 and 50 by another level.

He went on to describe what it is like to work in such a system:

> I'm finding that it uses a tremendous amount of my time. It is working well, but it's a drag on my available workload because it is long and needless.

The impression clearly conveyed is that the enormous demands of the administrative system distract people from the more substantive tasks of research, contemplation, and talking with colleagues about investments.

A further point to be made about ProductCo concerns the nature of organizational change. Change does not take place in a vacuum. When a pension fund changes its approach to investing, it does not obliterate its past. At ProductCo, notwithstanding the sweeping changes made in the last 10 years, there are still people in important positions who worked under the former system, and who may have varying degrees of comfort with the new one. The chief executive pointed out that some aspects of the current decision-making structure were put in place specifically to improve the comfort level of such people. These compromises had little to do with the logic of investing. Their legacy is a formidable set of political hurdles to be overcome if ProductCo should decide to change its investment approach again.

Case 5: State A

State A is a large governmental pension fund, with assets in excess of $10 billion. The executive staff of the fund consists of only a half dozen or so people, all of whom are compensated on a civil service scale. Most of them have worked in government through their entire careers; one or two worked in private sector jobs before coming to work for the state government.

State A differs from the other four funds we have discussed, as well as from most private funds, in that the majority of its equity investments are indexed. It puts about 80 percent of its equity assets into a self-managed index that its employees describe as a "South Africa-free S&P 500." Because state law forbids investment in companies that do business in South Africa, State A must delete certain S&P companies from its index and substitute others. The use of the S&P 500 as the benchmark for the index means that the total equity portfolio is heavily weighted toward very large companies. Primarily because of concern about putting too many eggs in the large-company basket, the remaining 20 percent of the equity portfolio is distributed among several outside managers with diverse strategies.

The choice of a passive strategy determined State A's structure. About five years ago the fund decided, based on prior experience, to avoid outside managers to the maximum extent possible. On a practical level, because staff and salary limitations precluded active internal management, avoiding outside managers meant a consistent, passive index approach. Thus, the single decision to avoid outside managers immediately determined both the active-passive and consistent-cafeteria choices.

In explaining their decision to index, executives at State A talk not so much about the virtues of indexing as about the comparative advantages of being rid of external managers. They emphasize the difficulties of selecting them, supervising them, and firing them. One of State A's pension executives described the transition to indexing in these terms:

> It's made it more mechanical, and it certainly has made it easier. The process of hiring managers is, at least particularly on the public side, not easy, because you've got to go through a bid process or evaluation process. So you go through this enormous pain to make sure that everybody that should have been looked at had a chance to be looked at. And then you whittle them all down, you've got to interview them, then you've got to pick them, then you've got to negotiate the fee, negotiate the contract, then you've got to monitor his performance. If he doesn't do well you've got to bring him in and ask him why he's not doing well, and if he doesn't do well for a long period of time then you can fire him, then when you fire him he's got $300 million worth of assets, and then what do you do with the $300 million worth of assets? So for a whole lot of reasons, we don't like managers.

Additionally, indexing eliminates many difficult investment decisions. Buy and sell decisions are required only when companies move onto or off the S&P 500, or when an S&P company enters or exits South Africa. These kinds of decisions can be made by computer programs. The primary human work, and the primary human responsibility, is to oversee the efficient working of the process. The same executive continued:

> You run the computer, and it says to put $200 million in, you need to buy these names. So my staff will sit down, and they'll buy those names. You can put $200 million into the market in days, rather than going through all the work I've just described to pick somebody who may be performing well, and maybe not.

The most succinct statement of the attractions of indexing came from State A's chief pension executive:

> I've always had my huge suspicions about Wall Street. The fact that most of my friends are there hasn't changed my version of what they really do. Somebody said, "Here's an idea: You don't give your money to money managers, they don't perform too well anyway. Just get a computer and match the market with it." Socko! It was the easiest decision that I've ever made. Easy.

IMPOSING DISCIPLINE ON THE FUNDAMENTAL DECISIONS

We found it surprising and sometimes disturbing that pension funds take such an unsystematic approach to the decisions they have to make in structuring their equity portfolios. Little effort is made to analyze the implications of each decision, maximize freedom of choice, and avoid redundant effort. As we will see in the next chapter, even the crucial selection of an investment philosophy is sometimes not a matter of careful choice. We have studied some funds that adopt a cafeteria philosophy because of a general belief that this is what pension funds ought to do, and others that take a consistent approach because they happened upon a certain strategy and it seemed to work. The point is not that these answers are wrong in individual cases, but rather that the question is one that deserves to be asked and answered in an analytical and deliberative way.

Our larger point relates to the concept of *discipline*, a word currently in vogue in the investment world. Pension fund executives talk constantly about the discipline that results from having committees reassess asset allocation decisions, or from evaluating outside managers against relevant benchmarks. Yet there seems to be little discipline imposed on the most basic undertaking of all: shaping the entity that will be responsible for the money. It seems not to have occurred to the people who run pension funds that they lack discipline in this area, or that it could benefit them as much as they believe it does in other, less consequential areas. Reasonable minds might differ on what form this discipline should take, but it seems beyond dispute that some form of conscious, disciplined analysis is in order.

ADDENDUM: THE OTHER FOUR CASES

The five funds discussed thus far reflect the range of variation in the basic investment options available to large pension funds. The other funds that we studied will be analyzed in detail in subsequent chapters. Here is a preliminary sketch of each of them.

State B

State B is a large public employees' retirement fund. Its assets exceed $10 billion. It manages its equities in-house and does not index. Like IndustrialCo, it does so with a small staff. It favors long-term value investing, but makes some use of other strategies as well.

State C

State C is another large public employees' fund, with assets in excess of $10 billion. It indexes a majority of its equities. It also places a portion of its equity portfolio with outside managers who pursue a variety of strategies.

TransCo

TransCo is a large transportation company. TransCo sponsors both a defined-benefit and a defined-contribution pension plan. The assets of the total fund exceed $1 billion. The company has established a separate corporation to run the pension fund. The fund places all its equity assets with outside managers who execute a variety of strategies.

MaterialCo

MaterialCo is a producer and processor of raw materials. The assets of its pension fund exceed $1 billion. The fund is under the direction of the sponsor's chief financial officer. Like many other funds, it delegates the management of its equities to a diverse group of outside managers.

NOTES

1. The funds we studied typically paid annual fees of 25–40 *basis points* for the services of outside managers. A basis point is .01 percent of the portfolio that the manager handles. Thus, at the 40-basis point rate, a fund will pay an annual fee of $4 million for each billion dollars it places with external managers.
2. One of the fund CEOs we interviewed used the term *cafeteria approach*. We found it apt and have adopted it.
3. The percentage in equities drops when the sample is expanded to include smaller funds as well.
4. With the decline of the junk bond market following the stock market crash of October 1989, pension funds have shown less interest in leveraged buyouts. Junk bonds have shown recent signs of renewed popularity and this may portend a shift in pension fund attitudes.
5. There is another view which holds that equity investments have performed well in the long term only for those who have gotten in and out of the stock market at the right times. See Louis Lowenstein, *Sense and Nonsense in Corporate Finance* (Reading, Mass.: Addison-Wesley Publishing, 1991), chap. 11. An additional criticism of indexing is that when a stock joins the S&P 500, the flood of

indexers who now need to buy it drives the price to an artificially high level. Thus, the indexers who buy it later rather than sooner pay too much. The same process operates in reverse when a company drops off the index. Accordingly, some indexers may end up buying high and selling low.

6. A few public funds evade these restrictions by hiring investment experts as independent contractors or consultants rather than employees.

CHAPTER 4

WHAT DRIVES INSTITUTIONAL INVESTMENT DECISIONS?— CULTURAL FACTORS IN THE ECONOMIC WORLD

When making carefully considered, on-the-record remarks, pension fund insiders portray their industry as a disciplined, unsentimental, bottom-line–oriented enterprise. When speaking anonymously and off-the-cuff, however, they convey a very different impression. In accounting for the structures they have created and the strategies they carry out, they give economics and finance second billing at best. Indeed, they freely admit that some of the things they do may be economically counterproductive. In telling their funds' stories, they emphasize instead such cultural factors as the quirks of history, the displacement of responsibility, and the nurturing of personal relationships.

As anthropologists, we believe this discrepancy between the official and unofficial accounts of fund management to be highly significant. Because the contents of unrehearsed and unconstrained narratives reflect the thinking of the speaker, we conclude that people told us about the cultural influences on their behavior because they believe these influences are real and important. On reflection, pension fund executives can usually (but not always) produce an economic explanation for their structures and strategies, and can sometimes demonstrate that they produce financially sound results. However, this does not alter the fact that the best available evidence—the executives' unpremeditated accounts—suggests that many of these structures and strategies owe their origin and maintenance to everyday kinds of concerns.

ASKING QUESTIONS

In order to evaluate our claim about the importance of cultural factors in the investment world, it is necessary to have a more specific understanding of how we carried out the research. In every interview that we conducted, the central questions dealt with how the organization invested money, why it did the things that it did, and how each individual fit into the organization. Our objective was to construct the metaphorical mind of the institution from the remarks of those who give it life.

The questions we asked should not have predisposed our interview subjects toward any particular answers. Our questions about fund structures and strategies could have been answered equally well in economic or noneconomic terms. For this reason, we attach great significance to the fact that almost all *chose* to answer in cultural rather than economic terms.

The simplest way to prove the point is to quote some of our questions verbatim. At IndustrialCo, for example, we began our interview with the fund's chief pension executive with such questions as "How did you arrive at that particular structure [for the pension fund]?"; "How did you come into this position?"; and "Describe for us a little bit about these strategies of managing money." Interviews with other employees typically began with, "Tell us a little bit about what you do here and where you fit into the structure." At ChemCo, as the chief pension executive described his fund's multimanager, multistyle system, we asked such questions as "What's the rationale for diversifying?"; "How do you evaluate managers?"; "When you say long term and short term, what do those terms mean?" And at ProductCo, our very first question to the chief pension executive was "Could you start by telling us, just generally, how the decision-making process is structured in this organization?"

These kinds of questions elicited lengthy narratives about such cultural issues as history, politics, and relationships, but little talk about economics or finance. Because the questions were as neutral as interview questions can ever be, we are strongly convinced that people raised the particular issues they did because these issues were foremost in their minds, not because we suggested them.

FINDING THE VOICE OF THE ORGANIZATION

An initial problem we encountered in many funds was simply finding someone to speak for the organization. This is not to say that the funds do not have official voices; all of them have chief executives and other designated spokespersons, of course.[1] These people rarely spoke authoritatively about matters beyond their own personal experience, however. Thus, we found few organizational perspectives, even in the statements of those whose positions suggested they should have been able to provide them. (Contrast an institution like a university. Despite the diversity among faculty and students, it can readily provide an official version of its position on such fundamental matters as academic requirements for graduation, majors, course offerings, and student life.) Instead, we had to piece together the highly personal and sometimes conflicting stories told by individuals.

The difficulty is that individuals' perspectives on institutional structures and strategies are constrained by the time horizons of their own careers. Individuals speak of the time before their own arrival in vague and general terms. It has the quality of folklore: They are aware of past events of symbolic significance and people of heroic proportions who preceded them, but the details of who, what, when, and where have been lost. By contrast, they remember in great detail events that they have participated in or witnessed. However, their perspective is not the bird's-eye view of the historian, management consultant, or financial adviser, but rather the fragmented view of those who are too busy living through an event to stop and analyze it.

Like other anthropologists, we consider the ways in which people describe phenomena to be reflections of the ways that they think about them. The fact that fund executives and employees rarely rise above their own personal perspectives to articulate a corporate vision suggests that one does not exist. This apparent lack of institutional coherence among such important players in the American economy is in itself a surprising and disturbing finding.

CORPORATE CREATION MYTHS

As we listened to the stories that pension fund executives told to account for their investment behavior, we were reminded of the creation myths that members of traditional societies recount to explain their origin and current state of affairs. Some of the most famous creation stories were committed to writing in the ancient world: for example, the Book of Genesis, the story of Zeus and the Titans, and the tale of Romulus and Remus founding Rome. In addition, anthropologists studying oral traditions have taken down comparable stories from more than 800 societies around the world.

Creation myths have several characteristics that are relevant here. First, they are myths. This does not necessarily mean they are not true (the archaeologist Schliemann found Homer's Troy right where it was supposed to be). It simply means that the events described in the myths are not the subject of precise historical reports, either because they occurred in the distant past or because those who have told and retold the story have distorted or embellished it to make a symbolic point.

A second characteristic of creation myths is that their truth is self-evident to those who hold them. A society's creation myth will be deeply ingrained in its members, and not open to question or analysis. A third and related characteristic is that the adherents of a particular myth find it difficult to consider alternatives. When truth is self-evident, looking for alternatives is a waste of time.

One famous creation myth (it seems to be especially popular among big-bang physicists, who have creation myth problems of their own) posits that the world sits on the back of a giant turtle. The turtle's peregrinations account for the rising and setting of the sun, the motion of the stars and planets, and, more subtly, for the vagaries of human history. When an anthropologist asked a member of the culture what was underneath the turtle, he replied with evident irritation, "Why, more turtles, of course!" The anthropologist had obviously asked a stupid question.

As we will see, the stories that pension fund executives tell to account for how they do business have all three of these characteristics. The details have often been forgotten or recast for symbolic purposes, giving the stories a mythic, folkloric quality. In addition, we were repeatedly struck by the lack of interest in questioning or analyzing the structures and strategies that had evolved. Comments about things being "instinctive" or "just part of the corporate culture" were common. And there was surprisingly little interest in considering alternatives. When we inquired about alternatives, more often than not the answer was the moral equivalent of "more turtles, of course."

Private Fund Myths

The creation myths we heard at private funds tended to be centered around important individuals and to convey the tellers' sense of the corporation's culture and personality. At IndustrialCo, for example, the pension fund is actually an independent corporation chartered and headquartered in a different state than the sponsoring company.[2] As we described in Chapter 3, the fund pursues a buy-value-and-hold strategy in which individuals assume clear-cut personal responsibility for buy and sell decisions. When asked to account for the fund's present structure, the chief executive told a story that goes back to the 19th-century robber baron era. He emphasized the personal role of the company's founder and the fact that the original logic of the fund's corporate structure has been lost in history.

> The company's founder established a pension fund for loyal employees. Early this century, he donated some bonds and said that the income would be used to provide pensions for loyal employees and widows and orphans. Well, it was totally at his discretion who got a pension—those he thought were worthy of pensions. Obviously this was one of the earliest pension funds. And it just sort of struggled along. At some point, it was incorporated into the current pension fund. . . . It was a pension fund for deserving retirees, widows of retirees, and disabled workers,

people who were disabled on the job. They actually had some rules. I mean, they just sort of made them up, but it was done nevertheless. You know anything like that was basically a charitable endeavor, and obligations were limited to the corpus of the fund. It's kind of hard to get a history on this, but at some point we set up a separate not-for-profit corporation to act as trustee of this early pension fund. And we kept it intact because frankly it was a very practical structure and suited the needs for a long time.

So the separate corporation structure goes back to the founder's day?
I think it does. I am pretty sure it goes back that far. I think that's the origin. Again, I can't pin that down definitively, but that's to my best knowledge. Actually, I don't have a document. But anyway, it was kept that way for a long time. In the late 1940s, the union workers won pensions as part of a bargaining contract close on the heels of some other unions, who won the first big contract. The separate not-for-profit structure survived all that, and we still use it. I think the main reason other people wouldn't do it is that it just sounds a little eccentric and kind of oddball.

He returned to the creation story a bit later in the interview, volunteering a comment about its mythic rather than historic quality:

Again, we're so many generations removed from the founding that there's not even really an oral history of it. The guys who would know that story have been dead for 20 or 30 years.

The present-day employees of the fund see a causal relationship between the physical separation of fund and sponsor and the way that the fund does business. In their view, the physical separation has led to a feeling of independence. They need not waste time catering to the demands of a corporate bureaucracy or giving an appearance of frenzied activity, as they might have to do if they were on the company premises. In this environment, their highly personal decision-making style and successful strategy of patient value investing have flourished. They are aware, however, that the environment in which they work and the strategy they pursue are the product of evolution rather than planning. As one of them said, "This point is so instinctive, it's so much a part of the corporate culture here I don't really know how it evolved."

Other pension fund insiders routinely cite IndustrialCo as a rare example of a fund that does things right. It serves its sponsor and its beneficiaries well by earning a good rate of return with a minimum of administrative expense. They also believe that it serves the nation's economy well by providing patient investment capital and taking a long-term perspective on the companies in which it invests. Thus, the ironic reality is that an eccentric and oddball structure that originated in a long-forgotten historical accident produces results that are envied throughout the pension world.

At ProductCo, officials told a different kind of story in explaining how and why their fund had developed its one-of-everything, frantically active investment approach. Rather than obscure history, their story features strong personalities and corporate politics in the more recent past. Despite these differences in detail, it resembles the IndustrialCo story in that cultural influences predominate over economic ones.

The story began some years ago, when the chief executive of the pension fund received a mandate for change from the CEO of the sponsoring corporation:

> Basically, he had given me a charge to turn the pension fund around, because it had not been producing good results. Its results had been horrible in comparison with the results of other major pension funds. He told me to find out what other companies did to produce better results and to try to make the changes that were necessary.

The head of the fund agreed that change was in order:

> Frankly, I was not too pleased with the way that the fund was going. It was, I felt, following some procedures and approaches that were 50 years behind the times.

Specifically, the out-of-date strategy was "basically to pick out good companies, buy the stocks, and then hold them." The thrust of the CEO's directive was to emulate a number of other "more up-to-date funds." Ironically, the pension executive's list of examples of up-to-date funds prominently included IndustrialCo, even though its strategy has always been the same buy-value-and-hold approach that he characterized as 50 years out of date.

From these founding premises, the fund moved quickly toward a more active and highly diversified strategy. A critical early decision was to try to manage a significant portion of the equity portfolio in-house. This decision was based less on a firm conviction that in-house management would yield better results than on the belief that it would be a learning experience for the fund, putting its people in a better position to evaluate outside managers in the future. Fortuitously, a particularly able private money manager was looking for a job because his employer had just been acquired by an insurance company—not a promising marriage, in the manager's view. Despite some opposition from influential members of the sponsoring company's board, the head of the pension fund hired him, and he immediately put together an in-house equity investment team.

Within a year, things were "off on a good footing." The team was functioning smoothly, and the early results were favorable. Then, unexpectedly, the equity manager announced his intention to move into semiretirement and spend only a few days a week in the office. He proposed a plan that would keep the equity team intact and functioning as before. The head of the fund was persuaded that it was workable and, from a financial perspective, clearly preferable to any of the alternatives:

> Since his approach had worked pretty well I hated to change it. You see, we didn't have anybody else that was clearly lined up to jump into his shoes.

The CEO of the sponsoring company intervened, however, and overruled him. The CEO decided that it was contrary to the corporate culture and "a bad principle" to have "an important job like this handled by a part-timer," and the manager was forced out. Another outsider had to be brought in, and again fortuity played a role:

> We just sort of lucked into it. There was an individual who had been out of work for nearly a year, having been ousted from the post of running the investment management operation at a large

insurance company a year earlier, for reasons that were mystifying to many people in the business. So we happened to learn about that just at this point in time and persuaded him to come here. That's how we solved that problem.

Despite the qualifications of the new manager, the unexpected transition was not without costs. The group hired by the original manager "was sort of turned off by this imposed decision to have him eliminated." The result was "a loss of the compatibility . . . of a working together nature of the thing." This intangible sense of loss had financial ramifications as well. The head of the fund observed a short-term decline in equity performance. Today, more than five years after the controversial events, performance remains equivocal.

Like IndustrialCo, ProductCo illustrates the significance, indeed the predominance, of cultural factors in the disposition of the trillions of dollars entrusted to pension funds. At IndustrialCo the controlling factors were historical; at ProductCo, personal and political. At IndustrialCo, the creation story has had a happy ending; at ProductCo, the outcome remains in doubt. What the two cases have in common is that neither management structure was established according to a rationally designed and rigorously tested economic blueprint.

Public Fund Myths

We heard creation myths in public funds as well. These also involved history and politics, but the history featured corruption and scandal and the politics was of the external sort. Once again, financial analysis was not a primary determinant of structures and strategies.

At State B, fiduciary responsibility for the fund rests with a board of trustees which includes both labor and public representatives. Some are political appointees and others are elected by employee constituencies. Historically, most have had professional investment expertise and have served multiple terms, which provides continuity. The board enacts regulations that deal with general policy matters and can hire and fire the chief executive. All other investment matters are delegated to the chief executive.

The current chief executive at State B has substantial Wall Street experience. He is assisted by a professional staff of about a half dozen and a very lean support staff. In its investment style, State B resembles a public version of IndustrialCo. State B manages its equity portfolio internally, with members of the small staff taking individual responsibility for buy-sell recommendations. Although authority ultimately rests with the chief executive, most decisions are made collegially. The general orientation is toward value investing, but the commitment is not as strong as at IndustrialCo.

According to the present chief executive, the roots of the organization lie in political scandal:

> Let me start with when the fund was formed and why it was formed, and what the peculiar circumstances of the interplay of the various parties were at the time, because their influence persists to this day. The fund was formed in the 1950s. It was formed as a result of a scandal that took place in the late 1940s. The nature of that scandal was that you had politically appointed people in the auditor's office, who did what politically appointed people do—they sold constituent service, basically, and friends of theirs would begin to do a little bit more business for the fund. There was no professional internal expertise; there was only a rudimentary oversight type of a function. That is to say, some people were supposed to get together on every second Tuesday and do something. But of course they didn't, because like all committee meetings, unless there is some formal structure to them, people have a tendency to drift away from them. There was no formal accountability mechanism. At that time, there were more than a dozen funds and several hundred million dollars. And at one of the funds in particular, one of the treasurers did a lot of business with a particular broker. And it was a very easy thing to do. I'm not suggesting that this was a venal form of a scandal so much as it was just falling into what are normal political practices.

The legislature responded to these practices with a package of laws designed to bring the pension investments under professional control. The chief executive described these reforms:

> I would say that the laws that were passed then wouldn't be passed now, for a whole lot of reasons dealing with the interplay between executives and legislature, not to mention the complexity and the

potential now for broader political involvement and the desire to have that take place. So in those days, there was a special committee formed. They were distinguished citizens in the state and they came out with some suggestions, one of which was to centralize all of the state's investments under professional management, and to provide for an accountability structure. That basically was it.

Once again, the story has many of the important qualities of a creation myth. It takes place at a time in the past—"in those days"—when things were very different from the way they are now. It involves people and their behavior—"the circumstances of the interplay of the various parties"—rather than abstractions like risk and rates of return. In fact, the system is an almost incidental result of this interplay among governors, legislators, brokers, and the like. As the chief executive characterized it later in the interview, "what was done was very interesting, because, whether consciously or unconsciously, I don't know, but a very interesting system was created."

As in the other cases we have studied, rigorous economic analysis is conspicuous by its absence. Throughout the chief executive's entire account of the fund's structure (more than a half hour of talk), he mentioned financial criteria only once—a parenthetical remark about the stupidity of the tax-exempt pension fund continuing to hold tax-free municipal bonds. As at IndustrialCo, the employees of State B are convinced that the system works. But in both instances, the system is the product of evolutionary pressures that have little to do with its present adaptability in the marketplace.

The point to be noted about all of these descriptions of structures and strategies is that the people who are managing a huge segment of America's capital markets, when asked to account for what they do, do not do so in the first instance on economic or financial grounds. This is not to say that they do not consider economics, but only that they choose to talk about other things first and more often. Most (but not all) executives of large pension funds are conversant with the arcane terminology of investing, and at some point in nearly every interview we were given a technical, financial explanation of structures and strategies. These explanations had the quality of after-the-fact rationalization, however. In almost every interview, the speaker gave primary emphasis to the historical quirks and the details of local politics that are the stuff of everyday life in less consequential institutions.[3]

DISPLACING RESPONSIBILITY

In every interview we conducted, fund executives talked at length about assuming, assigning, or avoiding responsibility. As we listened to them, it often seemed as if the funds had been designed for the purpose of shifting responsibility for decision making away from identifiable individuals. They described four specific mechanisms for displacing responsibility and avoiding blame: burying decisions in the bureaucracy, blaming someone else, blaming the market, or claiming that their hands were tied by the law.

Burying Decisions in the Bureaucracy

Complex bureaucracies are typical of funds that have high rates of turnover in their equity portfolios. Obviously, a fund with a high level of trading activity requires more people to run it than a fund where few decisions are made. Perhaps not coincidentally, however, the involvement of a large number of people helps mask which ones make particular decisions. Based on what we have seen and had described to us, there seems to be a roughly inverse relationship between the level of trading activity and the ability to identify the individuals responsible for investment decisions. As the number of investment decisions (and, consequently, the likelihood of error) increases, so too does the complexity and resulting impenetrability of the decision-making structure.

At ProductCo, which manages much of its large stock portfolio internally, a complex committee structure oversees a range of investment strategies. The equity turnover rate in this fund is the highest of the nine funds we studied. The fund also invests small percentages of its portfolio (but significant dollar amounts, given the size of the fund) in such decision-intensive areas as real estate, mergers and acquisitions, and venture capital.[4] It took the fund's chief executive almost an hour, with the aid of many charts and spontaneous diagrams, to explain the chain of command for different kinds of investment decisions. In doing so, he repeatedly expressed his doubts about the efficacy of the structure. Just describing the decision-making process for allocating assets was a tedious exercise:

> This process which is designed to come up with the best asset mix is the key thing, but it's the process that I have a lot of doubts about. We're not sure that it works. I mean the problem with the thing, as you might have figured out, is you've got so many inputs from a dozen people plus all the outside people that they've talked to. . . . Ultimately we've got a group of five or six people on this committee who are trying to reach a resolution, and generally we don't all agree. And the question is whether this structure tends to force a compromise solution, a least-pain solution that might not be the best solution. And we have some serious reservations about it, but we don't have any instant answer to what's better to replace it.

He then meandered through the details of the rest of the fund's decision-making structure. Individual staff members are authorized to make decisions affecting relatively small dollar amounts. But the more money involved, the more people must approve, to the point where truly substantial decisions may be reviewed by multiple committees, often with interlocking memberships. The complexity is such that it would be virtually impossible for the management of the fund or its sponsor to assign credit for a major success or affix blame for a major failure. It may not be coincidental that this fund is dissatisfied with its past performance and uncertain about the success of its present strategies.

In other funds where trading activity is lower and decisions fewer, it is easier to locate those responsible for particular decisions. Such funds try to make decisions by consensus. When there is no consensus, however, a particular individual is designated to break the deadlock. The following commentary comes from an employee at State B, which manages its equity portfolio internally, but adheres to a consistent philosophy of patient value investing. Significantly, we never heard talk like this among the employees of the ProductCo fund:

> We try to make it as collegial as possible. I mean people have strong opinions on stocks. When you get down to the nitty-gritty on strong opinions about markets, we try to make our opinions known. But somebody has to make the final decision. I would say most of the time we're pretty much in agreement. At times, it can be pretty sharp disagreement; and then the CEO of the fund has got to make the call. . . . You have to have somebody who is responsible for the final decision when you have a difference in opinion.

Blaming Someone Else: Outside Managers

A second means of displacing responsibility is to hire outside managers. There are many sound business and financial reasons for doing so, of course. First, many funds lack the in-house expertise necessary to manage assets efficiently and profitably. Second, many funds are unwilling to pay the Wall Street salaries that would be required to put together a top-notch internal management team. Civil service rules preclude most public funds from doing so, whereas many private corporations are reluctant to let the pension fund deviate from the company salary structure. Hiring outside managers allows a fund to purchase this expertise in appropriate units. Third, many companies are unwilling to try to make widgets and manage money at the same time. They see their primary business as complicated enough without taking on the burden of managing pension fund assets.

In addition to these factors, hiring outside managers provides the significant side benefit of enabling pension fund executives to deflect blame for bad investment decisions. As one outside manager put it, "The responsibility push is down at the point of attack. It's down at the portfolio manager." The fund officials remain responsible only for the hiring and firing of the external managers. When things go wrong, they can blame those who actually make the buy and sell decisions. If need be, the managers can be fired as well as blamed. The fund officials need not even accept responsibility for a bad hiring decision: They can say that the outside managers changed their stripes.

Conveniently, when the dust settles the fund's internal management team remains in place.

Blaming the Market: Indexing

A third structural device that serves to displace responsibility is indexing. Indexing appeals to public fund officials because it allows them to explain to the legislature and the press that the fund's success or failure depends on the performance of the overall American economy and is therefore beyond their control. Fund officials are culpable only insofar as they fail to implement the decisions mandated by the indexing mechanism.

Public fund officials believe that the press and the public are bored by pension funds, becoming interested only when disasters occur. Thus, indexing—which hitches the fund to the market—offers an attractive way to preempt questions of responsibility. Initially, it can be justified on the complementary grounds of the difficulty of managing money internally in a civil service environment and the allegedly spotty performance of outside managers. Thereafter, when the fund suffers serious losses, as many did in October 1987 and October 1989, responsibility can be displaced onto the market as a whole.

The chief executive of State A explained the enormous attraction of indexing by reference to the newspapers' ongoing quest to discover and expose bad decisions. He complained about their parallel indifference to successful investment decisions:

> We're in a public domain, and the rewards for doing well in the public sector are not great. Newspapers don't exactly print "Fund Executive Has Dynamite Year" in the stories. But if I ever fell out of bed, they would be happy to print it. So public systems operate a little bit more conservatively, take less risk, take less chance, than do their private counterparts.

Blaming the Law

A fourth mechanism for managing blame is to displace responsibility for decisions onto legal requirements. The fiduciary responsibilities of private pension funds are regulated by ERISA, a federal statute, while public funds generally operate under the common law of trusts. In the view of many legal scholars, the two sets of standards are not materially different. Both establish a general requirement of well-informed, prudent judgment exercised in the interest of the plan's beneficiaries.

In spite of the absence of specific rules governing specific situations under either standard, fund executives repeatedly told us that particular decisions were mandated by law. In the next chapter, we examine in detail how the law is used to justify investment decisions. For present purposes, it is sufficient to recognize that whatever law is applicable and however it is interpreted, the opportunity to blame the law for one's actions is highly valued in the investment world.

MANAGING RELATIONSHIPS

A third cultural factor that helps to determine structures and strategies is the desire to foster personal relationships. At some funds, a concern for people's feelings has led to internal decision-making processes that admittedly do not yield optimal results. And those funds that use outside managers acknowledge that relationships are often more important than the bottom line in evaluating and deciding whether to retain managers.

We have already made several references to the elaborate committee structure at ProductCo. We argued that it helps to diffuse responsibility for the innumerable decisions that characterize this fund's frantic investment style. A further rationale for maintaining this cumbersome structure is that it gives employees a sense of participation in important decisions, albeit an illusory one.

Earlier in the chapter, we quoted ProductCo's chief pension executive describing the process for allocating assets. He expressed his doubts about the efficacy of the process, admitting that "I've got some serious questions about it." As he continued, it became clear that the fund had abandoned its earlier, less formal system not because of any demonstrable failure to produce good results, but because some people felt left out. Pointing to an elaborate decision-tree diagram he had drawn during the interview, he told us:

> At first we didn't have this part, we just had this part. And that meant that some of the people didn't get a chance to input through

the process, or they felt that they didn't. And then I guess before we even set that up, we just had sort of a more or less informal ad hoc thing. Well, that had faults too, because it meant that the person who was the loudest or the most articulate might get his way and the other people didn't get a chance to get their views expressed.

We do not mean to suggest that the feelings of employees are not a relevant management concern. On the contrary, it seems self-evident that personal satisfaction and productivity are correlated. The problem, rather, is that feelings often displace finance as a criterion for evaluating the decision-making process. Pay close attention to what the speaker did and did not say: He evaluated a series of structures from the standpoint of participant satisfaction, but nowhere in his account did he offer any evidence of which one produced better outcomes.

The importance of relationships is also a major theme in fund executives' accounts of the process of evaluating outside money managers. At ChemCo, the fund employs 21 external managers and thus has vast experience in finding, hiring, and evaluating them. In describing the process for making the final selection of managers, the chief executive emphasized personal factors:

> When it really comes down to which one do you still like, it gets to be a very gut type of situation, gut level of comfort. It's almost like, if I feel more comfortable with that guy, I think I'd rather do business with that guy.

In turn, he expects the managers to rely on comparably intuitive factors when making their investment decisions:

> They do get a good deal of their information from reports, but they also go out and look—the buzzword is *kick the tires*.

One of his colleagues then added:

> The thing that the money managers get out of going to a company is a feeling for the management, meeting with people one to one and talking with them and gauging their confidence, and their vision, and their energy level.

At all of the funds we studied, the evaluation of outside money managers goes beyond a simple bottom-line comparison. In fact, it is difficult for fund executives to figure out just what that comparison should be. Most funds measure managers' performance not against the market as a whole, but against the performance of other managers with a similar style. Accordingly, when a manager does poorly, it can be hard to tell whether he is managing badly, or is doing as well as can be expected with a currently maladaptive style. One of the outside managers recounted an anecdote that reflects this dilemma:

> The chairman of the committee [in charge of evaluating managers], who I think is their personnel officer or something, says, "I have good news and bad news." And I said, "Well, give me the bad news first." He said, "You did the worst of all our managers and you weren't even close to the next to worst one. But we've decided that we hired you for all the right reasons and that the way you invest was just out of style, we guess, in the last 18 months, so we're doubling the size of your account." It never happened to me before or since. I've never heard anybody describe that process.

Under these circumstances, funds turn to the look and feel of the manager's firm—whether the same people are still in place, whether there have been any changes in investment style or decision-making processes, and whether there is regular communication with the fund. One outside manager even recalled being told how to dress:

> The pension officer that preceded the current one said, "You know, I see how you dress and it really doesn't look too good for the committee." So I went out and bought a suit, which I called my ChemCo suit.

The result of all this is that dismissal of a manager is an exceedingly rare event. For example, at ChemCo we were told that no manager had been fired for more than four years, and the reports from other funds were consistent. In view of the competition among managers to land new institutional accounts, this is an extraordinary fact. Either the funds we studied are remarkably—indeed, uniquely—successful in choosing managers, or they are seeing what they want to see in the quantitative evidence to avoid admitting a mistake and going through the burdensome process of changing managers.[5]

The outside managers themselves are keenly aware of, and occasionally cynical about, the significance of relationships to their continued employment. One manager talked at length about the difficulties of marketing his services to pension funds. The basic problem, he said, is that "the pension fund CEOs of the world are not, I don't mean this in a negative sense, they're not investment professionals." To compound the problem, heading the pension fund in a corporation is not a prestigious assignment: "It's usually a way-station. . . . There's not much status, et cetera, connected with it." As a result, he said, pension CEOs will be unable to understand the presentation "if you go in and start talking in terms that make it sound like an art form." Instead, one must emphasize in the simplest possible terms "a philosophy . . . a process, and then an implementation." At best, he concluded,

> Most of them are going to read the first couple of paragraphs of a prospectus. So you wanted to give them a simple handle on what you did. We finally got it down to a couple of charts.

Another manager was even more blunt about the hiring process:

> They want to know that if they hire you, you're going to make them look good. But most of all, you're not going to make them look bad. And in that sense it's not any different than any other decision-making process that would go on in any kind of hierarchical structure. Corporations don't tend to be great fountains of independent thinking.

Once hired, this manager emphasized, "we feel very, very strongly about the relationship." The reason for this strength of feeling is survival:

> We know statistically that all of our trends [i.e., of all money managers] will move to the mean, and this is an awful lot of money to make for the mean. If somebody has to go, we want it to be the arrogant guy that didn't pay any attention. That's basically the business strategy.

A third manager described a "mentality" in pension funds that makes it difficult to pursue investment objectives in an efficient way, even though the relationship may be "fun":

> I think that what it's spawned out of is the corporate culture. The pension CEO is probably facing a similar set of return parameters

as, say, some line guy, the local products manager or something like that. So he may have a set of criteria laid down, and there may also be whatever the planning horizons are within the company, or his own performance bonus evaluation horizons may be affecting how they structure investments and how they look at managers. I'm not saying that they're all hair-trigger and that they're really short-term. I'm just saying that I don't think the business quality in pension funds is as high as it is in individual investors. We have a great long-term relationship with one fund, it's probably one of the best, you know, a fun relationship. I think it's a fun relationship with the executive and his predecessor, but it's still different than working for a retired investment partner in New York or something like that.

This manager has stopped working for public pension funds entirely because, in addition to all of these problems, "they have high turnover on their committees, and their committees are generally highly politicized."

The dominant feature of the relationship between fund and manager is the illusion of control that each has. Fund executives would have you believe that they control the quality of their managers' work through a rigorous program of selection and evaluation. At the same time, managers talk of how they control the selection and retention processes by pandering to the ignorance and insecurities of these same executives. In fact, each group seems to be doing a successful job of patronizing the other, to their mutual benefit. The managers' performance typically hovers near the mean, so the fund executives are rarely embarrassed, while the managers are gainfully and profitably employed. Whether all this attention to relationships promotes the interests of the pension beneficiaries, the sponsoring corporations, or the American economy is another question, and one to which no one we interviewed had a very good answer.

NOTES

1. In addition, public funds publish glossy annual reports, but these typically contain only general statements of investment philosophy and quantitative summaries of performance. Private funds are

much more secretive, and the only materials available from most of them are their highly technical Department of Labor filings and the brief newsletters they send to beneficiaries. The performance data they provide to plan sponsors is considered proprietary, and they do not release such information to any outsiders. Thus, we are not able to compare funds with regard to the interesting issues of short- and long-term performance.

2. Establishing a separate corporation for the pension fund is unusual but not unprecedented; two of the funds we studied have done so. Pension funds are typically run out of the corporate treasurer's office. The geographic separation of fund from sponsor at ProductCo is unique.

3. One might ask whether the lack of emphasis on economics was simply a reflection of the executives' belief that we, as nonspecialists, would not be able to understand an economic explanation. There are two reasons to reject this hypothesis. First, almost every executive did speak in relatively technical economic terms at some point in the interview, demonstrating that our lack of expertise was not a total deterrent. Second, if the executives had wanted to give priority to economic concerns, they presumably could have said something like, "We do this for economic reasons, but I won't go into the details because you wouldn't understand."

4. An interesting question is why a prudent fiduciary would bother with such investments, since they consume a grossly disproportionate amount of administrative resources. The answer always given is *diversity*. However, since the objectives of diversification are economic, does it make any sense to do uneconomical things in the name of diversity?

5. The difficulty of measuring performance is itself a disincentive to change, because hiring a new manager might mean setting up a new benchmark for evaluating him. In the course of describing the qualitative side of manager evaluation, the chief pension executive at ChemCo expressed concern that firing a manager would "screw up all my measurement systems." One of the outside managers pointed out that there are also economic costs to changing managers:

> The guy who takes over dumps all the securities that the other guy had. And he doesn't understand them very well, so he probably sells them badly, and there's a cost of getting into his securities.

CHAPTER 5

IN THEIR OWN IMAGE AND LIKENESS—RESOLVING THE INDETERMINACY OF THE LAW

When talking about their professional lives, pension executives say surprisingly little about economics. They talk constantly about the law, however. The law is a pervasive influence in the pension world. As we moved from fund office to fund office, lawyers were never far away. Sometimes a fund's in-house lawyer sat in on our conversations with the chief pension executive; at other funds, the chief executive suggested that we speak separately with his lawyer in order to get the latter's critically important perspective. Even when lawyers were out of sight, they were never out of mind: Fund executives made frequent references to what inside or outside counsel had opined on this issue or that.

Beyond the frequent talk with and about lawyers, we also heard a great deal about the law itself. Fund executives spoke often about the role that the law plays in shaping their actions. In many instances, they cited the law as a positive force that required them to make a certain decision or to take a certain action; in others, they said that the law precluded a course of action that they might otherwise have preferred to follow. In fact, among all the various motivations for the things that they do (e.g., financial considerations, administrative convenience, internal politics, ethics), the pension fund insiders we spoke with talked about the law more than any other factor.

WHAT IS A FIDUCIARY?

Most of this talk about law centered around the concept of fiduciary duty. In the most basic sense of the term, a *fiduciary* (or *trustee*, a near synonym) is a person who holds something in trust. In legal usage, a fiduciary is usually a person or institution who manages money or property for the benefit of another. Examples include a guardian who looks out for the affairs of a minor child, a conservator who manages the property of an incompetent person, and a trustee appointed under a will to manage the decedent's money and dispense income to the chosen beneficiaries.

The people who manage pension funds are also fiduciaries. They manage large sums of money for the ultimate benefit of people who expect to receive pensions. Clearly, pension fund fiduciaries have a duty to act in the best interests of those people. Once we move beyond this truism, however, the duties and responsibilities of pension fiduciaries become less clear. In the examples in the preceding paragraph, the lines of responsibility are well established. In the instances of the child and the incompetent, the money belongs to that person, and the fiduciary has an unambiguous duty to act in his or her best interests. In the will situation, the duties and responsibilities of the trustee are typically spelled out in the will itself.

In the pension situation, however, the fiduciary's role is fraught with ambiguities and potential conflicts of interest. There are many questions that do not have simple answers. Whose money is it? Does it belong to the employer that has the responsibility for paying the pensions, or to the present and future pensioners? How are the interests of the beneficiaries to be defined? Can the fiduciary consider things beyond the pensioners' strict financial interests—for example, their presumed interest in a prosperous and healthy society? In making decisions about investment and corporate governance, is it proper for the fiduciary to take the employer's interests into account? If there appears to be more money in the fund than will be necessary to meet the pension obligations, can the fiduciary permit the employer to take back the surplus?

The pension fund executives we interviewed seemed not very attuned to these ambiguities. On the contrary, a consistent characteristic of their talk about law was the certainty of their answers to questions like these. When law professors and other independent legal experts respond to such questions, they qualify their answers (even more than lawyers always do in answering other kinds of questions). Pension fund executives do not. Each of them has a set of clear-cut answers—but they may differ from the ones given by a colleague down the hall. Pension fund executives shape their conduct according to strongly held, but often highly idiosyncratic, understandings of the law's dictates.

In this chapter we examine the ways in which the law influences the behavior of those who manage pension fund assets. We begin with a review of the basic legal issues that pension funds confront, with particular attention to some of the questions posed above. We turn then to a case-by-case analysis of how the law's requirements are understood and carried out at several of the funds we studied. The issues we consider include who owns the fund's assets, what the proper relationship is between the fund and the beneficiaries, how much investment diversification is necessary, and whether the fund may use its investments to promote social objectives.

FIDUCIARY STANDARDS: THE COMMON LAW AND ERISA

The standard of conduct to which a fiduciary is held has an ancient pedigree. The basic idea of the trust—one person holding property for the benefit of another—first emerged in medieval England in a context unrelated to pension funds, as a device for circumventing restrictive inheritance laws. Its evolution proceeded as part of the development of the Anglo-American common law—the law made by judges in the course of deciding individual cases, as opposed to statutory law enacted by legislatures. In this country, the most authoritative statement of the common law of trusts is the Restatement of Trusts.[1] A few of its central provisions are worth noting in some detail.

The Restatement provides that any trustee, including a pension fund executive, is obligated to manage the money entrusted to him "solely in the interest of the beneficiary." The phrase "solely in the interest" is not further defined. In all matters pertaining to the trust, "the trustee is under a duty to the beneficiary . . . to exercise such care and skill as a man of ordinary prudence would exercise in dealing with his own property." In making investment decisions, the trustee is obligated "to make such investments and only such investments as a prudent man would make of his own property." In addition, "the trustee is under a duty to the beneficiary to distribute the risk of loss by a reasonable diversification of investments, unless under the circumstances it is prudent not to do so."[2] According to widely accepted principles of investment practice, a fiduciary's prudence is to be evaluated with reference to the entire investment portfolio. Thus, a fiduciary should not incur legal liability if one or two investments in an otherwise sound portfolio prove to have been unwise.

In the view of most legal scholars, these principles do not provide definitive answers to the most vexing questions that pension fiduciaries face. In particular, they provide little guidance on the issue of what things the fiduciary may consider in determining the best interests of the beneficiaries. Is it in their best interests, for example, that their employer remain stable and profitable, or that there be racial equality in South Africa? The diversification requirement is also vague: Must a pension fund employ a diversity of investment strategies, or is it enough simply to spread the investments among a number of companies, and, if so, how many?

In 1974, Congress enacted ERISA, the Employee Retirement Income Security Act. ERISA is now the governing law for private pension funds. Most public funds remain under the common law of trusts. Some states, however, have enacted statutes that track the language of ERISA and apply the ERISA standards to public funds operating within their borders.

ERISA's fiduciary standards are similar to those of the common law. As under the common law, the trustee is under "a duty to the beneficiary to administer the trust solely in the interest of the beneficiary."[3] ERISA expands on this principle, stipulating that "the assets of a plan shall never inure to the benefit of any employer and shall be held for the exclusive [purpose] of providing benefits to participants in the plan."[4] ERISA follows the common law in adopting a prudent person standard of conduct and imposing a requirement that investments be diversified.[5] The critical questions about the nature of the beneficiaries' interests and the scope of the diversification requirement are no better answered than in the common law. There have been a few court cases on the issue of whether a pension trustee can invest for social or political purposes—for example, refusing to buy stock in companies that do business in South Africa or have poor environmental records. These cases seem to permit the trustee to take some account of noneconomic objectives as long as the investment in question yields a market rate of return.

ERISA also adds to the common law in some important respects. ERISA's definition of who is a fiduciary goes well beyond the common law's. Under ERISA, the category of fiduciaries includes any person who exercises any authority or control over a pension fund's assets, anyone who is directly or indirectly compensated for giving investment advice to a pension plan, and anyone who has any discretionary authority over the administration of a pension plan.[6] Whatever ERISA's fiduciary standards mean, it is clear that they apply to almost everyone involved in a professional capacity in the management or investment of pension fund assets. Fiduciaries who fail to live up to the standards are personally liable for losses that they cause.[7]

Notwithstanding its all-embracing definition of fiduciary, ERISA does permit some delegation of duties and responsibilities. The plan sponsor (i.e., the employer), which is itself defined as a fiduciary, places overall direction of the plan in the hands of a "named fiduciary," who in turn can delegate investment duties to other fiduciaries. As a number of fund executives emphasized to us, the extent to which one fiduciary can escape legal responsibility by delegating duties to another is unsettled.[8]

As we observed in Chapter 1, the primary impetus for enacting ERISA was the collapse of the Studebaker pension plan in the early 1960s. Accordingly, it is not surprising that ERISA establishes detailed rules for funding pension obligations. (Some of the ERISA rules work in concert with certain provisions of the Internal Revenue Code.) The basic rule is that pension plans that promise fixed benefits (defined benefit plans) must be fully funded, meaning that the sponsor must set aside enough money from year to year to meet the future obligations that it has incurred. How much to set aside is determined by actuaries. Each year, they estimate the plan's future obligations and value its current assets, then calculate how much (if any) money the sponsor must contribute to ensure that enough will be on hand to pay the obligations as they become due.

A critical element of this calculation is an educated assumption about the likely rate of return on the plan's investments. A 1 percent adjustment in the estimated rate of return can affect the long-term cost of funding the plan by as much as 25 percent. For obvious reasons, the rate of return that the actuaries assume can be a source of conflict between a plan's sponsor and its actuaries. For example, over the past couple of years there have been numerous press reports about the efforts of public officials in New York City to persuade pension fund actuaries to assume more optimistic rates of return in order to reduce the city's near-term funding obligations. Such conflicts have not been limited to the public sector.

The amount of contributions needed will vary from year to year, depending on the benefits paid out, the new obligations incurred, and, above all, the performance of the plan's investments. When ERISA was enacted, many pension funds, large as well as small, found themselves seriously underfunded and had to make large contributions for several years. During the bull markets of the 1980s, many sponsors found that the appreciation of their assets more than compensated for the growth of their pension obligations, with the result that they were required to contribute little new money. The trend for the 1990s has yet to be established, but brokers, investment advisers, and others who depend for a living on the investment activities of pension funds are watching with interest.

FILLING IN GAPS IN THE LAW

At each of the nine funds we studied, all of the upper-echelon employees were well-versed in the rhetoric of the law. We heard repeatedly that everything they did was done in the interests of their beneficiaries, and we were occasionally challenged when

---

BOX 5–1
Corporate Pension Funds: Can They Meet Their Payout Obligations?

- Only 73 percent of the largest 50 corporate pension funds were fully funded in 1989—they had more assets than projected benefit obligations.
- The average corporation in the top 50 had $4.95 billion in 1989 accrued benefit obligations, $5.79 billion in projected benefit obligations, and $7.1 billion in assets.
- The most "solvent" plans—those with the greatest surplus of assets in excess of projected obligations—have been, for three years running:

    AT&T, with excess assets of $11.4 billion.
    GE with excess assets of $8.2 billion.
    Du Pont, with excess assets of $5.1 billion.
    General Motors, with excess assets of $4.7 billion (one of two plans is overfunded).

  Other "solvent" plans include:

    IBM, with excess assets of $7.4 billion.
    GTE, with excess assets of $4.3 billion.
    Ameritech, with excess assets of $4.1 billion.

- The least "solvent" plans—those where 1989 projected benefit obligations exceeded assets by the largest amounts—were:

    Chrysler, with underfunding of $2.74 billion.
    General Motors, with underfunding of $1.87 billion (one of two plans is underfunded).
    Bethlehem Steel, with underfunding of $1.17 billion.
    Westinghouse, with underfunding of $620 million.
    Ford Motor, with underfunding of $349 million.

---

someone read into one of our questions even a hint of skepticism. But knowledge of the law's rhetoric is of little help to pension executives who must decide just how to pursue the beneficiaries' interests. A variety of concrete questions can arise. For example, can a fund be concerned about the impact of its investments on its corporate sponsor? Can a fund invest in below-market-rate mortgages that will be made available to its beneficiaries? Can a fund use its investment clout to modify corporate social behavior, as by divesting itself of companies that test their products on animals or do business in Northern Ireland?

Those who manage large pension funds confront these kinds of practical questions on a regular basis. The answers depend in large part on figuring out just what ERISA and the common law mean when they demand exclusive dedication to the beneficiaries' interests. Are the beneficiaries interested only in the appreciation of the fund's assets, or can they also be interested in improving the quality of life on a local, national, or even global level? Many of the legal authorities we interviewed believe that the law simply does not say—the law is *indeterminate*, in the current legal jargon. But pension executives must come up with practical answers to these questions in order to make day-to-day investment decisions.

We consider next three specific instances in which pension executives must fill in gaps in the text of the law: when refereeing competing claims to ownership of pension fund assets, when responding to demands for socially conscious investing, and when deciding how much diversification is enough. Two striking themes emerge: the extent to which well-heeled and well-advised people can read the same law and reach opposite conclusions, and the certainty and conviction with which they state those divergent conclusions.

WHOSE MONEY IS IT?

Both ERISA and the common law state unequivocally that pension assets must be managed solely in the interests of the beneficiaries. For some, this language can only be interpreted to mean that the money belongs to the beneficiaries. From a logical perspective, the beneficiaries would seem to have the most straightforward claim. It is their money in the sense that it has been deducted from their paychecks or, in the case of employer contributions, is a part of their overall compensation.

However, in the course of our conversations with fund executives we heard three divergent views on the question of ownership. Some contend that the sponsor is the true owner, or that its interests are at least entitled to consideration. They argue that the sponsor has an obligation only to pay the beneficiaries' pensions, not to turn the pension assets over to them; as long as that obligation is secure, there is no reason for the fund not to promote the sponsor's corporate interests as well. A second position is that the fund is an independent entity which looks out for the beneficiaries' interests, but as it sees fit; accordingly it should be immune from influence by either beneficiaries or sponsor. A third interpretation, applicable only to public funds, is that it is the taxpayers' money, so the fund's financial power can properly be called on to remedy social problems.

In examining how several different funds resolve the ownership issue, two fundamental distinctions must be made among the various funds. The first distinction, which is sociological in nature, is between private and public funds. In most private corporations, the pension executives have come up through the management hierarchy. As a result, they have little contact with and little in common with the production workers and other blue-collar employees who comprise the vast majority of the beneficiaries. Consequently, private fund executives see their beneficiaries as mere abstractions whose needs, wants, and—critically—interests can only be assumed.

In public funds, by contrast, even the most highly paid executives usually have extensive civil service backgrounds. Their experiences correspond more nearly to those of their beneficiaries. As a result, they perceive beneficiaries not as abstractions but as real people whose interests can actually be known. Moreover, public fund trustees are often elected by unions and other constituencies and are therefore in regular communication with beneficiaries.

The second distinction, applicable only to private funds, is that between defined benefit and defined contribution pension plans. In a defined benefit plan, the corporation is legally obligated to pay the beneficiaries specified monthly sums during their retirement. Accordingly, the investment performance of the fund can have a direct influence on the sponsoring corporation's bottom line. In a defined contribution plan, the employer's only obligation is to make contributions during the time a person is actually employed, at a level specified by a union agreement or an individual employment contract. After retiring, an individual receives whatever amount has accumulated (that is, the contributions plus income earned) in his or her account. As a result, the sponsoring corporation has no direct financial interest in the performance of the fund's investments. (It presumably has an intangible interest in the goodwill of its employees, and certainly has a legal interest in meeting its fiduciary obligation to invest prudently.) Conversely, the employees have a far greater interest in the performance of a defined contribution pension plan than in the defined benefit situation: If the fund performs well, they get more when they retire; if it does poorly, they get less. As one might expect, a defined contribution fund is likely to have a different kind of relationship with its beneficiaries and a different conception of its fiduciary status.

PRIVATE FUNDS

ProductCo

At ProductCo, the prevailing view is that the assets are the property of the fund. It must manage them in the interest of the beneficiaries, but it should be free from interference by either sponsor or beneficiaries. In the view of the chief executive of the fund, the law is perfectly clear on this point:

> ERISA views the fund, which no longer belongs to the corporation, as a separate legal pension fund which cannot be recovered by the sponsoring company until all the liabilities have been satisfied, so that it is there for the benefit of the beneficiaries of the trust and to provide them with retirement benefits.

He was particularly emphatic about his fund's independence from its corporate sponsor. He pointed out the fund must be prepared to go on long after the sponsor goes out of business. When we asked whether the fund felt any pressure to maximize investment performance in order to hold down the corporation's contributions, he reacted vehemently. Once again, he saw his conclusion as dictated by the unambiguous letter of the law:

No. No. I wouldn't ever say that even if it were true, because the law forbids us to say that. The law is quite clear. Under ERISA, the fiduciaries, the people that are running the thing, are responsible. The language says that they must behave in a manner solely in the interest of the participants and beneficiaries of the fund, not of the sponsor.

While in theory the fund is dedicated to the beneficiaries, they are not permitted to exert any influence on how it is managed. It is not that the law forbids such influence, but simply that the fund's executives never feel it and in fact cannot conceive of it. Most of the time, the beneficiaries are pure abstractions, not people capable of exerting influence. The only exception is when the executives think of themselves as future beneficiaries, but it would never occur to them that they might someday have an interest contrary to that of the corporation that employs them. We asked one of the chief executive's top assistants how he relates to the fund's beneficiaries. He responded:

> Well, admittedly, it's detached. The participants and beneficiaries are an abstract concept, but the way that I bring it back into reality is to remember that I am working for myself in a context of ensuring my pension promise—or in a sort of mix, in that I am working to ensure that pension promise, which also incorporates the corporation's ability to meet its obligations. So that by the fund's doing well, that means that I as a participant and beneficiary in this fund, have to worry less about ProductCo's being able to make its future pension contribution.

When he did manage to visualize a typical beneficiary, what he saw was a person interested only in getting his pension check on time—a person that he really cannot afford to think about:

> I don't try to personalize it too much, because of the level of sophistication that the average beneficiary has about what is actually going on in the pension funds, or about what he might like about junk bonds, or international investments in Japanese companies, or auto companies, or other things like that—maybe having a non-investment reaction. I can't allow myself to be dealing with the participant and beneficiary on that level.

Not surprisingly, communication with these beneficiaries is limited. Under normal circumstances, the fund speaks to them only to the extent required by law, by sending out an annual report in a form that satisfies ERISA's requirements. (Readers who receive such reports from their own employers will know how uninformative they are.) The beneficiaries rarely talk back, except when catastrophic events cause them to fear for the security of their pensions. Then, the fund may offer reassurance, at a level that it believes to be commensurate with the beneficiaries' understanding of the situation. ProductCo's chief pension executive told this story:

> In October of 87, there was a degree of fear on the part of retired people that the market had fallen so much, and they wondered if their pension benefits were in jeopardy. You know, there were horrible stories. Well, of course, their pension benefits were not in jeopardy at all. The market had fallen a lot, but it really hadn't fallen back much below the level that it was at the beginning of 1987. Now, they didn't understand all that, but we did put out, I think, some sort of press release.

The result of all this is a striking irony. For ProductCo's pension executives, the fundamental operating principle is the legal requirement of total fidelity to the beneficiaries' interests. But the same executives who are exclusively dedicated to the beneficiaries' interests rarely talk to them and have little idea of who they are.

IndustrialCo

IndustrialCo's pension executives have similarly limited contact with beneficiaries, but reach a radically different conclusion on the issue of the sponsoring corporation's right to influence the fund. Like others, the IndustrialCo fund speaks to the beneficiaries only to the limited extent required by law:

> *What kind of reporting to the beneficiaries is done every year?*
> The legal requirement under ERISA.
>
> *What does it look like on paper?*
> I'm trying to remember.

As at ProductCo, the beneficiaries rarely initiate communications; the chief executive could recall only occasional letters from beneficiaries, usually raising a technical question about entitlement to benefits. Even the powerful national union that represents most IndustrialCo line workers tends to stay out of pension affairs. As a result, the beneficiaries remain an abstraction to most of the IndustrialCo pension executives, as evidenced by the following colloquy with one of the investment specialists:

Do you ever have any contact with the beneficiaries of the fund?
None whatsoever.
It never happened?
None whatsoever.

Although similarly isolated from their beneficiaries, the IndustrialCo executives were less adamant than their ProductCo counterparts in disclaiming their sponsor's interest in the fund. One of them went so far as to abandon the usual rhetoric about the sponsor's bottom line being irrelevant to the fund:

I view the job as helping to make IndustrialCo the low-cost producer by helping drive down their costs as far as I can. And the [pension] cost has essentially been zero for the past six or seven years.

This statement—heretical to most pension executives and lawyers—implies a very different conception of the relationship among sponsor, fund, and beneficiary. In this view, the fund ceases to be a sacred and inviolable trust. It devolves into a mere financing scheme that the sponsor uses to defray the costs of meeting its pension obligations. If the fund succeeds, the company is saved the necessity of dipping into its operating revenues. The pensioners get paid either way, so they are perceived as having no interest in the mechanism.[9]

IndustrialCo's executives see no conflict between this concern for the sponsor's bottom line and ERISA. In their view, the interests of the sponsor and the beneficiaries are mutually reinforcing. If the fund performs well, it becomes a more secure source of pension payouts; by simultaneously contributing to the sponsor's balance sheet, the fund helps to make the sponsor a more reliable backup source.

This outlook, heretical as it might seem to some, reflects a carefully reasoned analysis of the competing claims on the fund's assets. Contrast the knee-jerk reaction of ProductCo's chief executive: "I wouldn't ever say that, even if it were true, because the law forbids us to say that." Does he protest too much? Is the IndustrialCo outlook widely shared, even though most people would not admit it because of potential ERISA problems? At the moment, these are questions on which we have little direct evidence. In any event, the IndustrialCo analysis avoids the apparent contradiction between unqualified dedication to the beneficiaries' interests and equally unqualified ignorance of who those people are.

A final point about IndustrialCo is that its executives have some reason to believe that what they are doing meets with the approval of the beneficiaries. Although here as elsewhere contact with beneficiaries is limited, at least one IndustrialCo executive has had the extraordinary experience of interacting with them. What he hears is a validation of his professional existence:

> I actually meet them once in a while, as I travel around the country.
>
> *What's it like?*
>
> They're very happy. The fund has a very strong reputation within the company, it seems, and they always say nice things. We keep the money coming. What I think of them is the obvious: they're people with limited means, and this is a fixed benefit. It is important to them, and it's important in their lives.

TransCo

Among the private funds we studied, there is an important distinction between defined benefit and defined contribution pension plans. In a defined benefit plan, the sponsor makes a contractual commitment to provide retirement benefits at a certain level. The better the investment performance of the fund over the years, the less the sponsor has to dip into its own revenues to satisfy its pension commitment. In a defined contribution plan, the sponsor has no explicit financial obligation beyond the point of contribution. The defined benefit/defined contribution distinction appears to correlate with some important differences in the

nature of the relationship between the fund and its beneficiaries.

The situation at TransCo illustrates how these influences
can work. TransCo's pension fund is actually an aggregation of
several different pension plans covering different categories of
union and nonunion workers. One of the union plans is a defined
contribution plan.

In thinking about his fiduciary responsibility for the defined benefit portion of the fund, TransCo's chief pension executive did not see the beneficiaries as having any role in defining
their own interests:

> For the fixed benefit plan, we've made a promise and a commit-
> ment to a certain level of benefits. We are going to fund it and
> manage it the way we think it best for them, and we don't invite
> their inquiries.

But if the beneficiaries are a remote concern, the sponsoring
corporation is an immediate and ever-present one. TransCo's
chief investment officer acknowledged the fund's solicitude for
the sponsor in terms reminiscent of what we heard at IndustrialCo: "We tie the investment policy of the pension funds very
closely to the financial considerations of the corporation." In his
view, the reason for this close relationship is the assertiveness of
the chairman of the sponsoring corporation:

> This organization takes its character from the chairman. I don't
> know what it was like before he was chairman because most of
> my career has been spent here since he's been the major influ-
> ence. . . .
>
> *How would you characterize his view of pension fund issues?*
> It's a cost center to him. You know, if you looked at everything
> the funds have ever done, the great investment decisions, if you
> back them out, were really corporate business decisions.

As at IndustrialCo, things have worked out well for the
beneficiaries, even if investment strategies have been dictated
primarily by corporate business concerns:

> And it's worked beautifully. It's done exactly what we wanted it to
> do, and these weren't really investment decisions as such. They
> were driven really from the corporate side.

TransCo's executives see no conflict between their attention to the corporation's concerns and ERISA's "solely in the interest of the beneficiary" rule. Indeed, ERISA is something that rarely crosses the mind of TransCo's chief pension executive:

> I personally don't feel that hampered at all. I think people were more afraid of ERISA in the early days, in the late 70s, early 80s, but the more people worked with it, the more exemptions that have been granted. We don't feel hampered in the least by ERISA.

The TransCo pension executives' perspective on the defined contribution plan is entirely different. The overbearing corporate interest is absent. Rather than being an abstraction whose best interests are determined by the fund, these beneficiaries are "very, very involved in the whole process." Indeed, "they look at it as their money," and the fund executives do not disagree; "we're somewhere in the middle." As a result, TransCo has established a consultative process not found in any defined benefit fund:

> We realize that it's their money, so we let the union representatives on the pension committee sit with us in discussing strategy and managers, and we've effectively divided decision-making processes into fiduciary decisions [that TransCo must ultimately make] and nonfiduciary decisions [that the union can participate in].

One might well ask why a similar process of consultation would not be helpful in administering a defined benefit plan as well. The uniform view among private pension executives, however, is that defined benefit beneficiaries have no role in fund management, whether consultative or otherwise.

PUBLIC FUNDS

State C

State C's executives have a very different perspective on their beneficiaries than their private fund counterparts. This difference results from the fact that State C's beneficiaries have channels for making their views known, and apparently do so with regularity. In addition, the investment and benefit functions operate in the same office at State C and most other public funds, whereas they are usually separated in private funds. Consequently, public fund investment officials, unlike their private sector counterparts, have daily opportunities for actual contact with beneficiaries as they come in to get help with benefit questions.

As is the case in many public funds, State C's trustees include public officials and representatives elected by unions and other employee groups. These trustees hear regularly from their constituents, and take their views into account when setting policy. In the words of State C's chief investment officer:

> Employee organizations are strong in this state and there are members of the board who represent employee organizations, and there are members of these organizations who are also ex-members of the board. There is a lot of communication there either through newsletters, personal letters, phone calls, that type of thing. And those interests do get expressed on the board. We would not invest in, for example, leveraged buyouts. One of the reasons —not the only reason, but one of the reasons—has been a reluctance on the part of certain board members to become involved in the area because of the interest they sense from their constituency, in response to closings and loss of jobs and that type of thing.

State C's investment professionals do not see this as a wholly salutary development. The chief investment officer continued:

> Frankly these [communications from beneficiaries] are not what I would call serious. They may be serious to the individuals who make them but they don't represent the majority views. It's generally a person with a particular axe to grind or some interest that they're trying to promote.

In any event, the trustees' concern for the beneficiaries sets a tone to which the investment professionals are sensitive. As a result, a good deal of the fund's time and energy is devoted to the individual concerns of the beneficiaries. State C's chief pension executive described it this way:

We try to [respond to] those concerns about the gray-haired lady who is out there counting on this pension fund. Speaking for the trustees, it is a very, very personal thing for them to have a high reputation. They are very sensitive about the image of the fund to its members. So when they go out and talk to beneficiaries and things like that, if it's appearing that we're not being responsive to beneficiaries in a certain area, they come back and they call me, and they bring that to my attention and we track it down. It's a very good shepherding process.

As is usually the case at public funds, State C's executives' sense of obligation to the beneficiaries is reinforced by their ability to identify with them. While those who manage private funds are also beneficiaries, there is a wide economic and cultural gap between the pension executives and the line workers who typify the private beneficiaries. At public funds, however, even the highest-ranking executives tend to have civil service backgrounds, and therefore to have a much clearer sense of belonging to the beneficiary class. When asked if he thinks about the beneficiaries of the fund, another State C executive replied:

I'm doing this for myself. I'm a member of the system, and I hope to get a retirement from this system. I think there's an obligation to better the system as a good fiduciary to those people. In the long run, that really is the ultimate goal of our system. It's not to make corporate America compete with the Japanese or to make them more accountable. That's not the ultimate goal. The ultimate goal is we want them to do those things so that we can get a better return, so that we can guarantee that the little old gray-haired lady, or my mother-in-law, or my brother, who is a policeman and a member of this fund, will have a retirement. Because as you know, these systems have become the primary savings function of America. We don't in our society save a lot of money. We are the savings funds now of a lot of people and that's all they have.[10]

Those in charge at State C have a clear sense that the fund is the property of the beneficiaries. Of course, at a public fund there is no corporation to compete for ownership. The competition comes from the taxpayers and from the elected officials who purport to represent them.[11] As State C's chief executive described it, the obligation to pursue the beneficiaries' interests requires constant vigilance against predatory politicians:

You expect to be able to retire, and then according to your age and salary and years of service, you expect a certain sum, which then will be given to you for the rest of your life. It is our security. It is like our home. There are things that politicians sometimes don't think about, in terms of what you can and what you cannot attack; and our retirement, our Social Security, our homes, our family, and our children, those are the issues that you cannot attack.

DOES THE LAW DICTATE INVESTMENT STRATEGY?

A second issue on which the law is less than precise is the choice of investment strategy. Both the common law of trusts and ERISA require prudent investment and diversification. Neither, however, defines prudence or specifies how much diversity is enough. In the pension world, answers to these questions differ from fund to fund and from executive to executive. Some see the glass as half full, emphasizing the range of things that the law permits; others see it as half empty, focusing on what the law forbids. Often, the law seems to have been called on after the fact to justify a strategy that was originally chosen for other reasons.

Some pension executives maintain that the law dictates nothing more than common sense, leaving almost everything else to the discretion of the fiduciary. To them, the diversification rule amounts to little more than a prohibition against putting all one's eggs in just a few baskets, especially if they are untested baskets. According to the proponents of this view, when ERISA was enacted in the 1970s, a brief panic ensued as pension insiders tried to determine what ERISA had added to common law; eventually, most of them concluded that the law remained as it had always been.

One of the outside managers we spoke with told us about how the early understanding of ERISA impeded his efforts to market his small money management firm to large pension funds:

I remember ERISA as an obstacle right after it passed. Because what it meant was that it had been born out of disaster: the market declined and some companies closed down and the workers never got their pensions. So it was a police action. It was something that you can get in trouble for violating. . . . So they asked the lawyers what to do, and whatever one thinks of lawyers, they don't think in terms of investment results. So, I think what they said is, "If you can find a guy who works in a building that's got granite on the outside of it and it says, 'Established a long, long time ago,' then you're probably complying with what *Marbury* v. *Madison,* or whatever the case was that established trustee law in Massachusetts in the 19th century, implied."

This interpretation of ERISA scared the funds away from small and untested firms like his. The prevailing interpretation changed over time, however, and a niche opened up for newer managers. Eventually, he told us, "ERISA became a nonfactor."

Many people working inside pension funds also espouse the view that ERISA did not really change anything. The chief pension executive at ChemCo put it as follows:

The primary area that ERISA dictates is prudence. I think any trustee, under the common law, has an obligation of prudence. Some people indicate, "Well, now that they've codified the word *prudence* it means more." But I really don't think so. I think if you're talking about prudence and where your loyalties were as a fiduciary of an employee benefit trust fund, any judge would have probably read into your obligations as a fiduciary for a pension plan as much as ERISA has codified in that area.

And some pension executives, such as this one from IndustrialCo, take the nonfactor interpretation of ERISA to such an extreme that they lose interest entirely:

I worked somewhere else for 10 years in investing, and I came here. And ERISA, personally, meant nothing whatsoever to me and to our process. . . . Basically we were, I would say, taking into account the fact that the world changed, and it always changes, and so the types of investing that you're doing also tend to change. But we really didn't have any trauma over ERISA, and my personal current understanding of it is that it's still an evolving and rather unknown kind of thing. And old-fashioned things like prudent behavior and common sense are going to pull me through these things.

Others read more specific commands into ERISA and the common law. In particular, ERISA is sometimes understood to compel the multistyle approach that many funds employ. An in-house lawyer at ChemCo, contradicting the chief executive's commonsense interpretation of ERISA, accounted for his fund's multimanager, multistyle approach in these terms:

> I think our philosophy is generally shaped by the law: ERISA. We have to invest at certain levels, and then we have to diversify. We diversify by getting different types of investments, bonds, equities, real estate; and in those areas get different types of it, get real estate in different parts of the country. We have five active managers in equities, and they have slightly different styles.

He also pointed out that in addition to being a sword that compels diversification, ERISA is a shield which insulates fiduciaries who employ outside managers:

> The other legal point was that when ERISA came in, if you delegated the investment of your pension fund to somebody who was a manager and you watched them in a prudent way, the directors weren't directly responsible for any losses. And that was deemed in the beginning to be an important consideration, and I don't know if anybody changed their mind since.

In fact, a number of people have changed their mind since, if they ever agreed with this proposition in the first place. The chief investment officer at IndustrialCo, for example, described it as "a very interesting and controversial proposition, as to what extent the ERISA responsibilities with regard to these management questions can be shifted." Nonetheless, it remains a comforting belief to those who hold it.

Significantly, the executives at ChemCo were never able to provide an economic rationale for their multimanager, multistyle version of diversification. The chief pension executive accounted for the multistyle philosophy as an effort to diversify, and then explained the desire for so much diversification in terms of reducing volatility. He was not able to tie either concept to fund performance, nor to refute the argument that this strategy amounts to nothing more than a high-priced index. Thus, the law is the only causal element in the whole ChemCo investment equation. From the evidence available to us, we cannot say whether the law was the original motivation or was subsequently discovered to be a useful explanation. In either event, it provides a convenient vehicle for displacing the responsibility for choosing an investment strategy that cannot be justified on other grounds.

SOCIAL INVESTING AND THE INTERESTS OF BENEFICIARIES

Perhaps the most vexing legal question that pension executives confront is how to define the interests of the beneficiaries that they serve. The question comes up most often in the context of social investing: managing a pension fund to promote social objectives, such as improving the environment, ending apartheid in South Africa or religious discrimination in Northern Ireland, or providing low-cost housing in American cities. The debate over these issues is frequently heated and is a source of great stress to many pension executives. Many states have enacted or are considering laws requiring divestment of companies that do business in South Africa, while individual politicians and various public and private interest groups put pressure on pension funds to apply social criteria in making investment choices.[12]

There are two basic views on the legality of social investing. According to the more widely held of the two, the interests of the beneficiaries include only economic interests; thus, pension trustees cannot be influenced by any factors not directly related to the financial performance of the fund. According to the other view, the interests of the beneficiaries to which the law refers include such intangible things as the quality of life in a person's community and the promotion of justice throughout the world. Under this view, as long as the overall performance of the fund is reasonably good, a trustee can do such things as invest in low-yield bonds to support the public infrastructure or refuse to invest in companies—even profitable ones—that do business in South Africa.

Those who argue that social investing is prohibited claim that the law is absolutely clear on this point. The chief pension executive at ProductCo talked about South Africa divestment in these terms:

> *How, when you're thinking about this responsibility that you've just described, do you deal with questions like, for example, the South Africa issue? What do you do with the problem?*
>
> We follow the ERISA rule—very simple. And under the ERISA rule that's not a matter that we could pay attention to, so we don't have to spend a lot of time thinking about that. . . . We don't have to face the issue, because our interpretation, and the interpretation of most private ERISA-governed funds, is that ERISA prevents a decision on our part that we are going to manage the assets of the fund to try to bring about a political result in South Africa or to satisfy noninvestment-related social objectives of our employees, or anything of that sort.

Under this chief executive's interpretation of the law, social considerations can become relevant only if they lead to economic consequences for a company whose stock the fund owns:

> Now, you do understand though that if, for example, an investment manager who was investing in equities reached a decision that it was bad business for a company to continue to do business in South Africa, and that it was likely to damage that company's reputation, or cause it problems and so on in the future, then that would be a perfectly legitimate reason for disposing of that stock.

The economic impact must be direct and obvious, however. If an ambiguous case were resolved in favor of social investing, it would open what ProductCo's chief executive called "a Pandora's box of special pleading. . . . You are not sure where it is going to lead."

This view of the law has interesting personal ramifications for those pension executives who hold it. In the first place, it simplifies life, by preempting any number of difficult decisions. Moreover, by positing the law as an unyielding higher authority, it relieves the executive of any moral responsibility for his actions in the social investing area. ProductCo's chief executive explained:

> It sounds like a heartless attitude that I'm expressing, but it isn't. . . . [The fund] is there for the benefit of the beneficiaries of the trust, and to provide them with retirement benefits, not to provide them with jobs before they retire, or to provide roads in the community where they live, or to provide them with the emotional

satisfaction that some of them might get from having this attitude or that attitude about a social question. So that's the purpose of the fund. It's an investment fund designed to produce investment results to provide retirement benefits for the beneficiaries of the fund. The law just says that that's the way it should be managed, and that you shouldn't be using it for other purposes.

Those who believe that social investing is improper can also bring economic arguments to bear. The fund at State B has recently been subjected to state legislation which prohibits investment in companies doing business in South Africa. The initial impact was to limit the investment options:

> Before, we had 88 keys on the piano, and then we ended up with 45 keys on the piano. We still make music. It may not be the same music, but it's music.

Over time, the fund has incurred two kinds of economic costs. First, selling South Africa–contaminated stocks and replacing them with others entails transaction costs: commissions on the trades and the impact of sometimes being forced to sell low and buy high. State B's chief investment officer estimated the effect on his multibillion-dollar portfolio:

> Obviously, if we had to sell $4 billion worth of securities, there is a commission cost involved, which is easily identifiable. We had to buy something back. This commission cost was involved, which is easily identifiable. The whole question of market impact is, everybody knows, there. The question of how much, we decided, was a half a percentage going out and half a percentage going back in.

In the second category are the opportunity costs associated with not being allowed to invest in a significant number of profitable companies. These costs are difficult to calculate. State B has created a "paper portfolio" of the investments that it had in place immediately before the divestment law took effect. After a couple of years of comparison between the paper portfolio and the actual, South Africa–free portfolio, State B's executives tentatively conclude that "it has cost us some money," but decline to estimate how much. (One might well ask why they spend the taxpayers' money running the paper portfolio, since the divestment law is a fait accompli. The answer appears to be that they are marshalling evidence to use the next time the legislature threatens to impose socially based investment restrictions.)[13]

The view that the law strictly forbids social investing is not universally held. Others see the law as less determinative, leaving room for—and, conversely, demanding—more individual judgment. There is disagreement both within and among funds. Even at ProductCo, whose chief executive is so adamant about the clarity of the law, some executives offer a more flexible view. One of the investment officers repeated his boss's official interpretation of ERISA, and then described "some situations where we had to compromise that for other goals." As part of a settlement with its unions, ProductCo "had to agree to have investments and mortgages in plant city areas"—surely a form of social investing. He also acknowledged that union officials "have provided us with lists of companies they would prefer that the funds not be invested in, which we gave to our [outside money] managers without comment."

Curiously, among the people we interviewed, lawyers seemed more inclined toward this flexible view of social investing, suggesting that the more one knows about the law, the more ambiguous one finds it to be. The most concise statement of the flexible interpretation came from an in-house legal counsel at State C. Note that he, coincidentally, used the same example—investing in roads—as ProductCo's chief executive, but reached an opposite conclusion:

> I'm not sure you have to maximize—see, I don't like that word *maximize*—your profits, which, you know, gives the view that you can't look at anything else. Let's say this state is reaching a gridlock with its highway system. And so, the legislature and the governor say to us, "The economy is going to fall apart unless you and some of these other huge funds invest in roads or high-speed trains." As long as you are getting a decent return, I think you can take those other kinds of things into consideration. In that regard, I think you don't have blinders on when you work as a fiduciary.

The chief executive of this fund does not share his lawyer's view. For example, he characterized environmental investing as "purely an emotional issue," and associated it with "crazies." He lamented that he, unlike his private counterparts, did not have

ERISA to shield him from social investing pressures: "If I had an ERISA standard there, I could head this off . . . because if we don't we are just going to get the crap beaten out of us."

Two things are interesting about this statement. First, it embodies the view that ERISA is absolutely clear on the issue of social investing, providing an impenetrable shield which enables a pension executive to deflect difficult questions without ever addressing them on the merits. Second, it reflects a remarkably imperfect understanding of the law. Because his state has a pension statute that tracks the language of ERISA almost verbatim, he already has the benefit of whatever protection ERISA provides. For this chief executive, ERISA has assumed mythic proportions, and the details of what the law actually says have become secondary.

What emerges from the examination of social investing is a picture of fund executives continually re-creating the law in their own image and likeness to support the judgments they make on contentious issues. The language of the legal standards is sparse and usually inconclusive, and legal experts readily acknowledge its ambiguity. Fund executives, however, rarely view themselves as engaging in an act of interpretation. Rather, they typically describe themselves as following explicit and detailed prescriptions—what ProductCo's chief pension executive referred to as "the clear-cut rule that's stated in ERISA." Questions of blame are preempted, and responsibility is fixed in advance on an unyielding external force. It is not surprising that people adopt this tactic. It is striking, however, that few of the pension insiders we interviewed—all of whom have access to sophisticated legal advice—have ever stopped to question the uncertain legal grounds on which their assertions rest. Apparently, the law is too useful to risk subjecting it to critical scrutiny.

NOTES

1. Restatements on various legal topics are issued by the American Law Institute, which works under the umbrella of the American Bar Association. Restatements are authoritative, but not neces-

sarily binding on particular courts. To find the real common law, one must research the judicial decisions in individual states.

2. *Restatement of Trusts (Second)*, secs. 170, 227(a), and 228.

3. ERISA, sec. 404(a)(1)(A)(i).

4. Id., sec. 403(c)(1).

5. Id., secs. 404(a)(1)(B & C). Some legal authorities view ERISA as setting a stricter prudent expert standard.

6. See section 3(21) of ERISA and sections 2509.75-8 and 2510.3-21(c) of the Department of Labor regulations that accompany it, which appear in Part 29 of the Code of Federal Regulations.

7. ERISA, sec. 409.

8. The relevant provisions are scattered through sections 402–5 of ERISA. They are summarized in John H. Langbein and Bruce A. Wolk, *Pension and Employee Benefit Law* (Westbury, N.Y.: Foundation Press, 1990), pp. 495–503.

9. The divergence of opinion between IndustrialCo and ProductCo on the question of sponsor interest yields yet another irony. In Chapter 4, we demonstrated that IndustrialCo's investment style owes much to its historical independence from its sponsor, whereas ProductCo's reflects the influence of the sponsor's chief executive. Here, however, IndustrialCo's executives emphasized their obligations to the sponsor, while ProductCo's stressed that ERISA precludes even thinking along those lines.

10. Interestingly, the employees of State C believe that this sense of obligation has not always been part of the fund's culture. Part of State C's creation myth is a story about how the fund emerged from a less enlightened past:

    I don't think that it was always that way. I think there were people running this system who viewed this as a little kingdom, who viewed the members as a necessary evil.

11. An instance of this competition has recently emerged in California. In the summer of 1991, Governor Pete Wilson tried to recapture some of the California Public Employees Retirement System's surplus in order to balance the state budget. To further his plan, Wilson asked the legislature to restructure the fund's board of trustees in a way that would give him control. CALPERS chief executive Dale M. Hanson resisted Wilson's initiative, characterizing it as "a hostile takeover." The legislature ultimately approved a compromise: Wilson was given $1.6 billion from the fund's cost-of-living account, but was not allowed to restructure the board. Despite initial speculation that Hanson's resistance would cost

him his job, he has survived. For accounts of this controversy, see Richard W. Stevenson, "California Battle Over State Funds," *The New York Times*, June 18, 1991, p. D1, col. 6; Michelle Osborn, "Politicians Coveting Pension Funds," *USA Today*, July 3, 1991, p. 4B, col. 1; and Alan Deutschman, "The Great Pension Robbery," *Fortune*, January 31, 1992, p. 8.

12. As yet, there seems to have been no movement toward repealing these laws in response to the gradual dismantling of apartheid.

13. One state pension fund has had to write off more than $100 million in investments in local companies that were made as part of a back-yard investment program. See James A. White, "Back-Yard Investing Yields Big Losses, Roils Kansas Pension System," *The Wall Street Journal*, August 21, 1991, p. A1, col. 1.

CHAPTER 6

PENSION FUND CULTURE—
DIFFERENCES BETWEEN PUBLIC
AND PRIVATE FUNDS

In the days and weeks preceding October 13, 1989, publicity about the proposed employee buyout of United Airlines drove the UAL stock to unprecedented heights. When the financing for the deal collapsed on Friday, October 13, the domino effect on the market was nearly instantaneous, and the Dow Jones average fell a couple of hundred points in less than an hour. The financial press, which had been surprised by the 500-point slide in October 1987, jumped on the story and played up the eerie coincidence of this event taking place almost two years to the day after the 1987 debacle. As the market hung on the brink of panic over the weekend, analysts began to point out that the crisis had resulted almost entirely from the UAL episode, and it gradually subsided with little lasting effect on either the market or the economy as a whole.[1]

These events set up a natural experiment that exposed some significant cultural differences between two of the pension funds we had selected for study. As the market began to collapse on Friday afternoon, we happened to be speaking with an executive at ProductCo. Then, and in later interviews, we were able to gauge how this private fund reacted. On the following Monday, we visited State A, where we saw a dramatically opposite set of reactions to the same event.

Our contact at ProductCo reflected the anxiety being reported in the media. We were told that there was frantic activity: The fund's management was monitoring the market minute-by-minute, holding high-level meetings, consulting outside managers, and making decisions about what to do to minimize the damage to the portfolio. There was no time to talk to anthropologists.

When we arrived at State A on Monday, we expected to hear similar things, and we were even prepared for the cancellation of our meetings. To our surprise, it was business as usual. The fund's three highest-ranking investment officials and its counsel spent more than half the day with us. The investment specialists stepped out of the room on a couple of occasions to glance at their computer screens, and then returned and calmly reported the latest market news. Although the fund is substantially indexed, billions of dollars are actively managed. But there were no frantic phone calls to outside managers, no urgent meetings, no discussions of short-term market strategies (nor had there been on Friday, according to their account). During the course of Monday afternoon, the head of the equity division observed that the fund's time frame was "just short of the hereafter," and dismissed the unfolding financial drama as an ephemeral aberration that the fund would largely ignore.

These observations in October of 1989 led us to ask: Do the differences we noted between ProductCo and State A reflect general differences between public and private pension funds? As we pursued the question, three categories of differences emerged. First, different kinds of people work in public and private funds. Second, they work in different environments and approach their work from different perspectives. Third, they are held accountable for their actions in different ways. We ultimately concluded that there are fundamental cultural differences between public and private funds, and that such differences have practical investment consequences. In this chapter, we present the findings that led us to this conclusion.

WHO ARE THE MANAGERS?

At most large pension funds, both public and private, investments are managed by three levels of professional personnel: a chief executive, a chief investment officer, and a staff of specialists within each investment category, such as equities and fixed-income. Public and private chief executives come from different backgrounds. Those in the public sector are typically recruited from executive positions at other funds or from Wall Street, whereas those in the private sector almost invariably have come up through the hierarchies of the corporations where they work. At the two lower levels, both public and private funds recruit people from their own bureaucracies and from Wall Street, although only the public funds seem to hire staff from other pension funds. The backgrounds of individual pension professionals are simultaneously a source and an effect of cultural differences between the public and private funds.

BOX 6–1
Public versus Private Pension Funds

- In 1990, pension funds controlled 38.2 percent of the assets of all institutional investors. Pension funds now total $2.5 trillion dollars, up from $891 billion in 1981, and only $17.6 million in 1950.
- The percentage of total institutional investor assets controlled by private pension funds fell slightly, from 31.8 percent in 1981 to a still significant 26.6 percent in 1990. The faster-growing public pension funds increased their share of total institutional investor assets from 10.7 percent in 1981 to 11.6 percent in 1990.
- Public pension funds are accounting for a larger and larger share of total pension fund assets. In 1990, private pension funds held $1,737 billion worth of assets, which represented 69.5 percent of the assets of all pension funds—a decrease from the 1981 figure of 74.8 percent. By comparison, public funds held $756.3 billion in 1990, and their share of pension fund assets rose from 25.2 percent in 1981 to 30.5 percent in 1990.
- Asset allocation comparisons between public and private pension funds reveal that private funds have much higher equity holdings than public funds.
- Private funds (excluding funds placed with insurance companies) invested 55 percent of assets in equity in 1990. The comparable

---

Box 6–1 *(continued)*

figure for public funds was 37 percent. This gap will likely shrink as state and local pension funds adopt more aggressive strategies and increase their holdings of equities.

- Between 1980 and 1990, state and local funds increased their share of assets invested in equities from 22 percent to 37 percent, whereas private funds shifted more gradually from 48 percent to 55 percent equity.

- These trends reinforce the notion that rapidly growing pension funds, and public funds in particular, will increasingly control corporate equities.

1990 Asset Structure: Public and Private

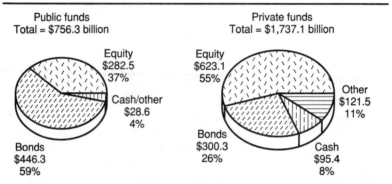

Public funds
Total = $756.3 billion

Equity
$282.5
37%

Cash/other
$28.6
4%

Bonds
$446.3
59%

Private funds
Total = $1,737.1 billion

Equity
$623.1
55%

Other
$121.5
11%

Cash
$95.4
8%

Bonds
$300.3
26%

Private fund data covers funds managed by trustees, with a total of $1,104.4 billion. Another $632.7 billion is managed by private insured funds.

Source: Brancato & Gaughan, Columbia Institutional Investor Project.

Private Funds

At the six private funds we studied, each of the chief pension executives is a long-term employee of the fund or its corporate sponsor. The majority of the chief executives have had experience in the corporate treasury department as well as the pension fund. One has worked exclusively in pension management and has had only limited contact with the corporate bureaucracy. Another worked in manufacturing before moving into pension management.

Pension fund management tends to be a corporate dead end. Although a couple of the chief executives we spoke with seemed to have aspirations to move up the corporate treasury ladder (and some prospects for doing so as well), for most, running the pension fund is a more or less permanent position. It is a reasonably remunerative job, and the incumbents see the work as interesting and often satisfying. Nonetheless, it is not a position that the most ambitious corporate stars seek, and they are rarely asked to assume it.

As one might expect from their backgrounds, pension chief executives usually bring to the job an extensive knowledge of the culture of the sponsoring corporation and considerable skill at corporate politics. They vary widely in their knowledge of investing. Most understand the major concepts and use the jargon of the investment world with reasonable facility, but depend on experts to analyze and execute the details of their funds' strategies.[2]

In the private sector, investment professionals at the two lower levels come from treasury and finance departments of the sponsoring corporation, other institutional investors (e.g., banks or insurance companies, but rarely from other pension funds), and Wall Street firms. Those coming from Wall Street usually take a pay cut, or at least lose the opportunity for the "big score." In exchange, they get relative job security, less pressure, more manageable hours, and, in some instances, the opportunity to run a large investment operation.

We met some investment professionals who had moved voluntarily from Wall Street to a pension fund and others who had been laid off or fired. In still other instances, it depended on whom one asked. At ProductCo, for example, the chief pension executive told us that the head of the equity division had been hired after "they forced him out" at a large insurance company. When we interviewed the individual in question, he told it differently: "I built and set up the whole investment operation at an insurance company. I came over here and I retired from the insurance company."

The outside professionals who join pension funds bring the detailed investment knowledge that those who have risen through the corporate bureaucracy may lack. They also have a sense of independence from the corporate culture; in fact, those coming from the performance-oriented world of Wall Street may be unfamiliar with the whole phenomenon of corporate cultural influence. This sense of independence has important consequences for fund management. On the one hand, it leads fund managers to focus on decisions from a purer investment perspective. On the other, it can cause them frustration when economic logic must yield to cultural or historical imperatives. At ProductCo, for example, we heard complaints from a Wall Street veteran about the degree to which the pension fund mimics the corporation's bureaucratic approach to decision making.

A characteristic of jobs at private pension funds that we had not expected to find is their permanence. We heard much talk about pressure to perform, but saw little evidence of sanctions for failure to do so. The one firing story that we heard—the one about the equity division head at ProductCo—involved not poor performance, but a dispute over style with the sponsor's CEO. The equity manager, who was not a long-time corporate insider, performed well but did not do things the ProductCo way. Notwithstanding the rhetoric to the contrary, most jobs in a corporate pension fund are virtually tenured positions. At many funds, one of the sources of this job security is the fact that responsibility for poor performance can be displaced onto external money managers.

These external managers are an important component of the management teams of the funds they serve. They are typically recruited through consulting firms, three or four of which seem to have most of the large fund business. The consultants function much like corporate headhunters. The fund discusses with its consultant the range of investment styles that it wishes to implement, and how it wants to allocate its assets among managers. The consultant then collects quantitative performance data as well as qualitative background information on a large number of managers within each of the relevant styles. (Much of the background information will be drawn from the consultant's own experience.) From these longer lists, the consultant will choose a limited number of candidates, usually fewer than half a dozen, for the fund's management to interview for each slot.

The final decision about whom to hire usually comes down to such nonfinancial criteria as "gut feeling" and "kicking the tires." The outside managers understand the respective roles of consultants and fund executives and plan their presentations accordingly. They believe they need hard evidence of solid performance and internal stability to impress the consultants. Once they are allowed in the door of the fund, it becomes a matter of one or two simple performance charts, followed by a sustained effort to establish and nurture a personal relationship.

The rhetoric about the retention of outside managers is hard-nosed. Some of the managers we interviewed told of being fired by pension funds after a bad quarter or two. Fund executives also talked about the performance pressure they exert. But at the nine funds we studied, we saw very little concrete evidence of firing outside managers for poor performance. On the contrary, it seems to be a rare and distasteful event. The reality is that unless a fund decides to index and thus dispense with managers entirely, managers who perform at least respectably and who are attentive to their relationships with fund executives have some expectation of job security.

Public Funds

The top executives at the three public funds we studied came to their present executive positions via three different routes: politics, other public funds, and Wall Street. The CEO of one has a background in law and politics. Another chief executive had worked his way up through a variety of civil service jobs in another state. When he finally reached the number two job in that state's pension fund, he began applying for the top job elsewhere. The third left a Wall Street job for strongly personal reasons:

> I came here because of what were family disasters. I'm prepared to work like an anchor, just as long as I can keep close to home.

Because of government-in-the-sunshine laws, the processes by which public chief executives are chosen are generally public. There are few secrets about the candidates. All the dirty laundry from the selection process gets aired, which can be particularly difficult for an unsuccessful inside candidate who stays on with the fund. A member of one state's board of trustees gave a candid account of how the fund's current chief executive was selected. He emphasized the political pressures that influenced the choice. The board divided along employer-employee lines. Despite the politics, the selection has worked out well, in his judgment:

> It came to five finalists, two of them being assistant executive officers at this fund. . . . The employee reps and myself backed one of the inside candidates. The others backed the other inside candidate. Except that a newly elected state official, deciding it was early in the term, who didn't want to get burned by either side, decided to take a walk. And so he would not participate. So we had about three or four straight efforts for each of us to select our candidate with the vote always tied. I mean, there was nobody breaking it. Among the other three that were to be interviewed, a third, outside candidate very much impressed us in his interview. So it became very clear to two of us on each side of the camp that we needed to break the deadlock and go with a compromise candidate. And that was the outside candidate. But he turned out to be far more than just a compromise candidate. He turned out to be a very excellent CEO.

The chief executive of a state pension fund is rarely subject to civil service protection. Despite the rhetoric about performance pressures in the private sector, public pension executives are much more likely to be fired than their private counterparts. The cause can range from poor fund performance to scandal to political insensitivity to, in the case of elected officials, voter whim. In one state, for example, a scandal wiped out an earlier generation of executives. In another, a former chief executive who came from the private sector lacked the political skill to maintain good relations with the board of trustees. As a result, the board ultimately fired him. A board member who participated in the controversy described it as follows:

> He was very definitely from the private sector, and he had a lot of trouble relating to a board, much less a lay board, and so relation-

ships quickly deteriorated. And it got to the point where he would make statements like, "I don't know why in the world I have to go in there and get permission from this board that doesn't know what it's talking about." We would routinely force him to bring in his recommendations, and do exactly the opposite. We could overturn his negative recommendations. It was a most unusual and unique sort of circumstance. It was not that we were just doing something arbitrarily, getting ourselves in trouble. I don't mean to create that impression. But, for example, the former CEO had decided that he was going to have his own advisers here and not the ones that the board had selected for him. His real estate advisers nearly immediately got into a huge fight with one of the original real estate advisers we had here, who had this strong relationship with the board. So every time his firm would bring in a proposed real estate transaction, the former CEO would immediately try to kill it, and we would resurrect it and buy it.

The lower-echelon investment specialists are usually either career civil servants or what can only be called refugees from Wall Street. One of the equity specialists working for one of the state funds followed the civil service track:

I have a Bachelor of Science in finance. I graduated in the late 60s and spent two years in the service. I worked for an insurance company as a claims adjuster for a year, took a civil service exam, and came to work for the state.

His boss, the head of the equity division of the fund, had managed the main office of a national brokerage firm, selling, as he described it, "God, you name it, everything: boxcars, stocks, bonds, pork bellies." He saw the public sector as an escape:

Oh, I spent 30 years with a national brokerage firm. I retired. I felt that I had a fair amount of money, my health, and most of my brains were still intact and I felt that I'd had it.

Other executives found employment in public funds after being laid off by Wall Street firms. One of the equity specialists at State B had worked with two private mutual funds for 15 years. When asked why he had come to State B, he responded, "They were the only people that were willing to hire me at the time. . . . Something is better than nothing." When we interviewed him, he had been with the state fund for 15 years.

Those who work in state funds see a number of advantages that more than make up for the relatively low public salaries. For all but the top person, security is an obvious attraction. The CEO of one public fund took a jaundiced view of his subordinates: "Part of the problem with civil service is, you have a portfolio manager managing $10 billion and when he's not doing too good you can't fire him." In addition, there is a sense of power that derives from having responsibility for vast sums of money. One executive described his position bluntly as "a very heady trip." The chief investment officer at State A elaborated on these themes:

> These jobs are, at least, enormously satisfying. The ups and downs are a little imposition. We have, particularly in this fund, little or no turnover. It's just a nonissue. Most jobs in government seem to be just working with somebody else in government. You pass a form to somebody else. And these are positions where you almost exclusively deal with people outside of government. You have exposure, if you wish to have it. You get some sense of travel, to go from one end of the state to another, every week, whether you want to or not. And there's a certain pizzazz, or whatever it is. "What do you do?" "I'm responsible for 40 billions of dollars." Whether you are or not, people think it sounds important.

Public fund employees also made frequent reference to the collegial decision-making style at their funds. Many of the public sector people we interviewed contrasted this with what they perceived to be the class structure of private funds. As one of them described it:

> They've got two or three classes of people. They've got the guy at the top that runs the shop. And then they've got two people under that. You're a portfolio manager, which means you're the guy that's on the line every day. At least for me personally, that's not my make-up. They've also got a marketing guy. And the marketing guy's out there trying to sell you, day after day, on why you ought to buy his money management firm.

Because of the recruitment patterns, there are people at all levels of public funds who have an intimate knowledge of how a state bureaucracy works. Many of the top people are experienced political infighters, skilled at jousting with governors and powerful legislators. Although many of the chief executives do not have technical investment backgrounds, the public funds' middle ranks are well staffed with people who are investment experts, as a result of a prior career on Wall Street or knowledge acquired in climbing the civil service ladder. All in all, despite low pay scales, the public funds we studied have managed to hire and retain people who, collectively, bring to the job all of the skills essential to managing the fund.

Many public fund executives view this state of affairs as fragile. Officials at each of the funds we studied believe that they have been uncommonly lucky in assembling their management teams, and are doubtful that they will be able to replace themselves with people of comparable quality. A typical assessment of the problem came from an executive at State B:

> I think maybe a part of the answer, and this may not be right, is that we were lucky getting the people that we did at the time we got them. When you look around this place, the problem is that we're all too old. So, maybe we have done a good job recently. We're all going to be gone in five years. Not all of us, but many of us. And many of the people will be gone. And maybe that was part of it. The people that got laid off on Wall Street, or they had enough of it.
>
> *Just got lucky here, to get these people?*
> I think so.
>
> *Can you attract new people, given the salary limits of the state?*
> No, that's what I'm saying. I don't know how you can maintain the quality of the people. And I'm not trying to flatter myself.

As he sees it, the only potential solution is to offer a superior working environment. In particular, he believes that public funds should stress responsibility and participation in the decision-making process: "We're trying to get the younger people as much involved as we possibly can and as quickly as we can."

THE NATURE OF THE WORK

One of the best ways to capture the fundamental difference between working at a private fund and a public fund is to analyze accounts of what happened during the October 1987 and October

1989 market crashes. For the current generation of investment
specialists, the 1987 crash represents the most dramatic single
event they have experienced in their professional lives. The
1989 crash, while less severe, was a frightening déjà vu, with
the added element of a weekend to worry between onset and outcome. Executives' recollections of what they felt and what they
did during these events is significant evidence of their values,
concerns, and priorities.

On the private side, the most vivid recollections we heard
were those of the chief pension executive at ProductCo about the
1989 crash, which occurred during the time we were interview-
ing him and members of his staff. His long and extraordinarily
detailed account given a few weeks after the crash emphasized
the level of activity, the tension, and the atmosphere of crisis at
his fund:

> I guess what I would say is that we do have, and we had back in
> 1987 as well, some overlay asset allocation strategies in place that
> depended then, and still do, on day-to-day market movements.
> Ours back then and now too operate more or less automatically. In
> other words, we got the funds established so that if the market
> goes up a certain amount, then we do this. If it goes down a certain
> amount, we do that. In a period of great sudden movements you
> might want to look at that and modify it, and that's essentially
> what we did on Friday the 13th. The thing was operating auto-
> matically, but when the market started to rapidly decline, and it
> happened very quickly, and I just happened to notice it on my
> screen, and I looked and saw that the market was way down. So, I
> went upstairs to the trading room where the people were execut-
> ing the strategy we'd agreed on just to try to find out what was
> happening. The futures contract went and hit certain circuit
> breaker points, and so on. The market was declined like this [*ges-
> turing to show steepness of decline*]. . . . So, I was trying to remem-
> ber now exactly when does that futures thing cut in, and what's
> going to happen, what it does, and so on. There were several people
> that were normally involved in this process that were out of the
> office. But those of us that were here just focused on what was
> happening and looked at the screens and so on. We basically con-
> tinued to carry on out the strategy as we had previously agreed to.
> . . . It was so quick. It all took place really in an hour or so. The
> circuit breakers were in effect a good part of the time. There

wasn't a lot we could have done anyway, but then what we did do was that over the weekend we thought, "Now, how do we think we want to behave on Monday morning?" We stayed around, several of us, until six or seven on Friday night. And I said, "All right, let's have an asset allocation meeting at 8 o'clock on Monday morning, and those of us who can do it will get in here earlier." We called all the people that we needed to who weren't still here on Friday afternoon and made sure that they were in here in time. One of the key implementers of this strategy, he got in here about 6:30 that morning, and started to make phone calls to find out how the people that he dealt with viewed the market. By 7:30 I was here, and talked to my boss and we agreed, "All right, we better have a meeting, a phone meeting of the fiduciary committee at 8:45." . . . And we agreed that . . . we would have a telephone conference call at 8:45, which would be our meeting. At eight we had here in this office the asset allocation group, which is my own staff, and we discussed it. By this point several of the people had already been in from, let's say, 7:30, and one guy had been in at 6:30, and they had talked to the people that they had talked to about the market falling. And, we had a pretty good sense of what we thought was going to happen when the market opened. And we already knew the evidence from what had happened in Tokyo and London, and things that were happening in the continental markets. And so, we discussed what we thought we should do, and then at 8:45 we . . . talked about the thing for about a half an hour. Before 9:30 when the stock market opened, we had decided what we wanted to do, and that's what we did. . . . During the day, as the day's events unfolded on Monday a week ago today, we changed our minds a couple of times. We had to get in touch with . . . a couple of the other committee members by phone to get agreement to change the strategy this way and that way, and we did that. And then, by the end of the day we put out a written report and faxed it to the members telling them what had happened. And then, I think, let's see, I can't remember. I guess we hung around here that evening and decided what we wanted to do. I think we did. We had a meeting at, let's say, about 5 o'clock, which lasted about two hours with my staff. We decided what we wanted to do for the next day. So then a couple of the people stayed and wrote a report, and the next morning we looked at that and we faxed that out to the committee members. We got their approval to operate that way for Tuesday and on. And that's where we've been since then. I think that we put out another sort of updating report on Tuesday night, and then on Friday we put out another report summarizing all of the events of the preceding five or six trading days.

The defining cultural feature of this account is the protagonists' apparent belief in their ability to *do something* about what was happening. They treated the crash as a problem to be solved rather than a storm to be ridden out. They met again and again, they discussed possible courses of action, and they executed a highly active strategy. Elsewhere in the interview, the chief executive wondered aloud about other things that might have been done—"brilliant steps" that became evident only in hindsight.

Contrast this with an account of the more serious 1987 crash that we heard from the chief investment officer at State A. The dominant features of this account are inactivity, a sense of powerlessness, and, ultimately, confidence that the crash meant little to investors with the long-term perspective of a pension fund. The 1987 account matches precisely what we observed when we were present in State A's offices during the 1989 crash:

> There wasn't anything to do. I mean you just watched. We all sat and watched the ticker. . . . It was very depressing. But there was nothing you could do in the middle of the day that was going to make it any better.
>
> *Did you start doing things?*
> No, we watched.
>
> *You watched?*
> Yeah. I think we have tried here to take the view that we're really in this for the long term and the purpose of this is to pay the benefits for people that are working today and those who have retired. I'm in my early 40s. I've got 20 years and that's where we ought to be looking. And one day, or one year, or two years shouldn't disrupt the long-term strategy, which is based on historical performance, that equities do well over time and that we ought to have a commitment to the equity market and we ought to have the courage, the conviction to ride out the bad times because the good times will be better.

These contrasting crash stories epitomize the most general difference between private and public fund culture: in the former, a perceived need to attempt to control events, and in the latter, a sense of resignation that seems motivated at times by powerlessness and at times by confidence. A number of other differences are also significant.

Private funds tend to behave like private corporations in matters of communication. They view the details of their investment strategies and performance as trade secrets. Throughout our interviews, we were given pieces of information on the condition that we respect their proprietary nature. (We have done so, of course.) There is little communication with other funds about these topics, even on a general level. Private funds typically subscribe to services that report the performance of all large funds, but with the names deleted. They can identify themselves and can therefore see where they rank, but they do not know how specific competitors are doing, or, more significantly, how well particular strategies are working in the pension world as a whole. The general lack of mobility of personnel from one private pension fund to another also helps limit the flow of information. As a result, private fund executives have little basis for comparing the efficacy of the various strategies among which they must choose.

The rhetoric at public funds is strikingly different. Chief executives repeatedly told us that their funds, because they are government agencies, must operate in the open, and that everything they do is a matter of public record. To back up this assertion, they sometimes produced written reports containing general information about asset allocation, return on investment, and other things that their private counterparts would never disclose. Consequently, public funds know a great deal more about each other than private funds. Additionally, private fund executives also know a good deal about the workings of public funds, although they frequently go to great lengths to distance themselves from some of the management procedures and concerns of their public brethren.

Public funds do not entirely fulfill the promise of this rhetoric, however. In the first place, because of the prevalence of indexing in the public sector, there is much less that is worth knowing. In addition, the lower-level officials who actually control the detailed information are much less forthcoming than their superiors. On a couple of occasions, we were caught in the middle of a difference of opinion between a chief executive and an investment specialist over whether a particular category of information should be made available to us. One issue that seemed particularly sensitive at one of the public funds was whether we would be permitted to observe the portion of a trustees' meeting at which investment strategy would be discussed. After consultation between investment professionals and lawyers, we were excluded. Despite these qualifications, it is fair to say that much more investment information is available from public than private funds.

A further point of distinction is that in all but one of the private funds we studied (the exception being IndustrialCo), there is a clear relationship between the particular culture of the sponsoring corporation and that of the fund. On the public side, by contrast, civil service culture exerts a more consistent influence on all funds. At ProductCo, for example, the bureaucracy and byzantine committee structure that characterize the fund also typify the sponsor's corporate culture. Recall as well the story of how ProductCo arrived at its present set of investment strategies. A critical event in the story was the sponsor's CEO insisting that an equity manager depart because his work habits deviated from the ProductCo way of doing things.

At TransCo, the corporate culture of the sponsor derives in large part from the strong personality of its CEO and his gospel of cost-cutting. As we heard repeatedly, his personality and its cultural emanations permeate the pension fund, to the point where the fund managers view their investment decisions as cost-wise corporate decisions. At MediaCorp, the sponsor's culture influences the fund in a very different but equally direct way. The fund's buy-value-and-hold philosophy is that of its sponsor's directors, some of whom have long-standing ties to the outside managers the fund has hired.

IndustrialCo stands as a striking exception to this observation. At least in part because of the fund's physical and legal separation from the sponsor, most of the fund executives we talked to have little sense of what the sponsor's culture is. On the contrary, some of them remarked on how lucky they were to be free of the constraints that they imagined to be endemic to the corporate environment. To borrow a metaphor from biology, the IndustrialCo fund is like Australia, its life forms evolving in splendid isolation from the environmental pressures that other private funds face.

A final point relates to the overall atmosphere at private versus public funds. At private funds, people look busy. A great deal of their time is spent managing relations. When asked a simple question about how they spend their working time, private fund executives talked about consulting with colleagues, attending internal meetings, managing external managers, and kicking the tires at companies whose stock they own. We do not mean to suggest that this time is not well spent. It is interesting, however, that meetings and other activities usually associated with government bureaucracies seem, in the pension world, to be much more common in the private sector.

Our observations at State A during the 1989 crash reflect the contrasting ambience of public pension funds. As first-time visitors to public funds, we were struck by two things. The first was how few people were there. The second was how little seemed to be happening.

Much of the inactivity can be accounted for in terms of indexing. Indexing requires little decision making and entails few relationships that need to be managed. As someone observed to us, an index cannot take you to lunch. But part of the explanation lies in the culture of civil service, because this kind of atmosphere evolves whenever any job is done by secure, modestly paid, and poorly supported public employees. Another way to frame the problem is to ask whether indexing is cause or effect: Does indexing help to create the culture of public funds, or does that culture lead public fund executives in the direction of indexing? We take up this issue in the next section.

ACCOUNTABILITY IN PRIVATE AND PUBLIC FUNDS

Another fundamental cultural difference between private and public funds relates to accountability. In all responsibly managed funds, there is a strong sense of accountability to the ultimate beneficiaries. The beneficiaries are remote, however, and likely to call for an accounting only if the fund were to collapse.

On a more immediate basis, private fund officials often talk about their accountability to the sponsoring corporation's bottom line, or at least to the sponsor's corporate notion of successful management. Their public counterparts talk instead about the press and the ballot box as the instruments of day-to-day accountability.

Accountability to the corporate bottom line was evident at IndustrialCo, where one of the executives bluntly stated that he viewed his job as reducing the cost of the company's products. In the same vein, at TransCo we heard repeatedly about how the abstract concern with costs is reinforced by a direct sense of accountability to the corporate CEO. TransCo's pension head described how he is called to account to the company's chief executive in informal, ad hoc meetings.

Surprisingly, however, this accountability to the bottom line seems to have few consequences. We heard only one story of a private fund employee being dismissed—and he was an outsider, a newcomer whose shortcoming was not poor performance, but his failure to assimilate the corporate culture. When the fund performs poorly, the favored solution is to blame outside managers whenever possible. But even in the case of outside managers, concern with the bottom line is largely rhetorical. We heard of few instances of outside managers actually being fired. When they were, it was usually for "changing their stripes." Poor performance was typically written off to the manager's particular style being temporarily out of sync with the market. As one of the outside managers noted, he and his counterparts are reasonably secure if they do nothing to attract adverse attention:

> They want to know that if they hire you, you're going to make them look good. But most of all, you're not going to make them look bad.

In the public sector, there is little sense of accountability to the sponsor's bottom line. On the contrary, public fund officials see it as an important part of their fiduciary duty to guard fund assets against rapacious politicians who would use them to balance the state budget.[3] Because of the prevalence of indexing, the bottom line of the fund itself is largely beyond anyone's control.

Public fund executives speak instead of the press and the ballot box as the primary agents of accountability. The outstanding characteristic of the press is that it is interested only in failure, and not success. State A's chief executive described his relationship with the press in these terms:

> Of course, there are no rewards. You beat the market, somebody's going to write it up? Forget it. Underperform? They'll be happy to. It's the environment in which we work.

He then pointed to his fund's annual report and asked rhetorically, "You think that a reporter would crack that book?" Given the nature of the press, the best way to survive its scrutiny is to avoid visible missteps. In addition to whatever financial merit it may have, indexing is an ideal way to achieve that purpose, of course.

For some public funds, the ballot box is a significant source of accountability. *Ballot box* (a term we heard from fund executives) can mean a number of things. In many states, the chief executive is elected by a board whose members are in turn elected, either by the voters at large or some special constituency such as a union. In a few others, the chief executive and/or fiduciary of the pension plan is an elected official such as the state treasurer or auditor. One public chief executive compared the ballot box to the bottom line in the private sector:

> In the private sector the bottom line is make or break. You make money or you don't.[4] That's the discipline: the market discipline. In the public sector, it's the ballot box. It's as simple as that, that's the discipline. And if you take away the ballot box, then you lose that discipline. That doesn't mean that people work any less hard, but there's a hell of a guarantee that just disappeared. It's just like in a socialist country, if there's no profit and loss statement, well, we've all seen what happens. I mean, we all see. You just don't get good performance.

The twin disciplines of the press and the ballot are such that public fund chief executives (but not their subordinates) can and sometimes do get fired. As a result, some chief executives report that they spend a great deal of time establishing and maintaining relationships with the press, their boards, and the various constituencies to which the members of their boards are accountable. The chief executive at State A described his early efforts to deal straightforwardly with the press, which were frustrated by the reporters' lack of interest in day-to-day competence:

> Once I called a press conference. It was my first complete year. It wasn't the best year the system ever had, and it wasn't the worst, but they ought to know. We'd put out reports. Nothing. Hadn't been a line about the pension system in the papers. So I thought, "Well, I'm accountable and I ought to do this." I'd called very few press conferences, so they came. I passed out the reports, and I gave it 10 minutes. Then I stopped. "Any questions?" There was a long pause. In the back of the room, one reporter put his hand up in the air and said, "Why are we here?" I said, "Because one little jiggle here, up or down, on this thing can save or lose more money than those bastards, the legislators, in six months of work for the state taxpayers. That's why you're here." Silence. One guy gets up and leaves. Another guy gets up. And then they all walked out. Just as it happened. Just as it happened.

As his career has progressed, this same executive has learned to deal with the press in subtler ways. He believes, for example, that he must be simultaneously open and cautious: open to scrutiny by the press, but cautious about giving reporters opportunities to misinterpret information. As an instance of this dilemma, he cited his concern about how the press reacts to changes in investment policy, however justifiable they might be:

> You put out a report that says, "Here's how we do it," and they say, "Fine," and throw it away. A year later, you decide to change, so you do it a different way. The reporter grabs it out: "Fund Executive Switches Policies on Eve of Desperate Reelection Try." Who needs it? I mean, I don't care. I tell everybody everything. I don't have drawers. I could, in my desk. Everything is here [on my desk top]. A reporter could walk in here and help themselves, as far as I'm concerned.

He believes that he has succeeded in managing this delicate relationship. In any event, the press is a burden he is willing to bear:

> I get along fine with the press. I mean, I might gripe that the nature of the press is to play up the negative and never the posi-

tive. But so what? If I didn't like that environment, there are a thousand guys that would steal or kill for my job, so I could easily leave it.

Another chief executive talked to us at length about his efforts to manage his relationship with a politically diverse board of trustees. After studying the difficulties experienced by his predecessor, he concluded that he was facing a "very explosive board: big fights between labor and management." He therefore decided "to focus on trust-building with the board"—or "my board," as he repeatedly called it. He then elaborated on this trust-building process:

> Dealing with boards is an art form. It's probably the most demanding part of your job, the care and feeding of the board. And I think I am very good at that, because I know how to work the board. And yet, I know that individual members of the board, when I'm not around, will say, "That so-and-so is doing such-and-such." And then they will badmouth you. But when you consider that you have a number of different individuals on there, if you can keep the majority of them in harmony, then you are doing an adequate job or maybe even a stellar job from that standpoint.

The purpose of working the board is twofold. Obviously, it promotes the job security of the incumbent chief executive. And it minimizes meddling in investment affairs by board members who are not investment professionals. By building the board's trust, and giving the members a sense of participation in investment decisions, the professionals hope that the board will defer to their recommendations on serious investment questions. One chief executive illustrated the point with reference to the fondness of board members for real estate investments:

> Real estate is the bane of every CEO in pension systems, because trustees love real estate. They can touch it. They can feel it. They can point with pride to it. And I used to joke in telling the trustees at the time when it was 5 percent of the portfolio, "See, it's 5 percent of the portfolio, and it's 95 percent in-house." A real major pain in the ass. They would spend more time concerned with that 5 percent than being concerned with the 50 percent or so that we had in equities, or the 40 percent or so I had in fixed income. Why? Who knows?

Public fund chief executives also report spending large amounts of time talking to the politicians who appoint some trustees and the union members, beneficiaries, and voters who elect others. Once again, this activity has a dual purpose and effect: to solidify the chief executive's position and to promote the image of the fund. Most of these people share with the press a voyeuristic interest in disaster and an indifference to solid if unspectacular performance. Thus, if they are persuaded that the chief executive is pursuing prudent policies and is showing sufficient interest in them personally, they are likely to think well of the fund and to leave the chief executive alone.

Another factor influences the relationship between fund executives and their political constituencies. A long-range objective of every chief executive we talked to, private as well as public, is to protect his fund against political incursion. On the private side, the fear is that Congress will tax profits and/or trading transactions. Public executives fear that state legislators will use pension surpluses to balance out-of-control budgets, or will encroach on the fund managers' ability to make independent investment judgments. One reason that most public fund executives strongly oppose such things as South Africa–divestment bills is their concern about opening the door to other kinds of constraints. If the politicians can get away with this, they reason, what will they tell us to do next? As a result, executives of large private funds spend significant amounts of time preparing and giving testimony to various congressional committees, while their public counterparts work behind the scenes to attend to the sensibilities of governors, state treasurers, and powerful legislators.

It surprises us that fund executives are not making greater use of the press in this ongoing tug-of-war. We find no evidence that they are making a concerted effort to induce the press to educate the public about the dangers of political encroachment, in the hope that the public will then pressure the politicians to leave the pension funds alone. It may be that they are trying, but the press is not interested in the story. It may also be that the fund executives have decided that the public will not understand the argument, or, if it does, will not agree with them.

THE INVESTMENT CONSEQUENCES OF CULTURAL DIFFERENCES

Indexing is the most important product of the cultural differences between public and private funds. Investment professionals vigorously debate the economic merits of indexing. Those who favor indexing argue that specific individual investments are so unpredictable and active management is so costly that it is more efficient to assemble a portfolio that replicates overall market results. Those who oppose indexing contend that the potential gains from outperforming the market far outweigh the costs and risks of active management. We lay no claim to being able to resolve this debate on the basis of the evidence we have collected. Our point, rather, is that the way in which a particular fund responds to the arguments for and against indexing is likely to be conditioned by cultural factors. On the public side, many cultural factors mitigate in favor of indexing, and few if any mitigate against it. Since the objective of maximizing profits lies at the very heart of capitalist enterprise, the cultural environment of private funds is generally hostile to indexing.

The attractiveness of indexing to public funds can be summarized as follows. First, it saves expenses, an important objective in a civil service environment. It can be done with a small and modestly paid staff; it requires no high-priced Wall Street wizards. Second, indexing is well adapted to the mechanisms of public-sector accountability. Although it is unlikely to produce notable successes, it is equally unlikely to yield notable failures. Because those to whom the fund is accountable—press and politicians—pay more attention to failure than success, the use of indexing means that such people will rarely pay any attention at all. When the fund does perform badly enough to attract attention, the management will be able to point out that the entire stock market is doing just as badly.

Third, a commitment to indexing requires an implied admission that one cannot beat the market—in effect, a statement that mediocrity will be good enough. In a civil service culture, this is an unremarkable kind of statement. If security, not success, is the paramount value, indexing is a perfect choice.

This attitude is difficult if not impossible to adopt in a corporate culture. A person who wants to get ahead does not want to be perceived as lacking confidence or shirking challenges. Such a person will be reluctant to admit that he can do nothing of an affirmative nature to improve the corporate bottom line. Thus, even if one believes that indexing is the best investment strategy, it is hard to say so in a "can do" corporate environment. This may help to explain why two of the three public funds we studied index more than half of their equity portfolios, while none of the six private funds use indexing to any significant degree.[5] It is clear that the people who manage these funds are conversant with and influenced by the economic arguments for and against indexing. It seems equally clear, however, that their receptivity to those arguments is conditioned by the cultural environments in which they hear them.

NOTES

1. The most significant effect of the crash was to undermine the junk bond market, which drastically reduced takeover activity.
2. This is not to suggest that hands-on management is necessary or always desirable. One of the funds that is recognized as especially well-managed has a chief executive who takes pains to point out that he is not an investment professional, and does not attempt to function as one.
3. For an account of some of the battles, see Maggie Mahar, "The Great Pension Raid," *Barron's*, December 2, 1991, p. 8.
4. Elsewhere in the interview, this same executive asserted that private funds are "in the business to make money for their companies."
5. There are a few large private funds that are heavily indexed, and some other governmental funds are more actively managed than the three we studied. But on the basis of our understanding of how other funds operate, we believe that the conclusions we advance are applicable to the majority of public and private funds in the United States.

CHAPTER 7

THE LANGUAGE OF INVESTMENT

Anthropologists have found that language is far more than a transparent medium for conveying facts and other substantive information. Language is itself a form of data, because the way that people speak about an issue provides important clues to the way that they think about it. All too often, language is treated merely as a window through which things can be seen. Our approach is to pause and look at the fingerprints on the glass.

In order to explain the relationship between language and thought, anthropologists frequently use the example of the Eskimo language. It has many words for the meteorological phenomenon that those in the temperate zones describe by the single word *snow*. The Eskimos' richer vocabulary reflects the fact that they are called on to think about the topic much more often. (An exception that proves the rule is temperate-zone ski enthusiasts, whose lexicon includes *frozen granular*, *packed powder*, etc.) If this were the only thing we knew about Eskimos, we would nonetheless be able to make some significant inferences about their environment and their culture.

The language available to talk about something can also limit the ways in which people think about it. It has been argued, for example, that one reason for the slow pace of economic reform in the former Soviet Union is that Soviet economists and policymakers have no tradition of speaking and writing about economic planning in units of less than five years. We will consider in this chapter whether a comparable phenomenon may be at work in the American investment world, where those who try to take a long-term perspective find themselves constrained by a vocabulary of financial analysis oriented almost exclusively toward the short term.

We turn now to the detailed analysis of the language of investment as we heard it spoken. We shift our focus from the substantive issues that lie behind the glass to the glass itself, searching for clues that will contribute to our understanding of the culture of capital. The language we analyze deals with three broad topics: the nature of the investment business, the different approaches of men and women to investment problems, and time horizons.

THE NATURE OF THE INVESTMENT BUSINESS

All the people we interviewed offered us their personal perspectives on the investment business. They talked, usually at great length, about how they got into the business, the kind of work they do, their professional philosophies, and the people with whom they work and against whom they compete. These were obviously matters of great personal concern to the speakers, and the talk was often intense, emotional, and colorful.

One of the most striking details of this talk was the pervasive metaphorical language comparing one thing to another, as in the first line of Alfred Noyes's poem, "The Highwayman": "The moon was a ghostly galleon tossed upon cloudy seas."[1] Metaphors can be explicit, as in Noyes's famous line, or implicit, as when someone compares one activity to another by adopting the language of the other activity. During the Persian Gulf War, for example, the press spoke of *surgical strikes*.

Metaphorical language is often more than a mere rhetorical flourish. The metaphors that individuals choose can be significant indicators of how they conceive of particular issues.[2] As metaphors spread through a culture, they not only reflect patterns of thought, but help to shape them.

Consider the commonly used phrases *break down* and *break up*. Each is a metaphor that describes some event by reference to a physical process. The two phrases are used in different contexts. Cars, negotiations, and people break down. Things that break up include ships on rocks, meetings, and marriages. The implications of the two metaphors are quite different. *Break down* is a mechanical metaphor: When a machine or anything else breaks down, the presumption is that it will be possible to pick up the pieces and put it back together again. *Break up* has a connotation of permanence: Things break up into little pieces that, like Humpty Dumpty, are beyond reassembly. (Think about using the two phrases as transitive verbs: One breaks down a bicycle to fit it into the trunk of the car, but breaks up rocks in the garden.)

Thus, if a person describes something in the investment world as breaking down—say, the internal quality controls at a money management firm—the listener may infer that he is describing a reversible process of disassembly. By contrast, if someone talks about a business partnership breaking up, the listener is likely to assume a permanent split. As the description of a particular event spreads through the culture, popular perceptions can be conditioned by the metaphor used. Ultimately, if a particular metaphor becomes pervasive, it may be difficult to persuade people to think about the event in any other way, regardless of how the facts unfold. Recall, for example, how metaphorical images have influenced recent political campaigns: Jimmy Carter as a hostage in the White House, Michael Dukakis as the patron of Willie Horton, and the like.

Sports Metaphors

The vast majority of the metaphors used to describe the investment business relate to sports and games. Our initial hypothesis was that this simply reflected the fact that investment is a masculine domain, and men talk about sports. We thought, however, about other areas we had investigated that were equally male-dominated—the culture of lawyers, for example—but were rarely described in sporting terms. We were also overwhelmed by the frequency of these metaphors and the detailed consistency we found from speaker to speaker. We suspected that something more significant was involved.

At the most general level, people use sports metaphors to describe two fundamental attributes of investing: its competitiveness and the fact that it is possible to identify winners and losers with considerable precision. The chief investment officer at State B made the point succinctly with a baseball analogy:

> It's a competitive thing. I mean, it's like you're out there playing baseball or something, you want to win the game. And they've got a scoreboard out there and after three or five hours, or a two-week series or whatever, you look up the score and say, "Did I win or did I lose?"

An internal money manager at IndustrialCo made the same point in a subtler way. He likened his work to chess in order to distinguish the financial rewards of investing from the competitive satisfaction that he finds more significant:

> The fun part, I guess, is supposedly making a quick, easy buck even though it's not so easy, but it's like a mental chess game competing against 50 million other investors out there.

In yet another variation, the head of equities at ProductCo contrasted the sporting appeal of pension investing with the more businesslike approach he had had to take in his prior position as investment director for an insurance company. He emphasized the fun of pure investing and the pleasure he takes in competing with his own fund's outside managers:

> I would say that in terms of pure fun, the pension fund is more fun, because it's a pure investment game. It's like going to a chess match, if that's your game. And you play hard, and you hope to win, and the other is more of a business thing. And you have these restraints, and it's like you had another additional set of rules laid on you that made the game a little more complicated and, maybe, more difficult to play. But then I guess you don't have the same element of competition with the insurance company that you do with the pension fund. Our equity portfolios that we manage internally, for example, are categorized as large cap U.S. equities, large cap domestic equities. Well, ProductCo has another 15 outside managers doing exactly the same thing that we do and we want to beat these guys. We love to beat these guys. It's fun.

In the preceding quotations, pension fund insiders analogize investing to baseball and chess, which are games of skill. Others see more of a connection with games of chance. The chief executive at State B, for example, used a gambling metaphor to explain his fund's patient investing strategy. His fund is like the house, earning a slow but steady income while the high rollers come and go:

> All of these markets are really like a gambling casino. There is a risk and return to it. But we are the house. . . . And the important thing is to just keep playing the game.

The chief executive at State A used a similar metaphor to express his disdain for money managers and his consequent preference for indexing:

> I am persuaded that money managers focus on the short-term performance. That's probably because they don't know how to pick stock. So they pick the wrong ones and get out of them as fast as they can. I think it is probably all hooked up to the behavior of the stock market. Well, we don't bother. That's why we index. I think it's all a big crap game played by guys in Brooks Brothers suits anyway, and we don't bother.

Investment professionals use highly specific sports metaphors to distinguish different investment styles. We have already examined evidence that pension executives are often more concerned with avoiding failure than achieving success. Many of the people we talked to made this point with reference to baseball, comparing the consistent singles hitter to the high-risk, high-yield slugger who either hits a home run or strikes out. The equity director at ProductCo, for example, gave a tour de force of mixed metaphors, moving from naval bombardment through horse racing before finally settling on the baseball analogy:

> These corporate pension managers want to have some sense that there's some kind of control. They don't want to be blown out of the water. They don't want to be surprised. You know, in the old days, you'd be out there and you'd be trying to hit a home run, and you'd try to really do something very spectacular and just move way ahead of the pack. And you'd stand out, and then you'd have a lot of attention, acclaim, and so forth. Now this is much less appealing. Now, these pension funds, they're just like in any other part of the business. They want to have some way that they can measure and keep control. If they don't hit the home run, they're willing to hit a couple of singles as long as they don't get struck out three times in a row.

He reiterated the point in a different context, describing how home run hitters are a vanishing breed being supplanted by more cautious types:

> In the old days, everyone tried to be like that. It was just the question of who could come in and hit the home run. Now, the kind of people are much more cautious. They have all these new techniques and quantitative approaches. They're less interested in being some kind of spectacular shooting star and they're more interested in just managing the risk, keeping everything under tight controls so that you don't get too far off the track. So it's a very different kind of person.[3]

Outside money managers frequently emphasized the need to stay calm and maintain a positive outlook in the face of financial setbacks. One of them made this point in baseball terms:

> *But do you continue to like doing this?*
> Yes, I love it. You have to have a strong ego. You've got to have some modest degree of intelligence and a nose for seeing, being observant about the world around you. And then you've got to have enough of an ego to be able to be wrong and take your lumps. It was tough last year, I was depressed, but you've got to be able to get up every day and swing. It's just like a baseball player who goes into a batting slump. He's got to be able to work his way out of a slump. And I think there are so many parallels to professional athletics in our business. It's fun. God, it's fun to buy stocks when they go down and watch them go up!

The people we interviewed spent a great deal of time talking about other people in the investment world. Just as the investment business is described as a sport or game, those who engage in it are often talked about as athletes, coaches, or other kinds of performers.

As just noted, there are two ways to succeed as a manager of pension assets: hitting many singles (and some doubles), or hitting an occasional home run. Because pension executives place great value on steady performance, they have more admiration for the singles hitter. As one of the executives said in reference to a highly regarded outside manager, "He has been one hell of a good money manager. We say he doesn't hit home runs, he hits singles and doubles."

Singles hitters are admired for two reasons: first, because consistently hitting singles produces a good outcome, and second, because trying to hit home runs all the time is an exercise in futility for most people. Nonetheless, it is recognized that in investment as in baseball there are exceptions, stars who combine power and consistency. An outside manager spoke with awe of the Mickey Mantles of the investment world:

> There's a certain star system in the business if you look at mutual fund performance—the Peter Lynches of the world, and others like John Neff, and others you see in *Barron's*. In baseball and in any professional sports there's a star system involved and it's always positively correlated with how much money they make. It's also a business where the great ball players are the guys who've had eight years of .300 batting average, you know, 25 home runs and 100 RBIs a year. Those are the great players, not the guys who had 2 good years out of 10; even though those 2 years may have been spectacular. The Mickey Mantles and the great money managers are very few and far between.

And in a rare deviation from the sports theme, a TransCo executive characterized outside managers as rock stars:

> This was not my career path, but I do have the perspective of how a manager thinks. And I don't let their b.s. affect me. You sit here after a while and you get a little cynical from the sponsor's standpoint. You just say, "You know, a lot of this is just showmanship. It's marketing. Each guy's got his little show. It's entertainment." Literally, I mean, it sounds funny, but it's very true. They're not much different than rock stars.

Given the widespread skepticism about inconsistent home-run hitters and the distrust of self-promoting rock stars, it is not surprising that the ideal pension investment organization is usually described as a team—and not just any team, but a team that works together unselfishly. In the words of an outside manager who plays on such a team, it is "like a basketball team that goes to the national championship, doesn't have three All-Americans, you know, on the starting five, but it has a very good cohesive team effort."

From the fund's perspective, the team approach is attractive because it is likely to yield steady if unspectacular results. From an outside manager's perspective, being a team player is worthwhile because it means that you are less likely to be called to account for a poor individual performance. The same manager who introduced the basketball analogy provided a detailed example of the advantages of team play:

> You've got some leeway. When we got hired by MaterialCo, we had a bad 1981, really got behind the eight ball, but in 82 we had an okay year because we matched the market, and then in 83, 4, 5, 6, 7, 8, 9 we just lit them up, and so we had a mediocre 1990 and we're starting off pretty well in 1991, so I'd say that relationship is solid. Plus it's the contribution you also make to the group in terms of asset allocation, but that's a very unique culture, and it's done well.

The Significance of Sports Metaphors

Why are sports metaphors used so frequently, to the virtual exclusion of all others? It could be that this is just insignificant locker room talk. But why, we asked, are these metaphors so much more pervasive in the investment world than in any other domain we are familiar with (including, interestingly, sports itself)? Perhaps investment people use sports metaphors because they actually see important parallels between what they do and playing games.

If so, what is there about sports that evokes these comparisons? Two straightforward points of similarity are the competitiveness of both sports and investing and the fact that both produce results that are readily quantifiable and easily understood. There is no difficulty in identifying winners and losers.

There are other significant parallels that are less obvious. Both sports and investing are zero-sum games in that for every winner there is a loser. If one investor buys a hot stock at just the right time, then another one has sold it too soon. When a money manager gets a new account, someone else has lost it. Both sports and investing also follow rules that are usually precise and often complex. The rules of investing operate at several levels. There are legal rules such as ERISA, the proxy regulations that relate to corporate governance, and the securities laws that govern the stock market. There are also rules of financial analysis: To be a real player, one must be able to turn volumes of financial data into a judgment about a company.

Both sports and investing have other conventions that anthropologists refer to as customary rules: informal, unwritten rules of practice that, for one reason or another, players generally follow. In both baseball and football, for example, it is a customary rule that the defensive players be positioned in certain ways in certain situations. Some of the investment people we interviewed analogized between these sports customs and the common practice in pension funds of having money managers with a range of investment styles. An outside money manager used a series of metaphors to explain the practice. He began with a psychological metaphor ("neatness fetish"), then shifted to engineering, and then moved to a detailed football analogy. His overall point was that adherence to the convention has become an end in itself, without regard to the financial consequences:

> Many of them have a neatness fetish. What they want to do is engineer these structures, and each person—it'll be like a football team. You've got your tight end, your split end, your tailback, the fullback, and the quarterback, OK? So the quarterback is the fund's CEO and then we're all the hired guys. Well, among the money managers, somebody's a split end. It may be the small growth-stock manager, because it's always "Go long, hit the deep ball." There may be a manager who is a very conservative value kind of guy, and so his portfolio volatility is extremely low, and he may have an above-average yield, below-average price-range ratio average, so his portfolios are going to move their way, and so he's got this neat little so-called scientific thing, and he may go to Barr Rosenberg and put it through their computer and look at what his most efficient universe is and all this sort of thing, and then when you change, you screw that up. It doesn't matter whether you've done a great job or not, you just foul it up.

One of the fund executives who employs this outside manager made exactly the same point with reference to baseball. His emphasis was also on the elegance of the structure and the ease of changing its components rather than the results it produces:

> This then is how we create the structure. I knew that what I wanted was more of a structure, kind of like a baseball team,

where you knew your positions, you knew the positions you wanted to cover, but you could remove a manager and replace that manager without affecting the whole bloody lineup. And I'd gone through one of these changes where just to remove a manager and go through a manager search was so disruptive and we had learned so much that selling stocks and so forth was really a very costly activity. So, by having a structure like this, we put more of a premium on the structure than we did on the actual players in the structure. Now if this guy screws up, we can remove him surgically and replace him with another.

Another characteristic of a sport or game—and perhaps the most significant one for this analysis—is that it is a self-contained universe. It proceeds according to its own rules and neither affects nor is affected by anything that happens in the outside world. In short, what happens in sports does not make any real difference, which is perhaps why so many people find it therapeutic to invest so much energy in them.[4]

A troubling question is whether the constant use of sports metaphors in investment talk reflects a similar attitude toward investing, a belief that it is a self-contained activity divorced from any external reality. We find no evidence that pension fund people take their work lightly—but then professional athletes do not take their work lightly, either. There is abundant evidence, however, that many pension people, particularly investment specialists, have difficulty looking beyond their immediate investment results to consider the broader consequences of what they do.

For example, we discussed in Chapter 5 the ways in which pension insiders talk about their beneficiaries, and we argued that most of them see the beneficiaries as an abstraction. In the same chapter, we documented the prevailing view that the social consequences of investment decisions are largely irrelevant.

There is evidence that the money being invested is also an abstraction. We were told that one must distance oneself from the enormous sums under management in order to avoid unbearable levels of anxiety. It is clear that for many of the investment professionals, the game itself has become the reward, rather than the compensation it yields. As the equity director at ProductCo put it:

I make more money than I'll ever be able to spend.
Right. Okay. So why? What do you do this for?
Because I love it.

Even when people cite compensation as a motivational factor, they emphasize the scorekeeping function of the money rather than its inherent value to the person earning it—as in the rhetorical question that one manager posed, "Was my W2 bigger than so-and-so's W2?"

Elsewhere in this chapter, we find pension executives deriding money managers as crapshooters in Brooks Brothers suits, and money managers contending that fund executives let neatness fetishes dictate their investment strategies. Everyone is accusing everyone else of playing games. In these terms, the accusation is probably overstated. Nonetheless, it is hard not to take people at their word when they insist on telling us, over and over, that pension investing can best be described as a sporting endeavor.

THE LANGUAGE OF MEN AND WOMEN

The world of pension fund investment is a man's world. At each of the nine funds we studied, we asked to speak to as many people as possible at every level of investment decision making. In each instance, we spoke first with the chief executive, and he selected others for us to interview. Those selected included chief investment officers, external money managers, and in-house specialists in different kinds of investments. Of the more than 50 people we eventually interviewed, only three were women— one in-house venture capital specialist and two outside managers.

Even with so small a group of women, we found some interesting linguistic differences that seemed to follow gender lines. Like the men, the women we interviewed often talked of sports and games. But they talked about different kinds of games, and they emphasized the differences between sports and investing rather than their similarities. Moreover, they spoke of feelings and relationships in words that their male counterparts never use.

A significant feature of the women's discussions was concern over access to the investment game. None of the men ever raised the issue of access; their comments assumed a right to play the game. One of the female outside managers, however, commented on how a recent economic trend (the relative scarcity of new pension money being put up for outside management) had made it difficult to break in:

> There hasn't been a whole lot of net new money put into the market. In fact, it's sort of a closed game, a closed circle.

Another woman contrasted the fairness of the game itself with the unfairness of being denied access to it:

> It's quite egalitarian and very much a meritocracy once you're in the game. . . . Getting in the game is very much a closed shop.

She then pursued the game metaphor to tell a self-deprecating story of a sort that we never heard from any of the men. Her point was that she had settled on a defensive investment strategy not because she believed in it in an affirmative way, but because she felt unable to compete with the people who were already playing the game with more aggressive strategies. Whereas many of the men described ego as one of the prerequisites for the profession, she talked about it as an impediment to be gotten out of the way:

> From time to time we really knocked the cover off the ball. I don't assume I will be mediocre. I don't aspire to it, but I don't run business as if I'm something special. I assume, first of all, the business is graded on the curve, OK? And the people playing the game are already pretty hot, so it's not like they graded on the curve and you're in with the guys from the Bronx. They're grading it on the curve and you're in with people who are really seriously smart and will do anything. So I think, "Gosh, if I'm in with people like this, the most important thing I have to do for myself so I can protect my clients is be realistic, get my ego out of the way. Don't fight the market."[5]

Her outlook on the investment game has led to a style of doing business that she believes is distinctly feminine. In the first place, her firm turns away business:

We try to really limit the number of relationships, because we want to make sure that we have the capacity to do what we do.

The firm expends an enormous amount of energy on maintaining relationships, in the belief that if they cannot outperform the competition, they can at least out-relate it.

The firm also has a business ethic that its principals see as distinct from that practiced by most money managers. The head of the firm used the example of brokers offering "tickets to the hockey game" to epitomize the prevailing investment ethic.[6] She jokingly characterized her own stricter ethical standards as "nuts," and then observed more seriously that only a certain kind of person could work for her:

> If we buy 300,000 shares of something, or 30,000 shares of it, every stock price in every account is exactly the same. None of our staff is allowed to be entertained by Wall Street. I mean we're nuts here. We're quite nutty. I'm concerned about them, I mean in the sense that I talk to them that what we want here is the best stock, I guess. That's all we want. We don't need tickets to the hockey game. That's not going to help you. It's not going to help our clients. It sounds very moralizing. You probably can see why there are certain people who are really thrilled to work here, and there are other people who go, "Oh, these women."

She ultimately rejected the sports and game metaphors that others use continually. She stressed, in a way that was unique in our hundreds of hours of investigation, that investing is not a game, but a serious pursuit undertaken with real money contributed by real people:

> When we deal with other people's money, this is where I can get on a soapbox. When we're dealing with our client's money, this isn't horseshoes. This isn't just getting the ball over the line.

This attention to the client has a significant practical ramification. All of the other outside managers we interviewed think that social investing strictures are an unacceptable distraction from the task of investing. Most refuse to accept money with such strings attached. This manager, however, has no difficulty following the client's directives on social questions and welcomes new clients with social investing policies.

Having interviewed only three women, we are, of course, reluctant to generalize about gender differences in the investment world. Nonetheless, some of the things that these women said at the very least raise some intriguing questions. For example, are men drawn to investing by the joy of playing the game, whereas women derive satisfaction from meeting their clients' needs? Does a greater degree of attention to the people behind the money have any consequences for the choice of investment strategy? Would the ethics of the investment business be significantly different if it were dominated by women rather than men? At the moment, these are interesting theoretical questions; as the representation of women on Wall Street increases, they will become equally interesting empirical questions.

TIME HORIZONS

Time is a crucial factor in all areas of business, and the investment business is no exception. All the people we interviewed talked at length about the relevance of time to the ways they think and act. Most of their talk was focused on the question, how much time is enough? This question can take a variety of specific forms. For example, how much time is enough to judge the efficacy of an investment strategy? What is an appropriate time for evaluating a money manager's performance? How much time should a company's management be given to prove itself?

The answers to these questions can have enormous practical significance. A widespread complaint of corporate executives is that the current generation of shareholders is too impatient. By demanding that a company's stock perform well from quarter to quarter, they say, the shareholders create incentives for management to take a quick-fix approach, and disincentives to attend to research and development, capital improvements, and other essential long-term needs. As evidence for the validity of their complaints, they cite the takeover epidemic of the 1980s: As soon as the value of a company's stock falls below the company's intrinsic value, it becomes a takeover target, and the incumbent shareholders are all too willing to take the quick profit and sell out.

Such complaints have struck a responsive chord in Congress and in the press. The alleged impatience of shareholders is seen as yet another example of the short-term thinking that plagues this country, and a major cause of corporate America's declining competitiveness in the world market. It is hard to get equal time for the counterargument that takeover specialists are agents of economic natural selection who target only those companies whose stock is chronically undervalued and whose managements have ignored their shareholders' legitimate interests.

In the public debate over the causes of short-term corporate thinking, institutional investors, particularly pension funds, have emerged as prime suspects. There are many reasons for this. On the simplest level, because pension funds are so big, they are inviting targets. It is also the case that large pension funds invested billions of dollars in the recent wave of leveraged buyouts, and the press has uncovered some disconcerting correlations between campaign contributions by LBO firms and the placement of public pension money.[7] Another argument starts from the premise that pension funds are strongly influenced by outside money managers and consultants. Since managers and consultants must continually market their services, they have a compelling interest in their own short-term investment performance. Depending on how they are compensated, they may also have an interest in generating a high rate of transactions.

However fair or unfair the targeting of pension funds may be, it continues unabated. The Senate Banking Committee recently held hearings on the short-term orientation of pension funds, suggesting its members' belief that there is a problem, or at least an exploitable political issue. Lloyd Bentsen, in his capacity as chairman of the Senate Finance Committee, has proposed a tax on short-term trading profits earned by otherwise tax-exempt pension funds. Supporters of such measures justify them both as revenue sources and as incentives to modify inappropriate investment behavior.

The response from the pension fund community typically has several components. Pension executives question whether there is any hard evidence of high turnover in fund portfolios. If there is, they ask, is there any causal relation between high turnover and short-term corporate thinking? They imply that the funds are a convenient excuse for the managers' own shortcomings. Some of the public fund executives acknowledge that there is a problem and argue that it is caused by the private funds. All of these points emerged in an interview with the chief executive of State A:

> *Why, for example, does Senator Dodd have to hold hearings on this problem? Why does Senator Bentsen think maybe we need a transaction tax?*
>
> Because of the private pension systems, the corporate pension systems who, of course, are going to give you all of these numbers and had such a rapid turnover. They put pressure on their own people. And they won't admit it.
>
> *How does that pressure work?*
>
> Well, I don't know. Ask these CEOs that stand up and give speeches at dinners, denouncing pension systems about the short-term pressure, that their stock turns over so fast and that money managers demand a quarterly performance. So they're going to dump their stock, and on, and on, and on. I think most of it's hokum and myth, but we don't have the statistics to prove that yet. There are plenty of people working on trying to disprove that theory, and mainly they're in the corporate pension systems who are now being accused by the likes of me, for causing the problem, the very problem that their own bosses squawk about.
>
> *Has the problem been proved to your satisfaction?*
>
> No, I don't know if there is any relationship between the rapid turnover of stock and the so-called American short-term outlook. I don't even know that there's even a short-term outlook. I assume DuPont's plowing plenty of money back into R&D, that sort of stuff. I'm not sure that this isn't all something *Business Week* needs to write about. I just don't know. I've not seen any of the statistics, but our stock turnover is 14 percent, California's is 10 percent, so whatever this evil is, the public systems are not involved.

Against this background, we turn now to a detailed examination of how people in the pension world talk about time. Their rhetoric is exclusively long term: In almost every interview, we were told that if there is short-term pressure on management, someone else must be causing it. As people talk about time horizons in greater detail, however, the rhetoric begins to break down. The picture that emerges is one of ongoing conflict

BOX 7–1
Pension Fund Turnover

- New York Stock Exchange block trading data indicate substantial increases in trading by institutions generally. Large block transactions (trades of 10,000 shares or more) jumped from a daily average of 68 in 1970 to 3,464 in 1989. This represents an increase from 15.4 percent of reported volume in 1970 to 51.1 percent in 1989.

- The Committee on Investment of Employee Benefit Assets (CIEBA) conducted a survey of 36 pension funds with assets of $259 billion as of September 30, 1989. The funds surveyed included 14 of the 25 largest corporate pension funds. The survey found that average turnover has been declining. Average turnover (defined as the lesser of sales or purchases divided by average assets) was found to be:

  33 percent from January to September 1989
  38 percent in 1988
  51 percent in 1987
  46 percent in 1986

- The CIEBA survey found that the average holding period for U.S. common stocks in these portfolios was approximately two and a half years.

- The Columbia Institutional Investor Project has sponsored pilot studies of the turnover in portfolios of major funds. The analysis is based on every individual transaction for the five years 1985–1989. Results for the first two funds—one public and one private—show the following:

  68.1 percent of the shares in one fund and 85.7 percent of the shares in the other fund were held longer than six months.

  43.9 percent of the shares in one fund and 76.7 percent of the shares in the other fund were held longer than one year.

  Of the shares still held at the end of the study period, 12.2 percent in one portfolio and 19.2 percent in the other had been held over five years.

between the philosophical commitment to long-term thinking and the day-to-day realities of managing a pension fund.

The Rhetoric of Time

In the typical statement of a pension fund's time horizon, the driving force is the long-term nature of the fund's obligations. The chief pension executive at ChemCo made the point in this way:

> What's my horizon? My horizon here is very long-term. We are funding benefits now that I will pay out 70 years from now.

This attention to the long term shapes the fund's overall orientation. In particular, we were told, it can have a direct influence on the evaluation of possible investment strategies. Some strategies are ruled out because they seem philosophically inconsistent with an overall commitment to the long term. For example, the chief executive at State C commented, "An LBO fund doesn't match. Our corporate philosophy, if you will, is patient capital."[8] In a similar vein, the head of the equity division at State A assured us that "we're not market timers, we're not trying to determine what rates are going to be six months, or three years, or four years from now." Later in the interview, he was even more emphatic:

> Our horizon is not the hereafter, but we have rather long horizons as do most pension funds, I believe. And the fact that the market goes down 150 points or up 150 points, or interest goes from nine-and-a-quarter to eight-and-three-quarters, so what?

The rhetoric of the long term also has a comparative component. A number of people told us that the opportunity to take a long-term view is one of the principal attractions of working in a pension fund. One of the equity analysts at IndustrialCo compared the pension fund environment to that of Wall Street investment firms, and then discussed Wall Street's influence on American business:

> What attracted me was the fact that I like working in an environment where the investment horizons are longer term. I've worked at four investment firms. Everything was geared to the next quar-

ter. And I personally think that that is one of the biggest problems of American industries today. Most managers are in here churning out what Wall Street wants to hear in the next three or six months. And they're not making enough longer-term decisions. And that was one of the reasons that I liked it here, because we could really get into an industry and know it well, stay with it. There's continuity, and we don't have to get so worried about an idea that, "Well, gee, the fourth-quarter earnings are 10 cents off of what the consensus is or was." "Gee, you made a terrible decision," or "Boy, why didn't one of us get out of that stock?" I think that that's what really appeals to me. If we can make the case, "Well, gee, maybe the earnings aren't doing all that well now, but putting A, B, C, D, and E together in a couple of years and given the certain economic assumption, this stock could do rather well for us." So that was a big selling point.

The strength and consistency of the long-term rhetoric make it hard to accept the claim that pension funds contribute to the short-term pressures on corporate management. Indeed, many pension fund executives dismiss management complaints as an effort to find scapegoats for their own poor performance. There are, however, a number of reasons to take a closer look at the funds' commitment to the long term.

First, the fact is that almost all large pension funds do pursue short-term strategies to some extent. Even at State A, for example, which is heavily indexed and thus committed to long-term thinking, about 15 percent of the fund is managed by external managers, some of whom pursue shorter-term strategies, and approximately 10 percent is allocated to nontraditional investments such as LBOs. The fund's chief executive is skeptical about these kinds of investments, but says that he must allocate some money to them to satisfy his fiduciary duty to diversify. Our point is not that these are bad investments; on the contrary, State A believes that its returns are quite good. We make the more limited point that if short-term investment strategies have a negative impact on the economy, then pension funds make a substantial contribution to that impact. Ten or 15 percent of hundreds of billions of dollars is a lot of money, even by macroeconomic standards.[9]

The other reasons for scrutinizing the funds' assertedly long-term philosophy are more subtle. As they elaborated on the theme of time horizons, the fund executives we interviewed mentioned a number of factors, both internal and external, that make it difficult for them to be as fully committed to the long term as their rhetoric would suggest.

Life Cycles

Fund executives' time horizons are strongly influenced by the demographic profiles of their funds. Many of them talked about the issue in terms of the *life cycle* of the fund. A fund with a relatively young group of beneficiaries (such as a fund sponsored by a growing company with few retirees and many young, newly hired workers) will not have to make substantial benefit payouts for many years. It does not need immediate access to large amounts of cash (i.e., its investments need not be highly liquid), and it can afford to make investments that will yield a return later rather than sooner. Also, since it is probably taking in more money in contributions than it is paying out in benefits, it will be a net buyer in the investment market.

A fund whose beneficiaries include large numbers of retirees and older workers faces a different set of constraints. It needs ready cash to meet its benefit obligations, so liquidity will be an important investment criterion. For the same reason, it may need to concentrate on fixed-income investments that promise a return in the near term. And because present payouts are likely to exceed contributions, the fund will be a net seller.

An equity specialist at ProductCo described in concrete terms how the life-cycle phenomenon affects his fund's strategy:

> The ProductCo pension funds are in a broad context of a pension fund's life cycle. We would basically describe ourselves as a mature plan where there is a degree of liquidity necessarily; that our payments to pensioners exceed by some small margin the contributions that are made into the plans. . . . So therefore, because of that stage in our life cycle, our time horizon cannot be 30 years into the future. It has to be something shorter.

He presented a contrasting portrait of the thinking at a hypothetical fund with a younger beneficiary profile:

> If there was no plan to begin with, they'd put it in place and the first payment out of that fund is not going to occur for many years.

I mean, even if you had people that were approaching retirement, they were all of a sudden included in the fund, any kind of benefit that they would accrue would be very small, because they wouldn't have the years of service. . . . Because it's early in the cycle and we start with nothing, the contributions you're putting in there are going to be relatively large with respect to the size of the fund that exists. There's not going to be any outflow, so that when that happens one is able to look out with a very long perspective and not be as sensitive to short-term risks; and, therefore, one would surely tend to say, "Well, I'm going to put my money into the higher returning assets that I think I can identify. And just put it in, and hold them."

The life cycles of individuals may also influence investment time horizons. Only one of the people we interviewed—the chief pension executive at ProductCo—remarked on this point, but his observation was so powerful that it bears repeating. He made it in response to a question about the proper time frame for evaluating his fund's investment strategy:

> *What kind of time frame do you think will be required to decide whether it really was worth changing to a more active investment style or not?*
> Well, my time frame is getting shorter and shorter as I pass time. I think that basically we've seen evidence that, as we have gotten rid of the bad managers and hired others, the averaging has improved. So, I think there's evidence that by constantly monitoring these managers and getting rid of bad ones and adding good ones, or so on, that we can improve the result.

As we noted in Chapter 4, individuals find it difficult to analyze how their fund worked before they arrived. Such history tends to be collapsed into stories that have the quality of folklore. ProductCo's chief executive makes a parallel point about the future. He implies that it is equally difficult to envision the fund at a time beyond one's own tenure. The result may be a tendency to insist on results that will be evident within one's professional life cycle. If others feel as he does, his comment is further evidence of the fragility of fund structures and their dependence on human idiosyncrasy.

Accounting Pressures

People are sometimes prisoners of their vocabularies. If there are no words available to talk about something, then it will also be difficult to think about it. In an arena like investing where all the action is verbal, it will be hard to act as well.

Pension managers who want to translate their long-term rhetoric into action confront this problem daily. The language of financial evaluation and accountability focuses almost exclusively on the short term: Companies issue quarterly reports, in anticipation of which the financial press salivates; the Securities and Exchange Commission requires quarterly and annual filings; the government issues key economic statistics quarterly or monthly; fund managers make quarterly or semi-annual reports to their sponsors. Short-term evaluation is necessary for many purposes, of course. The problem is that the language of the short term—and perhaps also the thinking with which it is associated—dominates the field. Thus, to focus seriously on the long term is an act of intellectual originality that goes against the cultural grain.

An equity specialist at State A captured the dilemma faced by a fund executive trying to reconcile a long-term philosophy with the constant barrage of short-term information about his outside managers:

> *What is the horizon in evaluating performance?*
> No one really knows. What we do is that it's calculated monthly. At the same time we provide fiscal year-to-date information, calendar year-to-date, and then one, two, three, four, five years, and inception numbers. All the information on a vast number of frequencies is available. Obviously it depends on how long the manager has been with you. You look at the long term, but if you see a guy that's coming up with a bunch of poor months you're going to have poor quarters, and you're going to have poor years, and poor years turn into three years' poor performance, and so on and so forth. But you do have to let it go for some period of time, and you hear things like, "What is that?" Well, nobody's really sure.

The chief investment officer at MaterialCo talked about the same dilemma, but seemed more confident of his ability to avoid making a premature evaluation in the face of adverse short-term data:

> I watch performance monthly. I prepare a report monthly. My boss gets a copy and I get a copy and that's about it. We look at it monthly, but we don't pull any triggers monthly. We tell our managers we'll give them a full market cycle. It's in our investment policy that they're expected to outperform the Russell 3000, over a full market cycle, and then we go on to say that's usually three to five years. As we come up on a calendar quarter, we'll show it first quarter, and then year-to-date. As we come up on June, we'll have last quarter, and then six months year-to-date, and the same with nine months and so forth. We go to our committees once or twice a year, usually once in February or March for the year that ended and usually once in the fall. We'll pick June, or maybe July or August, depending on how many months have elapsed, and we'll go to our outside committee with the report on performance. But we don't try to fire managers over short periods of time.

It may be significant that he said that he and his colleagues *try* to avoid firing managers because of short-term problems. Given the amount of short-term information available to them, the effort required to resist "pulling the trigger" must be considerable. One wonders whether they and other fund executives always succeed.

The Tyranny of Computers

It goes without saying in the investment world that one must have the latest in computer technology. What computers do, of course, is to store, organize, and reproduce information. To justify the existence of the machines, one must at least read the information as it is produced. We heard several suggestions that the availability of computers also creates pressure to act on the information they generate.

One of the external managers we interviewed made this point as he talked about the conflict between the rhetoric of the long term and the realities of manager evaluation. He made it clear that this conflict has an impact on his state of mind, if not his investment strategy:

Even though they talk about three to five years, I've had calls where the computing power at their hands is so great they can track you weekly, daily, monthly.

Do they do that?

Hell, yeah. One of the people we work for called me and said, "I heard you had a bad month. What happened?" "Well, you know, this, this and this, and this." I mean this is after seven years of 400 basis points a year compounded over the S&P total account, 500 or 600 basis points a year, equity-only numbers. I mean, one month is just not really relevant, but they're so surprised if something happens, they call you. That doesn't happen very often, and that's the exception, but we worry about quarters.

The head of ProductCo's equity division, who worked previously on Wall Street, was even blunter in describing the tyrannical power of information:

In more than almost any other job you can think of, what you do is absolutely measurable. And there is no question, no question, you work for those numbers. You don't work for this guy, or that guy, and you don't work so as to please him, or please that person. You work for those numbers, because what you do is absolutely quantifiable.

Comments such as these raise a serious question about whether a long-term philosophy can survive in an atmosphere of constant information updates. Something old—the short-term reporting conventions of accounting—and something new—the ability of computers to provide far more information than any human being can process—seem to be working in tandem to exert pressure on those who are philosophically inclined to take a long-term view of their investments.

Money Managers and Market Cycles

Several of the fund insiders we interviewed commented that the very practice of using outside managers makes it difficult to maintain a long-term perspective. An equity analyst at IndustrialCo defined the problem, arguing that his fund's long-term, value-investing approach would be much harder to implement at a fund that uses outside managers:

I think that the short-term pressures will probably increase.

They'll increase more?

Yeah. We're in-house, so we could take a very different perspective about most of it. I'm sure some of the other funds that you've visited are externally managed, and I'm sure that they review their portfolio managers every quarter. And if they don't beat the S&P 400 or whatever yardstick, they get their heads handed to them. And I think that's going to happen more and more, unfortunately.

In other words, the standard practice of quarterly reviews and the resulting pressure to act on an unfavorable review are factors that influence any fund that chooses to employ outside managers.

The funds that do use outside managers face the additional difficulty of deciding when to evaluate them. The prevailing view is that a fund with a long-term perspective should give managers three to five years before passing judgment on them. According to the chief pension executive at ChemCo, "A long-term evaluation of a manager would be over a five-year period; a short-term evaluation would be in the range of three years."

The stated rationale for the three-to-five-year period is that it represents a complete market cycle. One of the equity specialists at ProductCo explained the rationale in considerable detail. Note that he undermined the theory even as he developed it, first calling into question whether a market cycle can really be defined and then wondering about how well the concept applies to specific managers:

What's your time frame for evaluating the managers?

We generally talk about a market cycle, whatever that is. But I'd say, we are going to give them at least three years to look at their performance. I don't know whether that's still too short or whether it's too long. Sometimes, in retrospect, it may have been too long from the point in time that you first identify a problem and give them that long to work it out. But in general, I think it's fair. . . . We've gone to normal portfolios for our stock managers which are an attempt to define their habitat. . . . Even if you've gotten the cyclicality of styles of equity management out of the equation, there still can be periods of rather lengthy durations, six months, a year, when the managers can even underperform their normal, and you've got to try to gauge this when you're thinking too. So there's no really quick answer.

Others approached the manager evaluation–market cycle issue from different angles. Another equity specialist at ProductCo suggested that a fair period for evaluation might be somewhere between 5 and 25 years. The chief pension executive at TransCo talked of 5- to 10-year "investment cycles." Perhaps the most interesting comment came from an equity specialist at State A who asked rhetorically whether 1987 or even Friday, October 13, 1989, might not have been a market cycle in itself.

All of this talk evidences a logical dilemma. Three to five years is generally said to be a fair period for evaluating managers. The reason given is that this period is believed to represent a market cycle. But it is widely acknowledged that a market cycle can be much longer or much shorter, and some think that concept may not be relevant at all in today's market. What, then, happens to the three- to five-year evaluation period? Should it be retained simply because it seems like a good number? Alternatively, should the evaluation period be adjusted continually to reflect changing conceptions of the market cycle? However one resolves these questions, it seems clear that the unsettled relationship between manager evaluations and market cycles can only make it more difficult for fund executives to translate a rhetorical commitment to the long term into day-to-day reality.

Billions of pension fund dollars are knowingly dedicated to short-term investments. As for the rest, even those funds that claim a commitment to the long term face a host of practical and cultural obstacles in attempting to turn their rhetoric into reality. The strong implication is that pension funds, intentionally or unintentionally, are constantly making short-term judgments about investments, money managers, and companies.

The ultimate policy question is what effect any such short-term judgments are having on the corporations whose stock the funds own. In particular, do the funds take a sufficiently long-term perspective to be credible monitors of management performance? We turn our attention to this and related questions in the next chapter.

NOTES

1. A simile is a metaphor that uses a comparative word such as *like* or *as*; for example, the opening of Portia's famous speech in *The Merchant of Venice:* "The quality of mercy is not strained. It droppeth as a gentle rain from heaven upon the place beneath."
2. They are not always significant, of course. The delicate interpretive issue is distinguishing between meaningful metaphors and those that really are nothing more than stock phrases, or what linguists call *frozen forms.* George Lakoff and Mark Johnson's *Metaphors We Live By* (Chicago: University of Chicago Press, 1980) analyzes the pervasiveness of metaphors in social life. Readers interested in pursuing the relation between speakers' metaphors and the mental templates from which they are derived may wish to consult Naomi Quinn on "The Cultural Basis of Metaphor," in *Beyond Metaphor: The Theory of Tropes in Anthropology*, ed. James W. Fernandez (Stanford, Calif.: Stanford University Press, 1991), pp. 56–93.
3. In addition to sports metaphors, the speaker also refers to *shooting stars* and to getting *off the track.* These references draw on metaphors beyond the sporting world. The important thing to note is not the exclusiveness but the predominance of sports metaphors in investment talk.
4. In his famous letter to baseball commissioner Kenesaw Mountain Landis at the outbreak of World War II, Franklin D. Roosevelt emphasized this point in urging that baseball continue during the war as a source of national diversion.
5. This passage contains some surface features that linguists have identified as characteristic of women's language. They include the use of "intensifiers" before adjectives ("like really seriously smart") and the use of direct quotations to describe the speaker's thought process ("So I think, 'Gosh. . . .'"). For a fuller discussion of this issue, see Robin Lakoff, *Language and Woman's Place* (New York: Harper and Row, 1975); and David Graddol and Joan Swann, *Gender Voices* (Oxford: Basil Blackwell Ltd., 1989).
6. The chief executive at State B chose the same phrase to describe improper inducements offered to public fund officials by stockbrokers.
7. See, for example, Sarah Bartlett, "Gambling with the Big Boys," *The New York Times Magazine*, May 5, 1991, p. 38.
8. Most of the people we interviewed lump LBOs into the category of short-term investments. In doing so, their thinking is that LBOs are motivated by the desire to take over a company and then break it up for short-term profit. They see this as the antithesis of invest-

ing in a company for the purpose of prospering with it over the long term. However, LBOs can be, and sometimes are, used as vehicles for permanent acquisitions of companies.

9. Another disincentive to long-term thinking in the public sector is a factor that is rarely mentioned, but probably of great importance. In one of the states we studied, state regulations limit the contracts of money managers to three years. By this apparent effort to ensure regular accountability, state lawmakers have, probably unwittingly, forced their pension fund into a three-year cycle of evaluation, regardless of the behavior of the market or the specifics of an individual manager's style. Fund officials in this state acknowledge that three years may be too short a period for a fair and effective evaluation, and are pushing for a two-year extension.

CHAPTER 8

THE GOVERNANCE GAP— PENSION FUNDS AS CORPORATE OWNERS

The most contentious issue in the business world today may be the question of who is supervising the managers of America's large public corporations. The evolution of American capitalism has been marked by a widening gap between corporate owner-ship and corporate management. In the 19th century, legendary figures like Henry Ford and Andrew Carnegie, working in con-cert with powerful investment bankers like J. P. Morgan, founded, owned, and managed the nation's earliest giant manufacturing companies. These founding entrepreneurs gradually gave way to a class of professional managers. As America's corporate stock passed into the hands of a broad base of shareholders with vary-ing degrees of interest and expertise, power increasingly de-volved onto these managers. With the growth of pension funds and other institutional investors, this trend has accelerated. Now the ultimate owners of most of the stock of large public corporations are institutional beneficiaries who may not even know the names of the companies in which their money is in-vested.

Many observers argue that this environment presents cor-porate managers with irresistible temptation. With no one look-ing over their shoulders and asking hard questions, they are in a position to put their own interests ahead of those of the share-holders, their nominal bosses. The first step, the argument goes, is to pack the board of directors with insiders and other members of the corporate management club.[1] The passive board is then expected to acquiesce in measures that advance the interests of management at the expense of the shareholders. The most frequently cited examples are excessive executive compensation packages that are not tied to corporate performance, golden parachutes and other devices to protect executives against termination, and such antitakeover provisions as poison pills and shark repellents. Such provisions, it is argued, reduce management accountability by weakening the market for corporate control as a means for disciplining inept or self-aggrandizing managers.[2]

The efforts of corporate managers to insulate themselves from market forces have been aided and abetted by the enactment of laws in several states that inhibit hostile takeovers, either directly or indirectly.[3] There is widespread concern about the macroeconomic implications of hostile takeovers, especially leveraged buyouts. State legislators justifying antitakeover votes have emphasized the job losses that often accompany an unfriendly corporate restructuring. Some outspoken executives continually stress that they cannot concentrate on long-term business planning if they are liable to be taken over and thrown out whenever the stock price drops a few points.

As a result of all of these concerns, there is an ongoing search for a new class of activist shareholders to assume the task of monitoring management and close the perceived corporate governance gap. Institutional investors, particularly pension funds, have emerged as the most promising candidates—indeed, as the only realistic candidates. As large shareholders in individual companies, institutions have a compelling financial interest in how well those companies are managed. The very size of their holdings may make it difficult for them to "take the Wall Street walk" and sell out when they are dissatisfied with management. The institutions are also believed to have the expertise and the financial wherewithal to overcome the logistical and legal barriers that stand in the way of active shareholder participation in corporate governance.[4]

Among institutional investors, pension funds seem to be particularly well adapted for the watchdog role. They comprise the largest category of institutional investors, and thus have the best chance to get a hearing. The public funds are never far removed from the political arena, and they must therefore be attuned to issues of public policy. And all pension funds have strong common interests. Accordingly, they have some motivation to engage in collective action, which would magnify their influence.

Most of the commentary about the role of pension funds in corporate governance has been purely theoretical. Economists have speculated about their incentives to act, and lawyers have analyzed the barriers they would have to overcome and the ways they might do it. Little has been written, however, from the perspective of the people who manage the funds—their goals, strategies, and motivations have simply been assumed. Although a few episodes have gotten wide coverage in the press, no one has studied from a behavioral perspective what the funds are now doing in the area of corporate governance, why they are doing what they do, and what they are likely to do in the future.[5] It is to these questions that we turn in this chapter.

THE LEGAL BACKGROUND: CORPORATE DEMOCRACY

In theory, an American corporation is a democracy. Major questions of corporate policy are required to be submitted to a vote of the shareholders. Each share of common stock typically entitles its owner to one vote. The questions on which shareholders usually vote include fundamental changes in the nature of the corporation, such as mergers and acquisitions, and, most importantly, the choice of directors. The board of directors in turn elects the officers of the corporation to whom the day-to-day management of company business is entrusted. The officers usually seek board approval for certain particularly important business decisions, such as the opening or closing of a plant, the acquisition of another company, or the divestiture of a division.

The election of directors is the most significant opportunity for shareholders to influence the governance of their corporation. The opportunity to accept or reject a fundamental change like a merger is important, of course, but such events are rare in the life of a company. At least some of the seats on the board will be up for election each year, however, and the choice of the people who will fill them can affect the company's fortunes. If large numbers of shareholders fail to vote, or routinely endorse management's nominees, the result may be a board that acquiesces in whatever management wants to do, for better or worse. By contrast, a board dominated by able independent directors can give the officers an additional critical perspective on its most important decisions.

Procedurally, shareholders can participate in corporate governance in two principal ways. First, they can vote up or down on resolutions that management puts before them. For example, they can vote to accept or reject a merger or management's slate of directors. Yea or nay votes such as these comprise the great bulk of shareholder governance activity. Second, shareholders can seek to put their own resolutions before the other shareholders. A shareholder can, for example, nominate a slate of directors or propose to amend the corporate by-laws to prohibit paying greenmail to hostile suitors. The corporation's charter and by-laws and the law of its state of incorporation will determine how difficult it is for a shareholder resolution to succeed.

Shareholder votes take place at the company's regularly scheduled annual meeting and at special meetings called to deal with particular issues. Few shareholders actually attend meetings, of course; even the largest corporations usually draw only a couple of hundred. Instead, they vote by proxy. Most legal analysts believe that the proxy process is heavily weighted in favor of management. At the outset, shareholders are inhibited from communicating with each other by the Securities and Exchange Commission's proxy solicitation rules.[6] On the other side, the corporation's annual meeting announcement mailed to shareholders will contain a carefully prepared statement of management's position together with proxy cards enabling the shareholder to endorse it. A shareholder who wants to oppose a management proposal must conduct a counter-solicitation, a course of action fraught with legal and practical difficulties.[7]

A threat to file a shareholder resolution can sometimes be a lever to induce management to negotiate. Even if they are likely to win the election, a company's managers may want to avoid the embarrassment of a substantial number of votes being cast for a hostile position. They may therefore be willing to compromise their own position if they are persuaded that a shareholder proposal is likely to get on the ballot and draw significant support.

BOX 8–1
Shareholder Activism

- The 1991 proxy season was notable for its spirit of negotiation. According to the Investor Responsibility Research Center, 42 proposals were submitted but later withdrawn after negotiated settlements. Nevertheless, a record 272 major corporate governance proposals were on corporate ballots by August 29, 1991. As institutional shareholders have become increasingly concerned with corporate performance, proposals related to boards of directors topped the list. These proposals call for a majority of independent outside directors on the boards of such companies as Dow Chemical Co., National Semiconductor Corp., and Occidental Petroleum Corp.

- Shareholder voting data obtained by the Investor Responsibility Research Center, as of June 1991, indicate that governance proposals dealing with such longstanding issues as poison pill rescission, confidential voting, and golden parachutes tended to receive greater voting support than proposals dealing with newer issues such as board composition and executive compensation.

- The Securities and Exchange Commission has instituted an extensive review of the rules governing the proxy system. It has already issued one set of proposed revisions to open up the proxy process to dissident shareholders. Changes are likely to generate fierce debate.

- During the first half of 1991, 14 companies adopted a shareholders' rights plank calling for confidential voting, bringing the total number of companies to 66, according to the Investor Responsibility Research Center. Among those adopting confidential voting procedures were Weyerhaeuser Co., Baxter International Inc., Avon Products Inc., General Signal Corp., and W. R. Grace & Co. In some cases, confidential voting procedures have been adopted in exchange for shareholder agreements to drop resolutions to rescind poison pills and reduce golden parachutes.

Box 8-1 *(continued)*

Corporate Governance Shareholder Proposals as of August 29, 1991

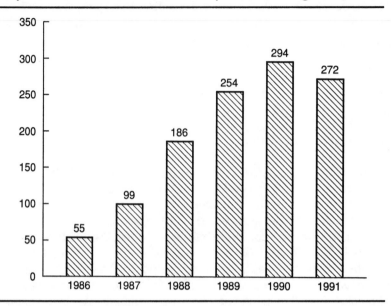

Source: Investor Responsibility Research Center.

Shareholder Proposals as of August 29, 1991

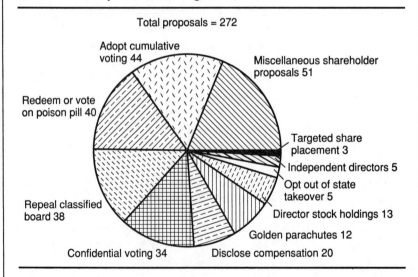

Source: Investor Responsibility Research Center.

AVON CALLING

In the case of an institutional investor like a pension fund, the ultimate beneficiaries of the stock never receive the proxies and have no legal right to vote them. The proxies are received by the fund's management or by an agent of the fund such as an external money manager or a bank acting as custodian of the stock certificates. The fund may retain the right to vote or may delegate it to one of its agents.

Until the 1980s, pension funds paid little attention to the voting of proxies. Proxies were viewed, in the words of an IndustrialCo pension executive, "as an inconvenience." They were either not voted at all or simply marked in favor of management and returned—often, we were told, by a low-level clerk in a back room. Thus, the largest single bloc of shareholders in America's public corporations effectively renounced their corporate citizenship.

Two things happened in the 1980s to change this attitude. First, shareholder initiatives on so-called social issues began to appear. Activist shareholders occasionally succeeded in bringing before the annual meeting a resolution on an issue like environmental stewardship or getting out of South Africa. While these resolutions were invariably defeated, they attracted media attention. Public pension funds, which must be sensitive to the political climate, began looking more seriously at these kinds of initiatives. At many public funds, this initial concern evolved into a process for systematically reviewing all kinds of proxy issues.

The legal counsel at State A described how this evolution came about at his fund. The fund progressed from an initial focus on social issues to a consideration of business issues as well, and ultimately developed a procedure for evaluating all questions in terms of their economic impact:

> A proxy review committee was begun in 1979, for the 1980 proxy season. . . . It was created by the chief executive, as I understand it . . . as an opportunity for the constituency of the fund to review what were basically social issues that were coming before it. Their policy recommendations for years were based on the consensus of the committee and their feeling about a given moral issue. In the mid-1980s there was an internal panel drawn up to look at man-

agement proposals, so that there was a separate body operating on management. As the corporate governance area grew in 1986–1987, suddenly you've got a proxy review committee dealing with poison pills and Delaware opt-out and other areas that take on an economic tone.[8] When the proxy voting came under my jurisdiction, I started the process of the economic impact statement to kind of meld the two together. So that we were, in fact, looking at all these issues for the economic impact they might have, while at the same time recognizing the concerns of the committee on the moral side of the issue.

By now, the prevailing view at public funds is that careful attention to proxies is a fundamental obligation. In the words of the chief executive at State B:

> If you're a shareholder, I think that it's part of your responsibility to vote, just as it is your responsibility to vote as a private citizen in this country. It's really a civic issue.

The second development was a growing legal concern over the possible conflicts of interest that could arise when private pension funds voted their proxies. This concern was triggered by the 1980s takeover boom. Legal regulators worried about the possibility of divided loyalties when a pension fund had to vote on a hostile takeover of a company in which it owned a substantial amount of stock. One of the outside money managers we interviewed provided a graphic characterization of the problem:

> Some guy's company was being taken over and he called his crony at some other company, who's the CEO, and he'd say, "Your pension fund owns 500,000 shares of our stock and I want you to vote in this crazy thing that we're sticking in to protect management forever." And so the CEO would come down to the pension officer and say, "Does one of our managers own 500,000 shares of Harry's stock?" and he'd say, "Well, yeah, as a matter of fact they do." The CEO would say, "Well, you tell them that I can't play golf with Harry next Saturday if we don't vote in favor of what Harry wants to do." And that's what brought this thing to a head.

Concerns such as these prompted the U.S. Department of Labor, which regulates private pension funds under ERISA, to issue in 1988 what has come to be known as the *Avon* letter. In a letter written in response to a question concerning a particular company, Avon Products, the Labor Department took the position that "the decision as to how proxies should be voted . . . are [*sic*] fiduciary acts of plan asset management."[9] Voting proxies, formerly an inconvenience to be avoided, had now become part of the investment process, and subject to the same standards of prudence and exclusive attention to the interests of the beneficiaries. In practical terms, this meant that private pension executives now had to take proxy voting as seriously as they had always taken investing; failure to do so could result in legal liability for breach of fiduciary duty.

The *Avon* letter went on to give pension executives two options for satisfying their duty to vote proxies. First, they (or, more precisely, the trustees to whom they report) can do it themselves. Alternatively, a fund that employs outside investment managers can delegate the voting of proxies to them. A fund that chooses the latter option must decide in advance whether it wishes to retain any right of supervision and must scrupulously abide by its decision.[10] It must also set up a process for periodic review of its managers' voting activities.

The *Avon* letter had an immediate and dramatic effect on the private funds' attitudes toward proxy voting.[11] Each fund took a formal look at what it had been doing, decided what it needed to do in the future, and then codified the new approach in a set of written procedures and guidelines. Each of the six private funds we studied arrived at a different solution to the proxy problem.

At MaterialCo, for example, the fund moved from allowing the outside managers to vote proxies within certain guidelines to voting in-house. According to the account given by the sponsoring company's chief financial officer, the change has had little impact on the substantive positions that the fund takes:

> We had an arrangement that we thought was what we wanted and worked. Basically, we let the managers vote proxies within guidelines, and said, "Well, we believe in most instances that management should be supported—if you own the stock you presumably made the judgment on management—but in those areas where you think they shouldn't, let's talk about it." It kept the bookkeeping and processing of paper to a minimum. We liked that, but the further we got into it, we finally said to ourselves, "Look, it's time

that we all stood up and said, 'Who really owns the fund?' True, it's for the benefit of the beneficiaries, but let's act as owners and let's vote." And everybody agreed that we should bring it in, even though we had sort of a quasi-arrangement that accomplished that—let's go the final mile. This retired corporate secretary set up the system and worked the guidelines and we've since expanded that and we've got a few more people involved, but we found that it's not a terrible chore. . . . The guidelines are fairly general, only three pages.

ChemCo has gone in the opposite direction. It delegates proxy voting to its external managers. According to the chief pension executive, the only requirement imposed on the managers is that they notify ChemCo whenever they intend to vote against corporate management:

> We consider the voting of proxies to be an investment decision. So the voting of the proxies is done by the investment managers. It's all part of their evaluation by ChemCo.
>
> *Do you issue any guidelines to them of any sort as to how they should be voted, other than what they think is appropriate?*
> No. We don't have guidelines for them.
>
> *Is there any review of what they're doing?*
> None per se. The only limitation that we have is that the investment managers who would be voting any of those proxies against the management's recommendation would let us know. They just have to advise us.
>
> *And have you had occasion to differ with them, and tell them to do it differently—ever?*
> I've had discussions with them, when they've called up and told me how they were going to vote. I've never told them to do otherwise.

ProductCo has taken a hybrid approach. It has set up an elaborate committee process to vote the stock in the internally managed portion of its portfolio. With respect to the externally managed portion, it delegates the voting to its external managers, but closely monitors their policies and performance:

> We have copies of their policy statements and copies of the practices that they follow. We look at the votes and we look to see if

there's anything in there that appears to deviate from those policies and practices. And if we see something in there we will exercise our diligence as ERISA and the recent Department of Labor statements have called upon us to do. We will not necessarily challenge it, we will not necessarily second-guess it, but we want to understand and we want to be assured that they are behaving properly, that they are not voting with an eye to some other business pressure.

PENSION FUNDS AS CORPORATE CITIZENS: THE PUBLIC–PRIVATE SPLIT

Both public and private funds are now acutely aware of the need to take proxy voting seriously. Political developments originally motivated the public funds to move in that direction; the private funds have been driven in large part by changes in the legal climate. Whatever the cause, all responsibly managed funds now pay far more attention to their roles as corporate citizens than they did even 10 years ago. This does not mean that public and private funds are equally active on the corporate governance front, however. A sharp split has developed between public and private funds with respect to how they conceive and carry out their corporate governance responsibilities.

Public Funds

Beyond the conscientious voting of proxies, corporate governance activity by the public funds has taken two forms: filing formal proxy resolutions and directing comments and demands to the managements of particular companies, sometimes through private channels and sometimes through the press. The proxy initiatives that many large public funds have undertaken in recent years have all been related to the conflict between shareholder value and management control. Funds have targeted companies that they believe to be underperforming and have filed resolutions directed at some of the most visible manifestations of management control—for example, seeking to prohibit poison pills or greenmail, or to require that boards have a majority of outside directors. The chief executive of State A described how this process began at his fund, which is heavily indexed:

> Two or three years ago, I put my people on the phone and I got the CEO of another state fund to do the same. We phoned . . . 10 of our biggest money managers and got from them the five corporations in the S&P 500 that because of their performance . . . they wouldn't own that stock. They just wouldn't own it because the company just doesn't have it and isn't going to have it for a long, long time to come. Then we took the five that popped up most and ranked them in order and the other CEO did the same. This came out of some lengthy discussions that he and I had about what are we going to do with underperformers when we are permanent holders.

All of the funds' initiatives have failed, we were told. Some, however, have gained enough shareholder support to get the attention of management. The funds have learned from experience, and have shifted their focus to issues on which they have some long-term prospects for success. State C, for example, now limits itself to about 10 resolutions a year. Like State A, it targets well-known and chronically underperforming companies, and selects its issues with great care. The fund's chief executive talked about some of his recent efforts and the management responses they have elicited:

> Confidential voting is one that we've gotten involved with simply because we've been thwarted in some cases on other items such as poison pills, where the company has called back, pressured individual shareholders, seeing how the vote is going, to change the vote. So we felt confidential voting was something that we should push for. Plus it's a very easy item for people to embrace as part of the concept of the voting process.

Some of the public funds' efforts to negotiate with corporate managements have been highly publicized. During the Texaco–Pennzoil dispute, for example, the California Public Employees Retirement System agreed to back Texaco's management in exchange for management's agreement to consider an independent director. (New York University president John Brademas was ultimately selected.)[12] In early 1990, the chief executive of CAL-PERS, Dale M. Hanson, and New York State Comptroller Edward V. Regan, who heads New York's public employee fund, wrote separate letters to the General Motors board. They expressed concern about the company's performance and asked for information about the process for choosing a successor to outgoing CEO Roger Smith. Regan's letter was leaked to the press and provoked a noisy controversy over whether the two funds were attempting to meddle in the day-to-day business of GM. Both Regan and Hanson took the position that they were simply exercising the fundamental right of shareholders to consult with the board of directors on major corporate policy decisions.[13]

Large public funds have occasionally combined the two approaches, using the threat of a shareholder initiative to induce management to negotiate. In late 1990, for example, CALPERS wrote to General Motors' new CEO, Robert C. Stempel. It advised Stempel of its intent to file a resolution to amend GM's bylaws to require a majority of independent directors, and to define *independent* to exclude anyone having any connection with GM, direct or indirect. After some initial resistance, GM's management came to the realization that the resolution simply codified a long-standing GM practice, and seized on the proposal as a public relations opportunity. GM and CALPERS exchanged mutually congratulatory public letters, and the resolution was adopted with management support.[14]

The public fund officials we interviewed were uniformly opposed to taking the governance initiative on social issues. State C's chief executive expressed the consensus view in these terms:

> I had people come and ask me to get involved with the *Exxon Valdez* thing and I said, "No, I don't want that issue, because it is purely an emotional issue." I'm certainly very sympathetic to the fact that they made a horrible mess with the environment up there, and there certainly is a major cost associated with the cleanup. But it's just not an issue I want to get involved with. We don't run resolutions on South Africa or Ireland or anything like that simply because we'd rather focus on the economic side. We think that it is more important.

Many of our sources knew of instances where other public funds had taken the initiative on social issues. Several different people cited the example of the New York City fund's reaction to the *Exxon Valdez* disaster, when the fund made a highly vocal demand for the right to appoint an environmentalist to Exxon's board. All of our sources, both public and private, were critical of this effort, and some of them questioned the motives of Harrison K. Goldin, the head of the New York City fund. In the view of State B's chief executive, for example, Goldin "was running for mayor."

The sole exception to this hostility to social activism is the situation in which a company's social policies have economic ramifications. Several public fund executives cited the *Exxon Valdez* example once again. They pointed out that they would have supported, or perhaps even initiated, a proposal like the one made by the New York City fund if it could have been shown that Exxon was losing business because of its environmental policies. As noted earlier, some funds now have formal procedures for assessing the economic impact of social initiatives.

Public fund executives claim the most modest of objectives for their corporate governance activities. Their stated interest is in ensuring that the directors do their job of supervising management. They expressly disclaim any interest in the day-to-day management of companies. State A's chief executive described his objectives as follows:

> The board of directors' job is to monitor management, and my job is to monitor the board, period. Nothing else. I never want to get involved with management at all. Ever. For any reason whatsoever. Only the board.

State C's chief executive said almost the same thing:

> We have been active in our firm belief that the owners of securities or shareholders should have an effective voice in how the company is run, not at the management level of the company, but at the level that the shareholders' interests are getting effectively represented on the corporate board.

When asked why they involve themselves in corporate governance, public fund executives often talk about their fiduciary duty. As fiduciaries, they claim, they have a legal and a moral duty to exercise their shareholders' rights diligently. But why, we asked, do they not simply sell out when a company is being badly managed? The answer was twofold. First, those funds that index would have to modify that policy in order to sell out. That, we were told, would be a complex bureaucratic process and would result in a loss of the benefits the fund thought it was getting from indexing. Second, even if a fund is not indexed, selling out a large position in a major corporation is difficult. The transaction costs are high, and the very act of selling may depress the price of the stock.[15]

The chief executive at State A described what he perceives as a fiduciary dilemma:

> I painted myself purposefully into a corner, in that I'm a fiduciary and won't sell. . . . I keep thinking about the issue of one, being a fiduciary, and two, being a permanent owner, and then three, how do I then discharge my fiduciary duty?

We call this dilemma the *fiduciary energy* problem. A pension fiduciary feels that he cannot just invest the fund's money and stand idly by; he must *do* something. To be doing his job, he must expend a certain amount of fiduciary energy. In many instances, the requisite activity takes the form of participation in the investment process, by buying and selling, or choosing investment strategies, or selecting and monitoring managers. But a fiduciary who indexes and thus forswears such participation may see governance activity as the only alternative. It is probably not coincidental that most of the executives who maintain the highest profile in the governance area work for heavily indexed public funds. A related point is that investment activity does not consume a great deal of time at indexed funds. As we reported in Chapter 6, there is not that much to do. Corporate governance activism may appeal to executives at such funds as a productive way to pass one's day.

Many people are skeptical about the goals and motives of those who take an activist stance on governance. Private fund executives and independent money managers repeatedly told us that they thought that Regan, Hanson, Goldin, and others in the public sector were promoting themselves and their political agendas. The word *grandstanding* was recurrent in our conversations. These critics dispute the *fiduciary energy* justification. As one independent manager put it:

I think it's a cop-out personally. They can sell. You could vote with your feet. And generally speaking, even though they own massive positions, they're in stocks like IBM and it may take them a while to get rid of them, but they can do that.

A ProductCo executive made the same point in more dramatic terms:

Generally we like the direction that the companies are going or we wouldn't buy them in the first place. Nobody is holding a gun to our head and saying that you have to be a permanent investor. I think it's really a lazy excuse for doing a lot of grandstanding. I think that it is an argument against indexing, first of all. Do you really want to buy a company that you hate? Why do you want to do that? Because it is an index? I don't have a lot of sympathy for people who index and find themselves captive to that strategy.

Having rejected the public executives' explanation for their activism, some critics go on to question their personal motives. Public fund officials are sensitive to these criticisms. The chief executive at State B, for example, went out of his way to disavow any personal motives for his activist stance on governance issues:

It means nothing to me to have any kind of public visibility at all on this corporate governance issue. So, I think what's driven me into it is really a sense of the passion of maintaining the purity of the pension funds, of really working for the beneficiaries. This has been my sole satisfaction in here.

But many see the public funds' greater involvement in social issues as creating an irresistible temptation to self-aggrandizement. According to one independent money manager:

The agendas unfortunately are very political. There's the South Africa issue. My sense is that it is inevitable, unfortunately, that it provides a forum for people whose personal motivations in pursuing these things are typically not necessarily the best interests of the beneficiaries.[16]

The critics also seem to ignore the distinction that public fund executives seek to draw between monitoring the board and micromanaging the company. An independent money manager commented:

We could sit there and criticize a company but we don't know all the facts. I can't tell Bob Stempel how to run General Motors. I can tell him, but I don't know probably one tenth or one thousandth of what he knows about the car business.

ChemCo's chief executive took a generous view of the public funds' motives, but he, too, questioned their competence:

I believe that the major state funds that have been involved in that are very well meaning. I think they think that they're a force for good there. What I just question is why do those people believe that they can run General Motors better than the independent directors of General Motors?

Whatever their true motives and objectives may be, public fund executives readily acknowledge the feeling of power that comes from their involvement in corporate governance. State C's chief executive remarked:

From my perspective, money is power. It really is interchangeable. . . . Just as I said to my wife, "Just always keep in mind that the friends that we've accumulated here are friends because of my job." When I leave the vestiges of this fund, how many of them will remain friends is something that you have to constantly be thinking about. It is very easy to lose sight of the fact that you and the fund are two separable things.

Later in the interview, he reflected again on the attractions of power:

It's a real heady trip. It's very, very heady to say that you are the chair or the vice-chair of the state pension system—a multibillion-dollar system. Just as it's heady for me to say that I'm the chief executive officer of one of the largest pension systems. Why do I do it? I certainly would make more money on the outside than I make with this system, but it's really a fascinating organization to be involved with. Fascinating in the fact that they're very receptive to cutting new ground in many respects. The corporate governance thing is one area. If you'd have told me when I accepted this job that I would be involved to the extent that I am involved with corporate governance, I'd have said, "You're nuts." When I told them the other day that we wrote a letter to the audit committee of United Airlines because we think it's a waste of corporate assets to pay more than 50-some million dollars for a failed management-led buyout, they understand what that's about and they get pretty rubbed up about that.

The ultimate question is whether this sense of power can be translated into real influence. That is, can public fund executives go beyond grabbing the occasional headline and play a significant role in the governance of the corporations they own? The evidence to date is equivocal.

The chief executive at State C believes that corporate managers are gradually changing their attitudes toward pension funds. He told a lengthy story to make the point that managers who formerly viewed fund executives as "crazies" now see them as serious contributors to the governance debate:

A year ago, I had dinner in New York City with the Business RoundTable [a management group] and the Council of Institutional Investors [a group that promotes institutional shareholder activism]. . . . We sat at the table. You would have thought you were looking at a painting of the Last Supper, almost to the extent that I was disappointed that I didn't see a halo behind the back of this guy's head. He was pontificating and I kept getting up and walking out of the room because I was getting nauseated. The whole thrust was trying to set up some dialogue with corporate America, to say, "We are not the crazies you think we are." In fact, if anything, it certainly seemed like, based on that dinner, they would have every right to walk away saying, "These guys are nuts."

Well, two weeks ago, we had a similar deal in Connecticut at Champion International's little mansion in the treetops. It was just the most superb meeting, because we started with the basic premise of "What can we do to work with corporate America?" because there are certainly a number of issues that we as shareholders and the corporations have in common, healthcare being one of them. It consumes an enormous amount of the corporation's profit, and certainly from our standpoint, it's a dilemma for us. Those are issues that we should be looking at. Where could we help them on regulation? Where can we help them on strike suits?—a number of areas. . . .

Shareholders have been asleep at the switch on the whole issue of corporate governance. They've abdicated a great deal to the corporation and particularly to the CEOs, and now they want to reclaim it. It's very, very threatening to CEOs, and in many cases, it shouldn't be.

This new spirit of cooperation has caused State C to change its governance strategy from one of confrontation to one of negotiation. It now resorts to formal shareholder initiatives only when informal negotiations fail. According to the chief executive, the corporations that State C targets settle short of a formal resolution about 75 percent of the time. He described the current state of affairs in upbeat terms:

> In the last year or so, I really have tried to emphasize that our approach now is more one, dialogue, and two, the proposal. . . . We're just absolutely delighted with the dialogue part of it. We're finding, particularly this year, that the companies have, for the most part, been a pleasure to work with.

Other public fund executives take a more cynical view of the new spirit of cooperation. They suggest that corporate managers have co-opted former adversaries by pandering to their egos, inviting them to carefully staged meetings and pretending to listen. In the experience of State B's chief executive, a request to talk to corporate management typically leads to a public relations show, but no serious discussion:

> We've extended invitations to companies, to talk with them from time to time. They immediately go to the lawyers. . . . The fact is, they don't want to talk with us. They want to address us as a public relations thing, just as you would a customer. But they don't want to talk to us as an owner. They don't want to treat us like an owner.

Regardless of how seriously corporate managers take them, there are some situations in which large pension funds can exercise real power just because of the size of their holdings. To illustrate this kind of power, one public fund chief executive recalled his response to Donald Trump's unsuccessful effort to acquire AMR, the parent of American Airlines:

> The CEO of a big corporation called me and said, "I'm really upset about Donald Trump trying to take over American Airlines and AMR." Then he says, "Why don't you guys do something about that?" And I said, "That's a valid question." Three days later, we had contacted the top 10 holders of AMR, and said, "Hey, we don't like AMR from the standpoint of how they deal with shareholders, because Crandall's [AMR's CEO] position is basically 'treat 'em

like mushrooms, keep them in the dark.' But you have to recognize that he has done a very good job of turning that airline around. Is Donald Trump going to be in a position to do that?" You know, I look at how much experience he has in airlines, which I know is the Trump Shuttle, and I say, "I think if they go to a consent solicitation, that if the top 10 shareholders say, 'Sorry Donald, we're not interested,' we could be a very powerful force."

This story is noteworthy not only because it demonstrates the extent of the large funds' behind-the-scenes power, but also because it shows that power being exercised in response to a request from corporate management. In addition, the public fund executive wielded his power to support an incumbent manager against a hostile takeover. The story is thus strong evidence of the new spirit of cooperation that some fund executives discern. However, it leaves open the question of whether that spirit results from a principled compromise or a successful program of co-optation. The story might be read as evidence that America's large corporations and their institutional owners have agreed that quick-buck takeovers are not in the country's best interests. Alternatively, it might be interpreted as an instance of a pension executive ignoring the economic interests of his shareholders in order to have a chance to play with the big boys.

Private Funds

The private funds have taken a markedly different approach to corporate governance. They have complied punctiliously with the requirements of the *Avon* letter. But they see governance as a burden rather than an opportunity, and have shown none of the activism of their public counterparts. Their objective seems to be to meet the requirements of the law while maintaining the lowest possible profile.

The whole idea of paying attention to corporate governance issues is irritating to some private fund executives. MediaCorp's chief pension executive, for example, gave this advice, contrasting his attitude with the apparent enthusiasm of some of the public funds:

> Don't spend a hell of a lot of time being like the state pension funds and focusing on who votes the proxies and this and that. Unfortunately, the Labor Department gets all wrapped up in that. It's very, in my opinion, very obfuscatory. . . . I don't care about the nuance of some particular proxy.

Notwithstanding such irritation, each of the funds we studied takes the *Avon* requirements seriously, and has set up procedures to implement one of the permitted proxy voting options. Some vote all proxies in-house, following a set of internal policies; some allow external managers to vote the stock they buy, but impose guidelines on certain sensitive issues; and others allow their outside managers total voting discretion, subject only to periodic review. Regardless of the procedure adopted, private fund executives are even more vehement than their public counterparts in their insistence that the only proper subjects for their concern are issues that have a direct impact on stock values.

According to an IndustrialCo executive, the task of pension fund management is "to enhance shareholder value." Pursuing other objectives is, in his view, an intolerable distraction:

> This is a tough enough and demanding enough job that if we start spending time getting involved in social and environmental issues as well, we're going to end up losing some of our focus.

The exclusive focus on shareholder value means that personal moral judgments must be put aside. Another IndustrialCo executive commented:

> We think ERISA is clear. . . . Apartheid, the Northern Ireland provisions, the animal rights provisions, nuclear weapons manufacturing, and all of those things, we don't think it's right to let any of our personal preferences enter.

Having defined social issues as beyond the scope of their legitimate concerns, private funds invariably defer to management when proxies present social questions. The IndustialCo executive continued:

> We feel that it's management's job to handle these. We don't feel that we can dictate to management a certain strategy or a certain tack on matters like those.

The rhetoric surrounding shareholder value issues is strikingly different. The attitude expressed is one of strict scrutiny and readiness to oppose management. A ProductCo executive contrasted the fund's approaches to social and economic issues:

> With ERISA considerations, the position that has been taken is that we are going to vote on the economic basis and, therefore, we generally find that proxies in the area of social and political issues are not in the economic interest of the participants and beneficiaries. But in the area of executive compensation packages, shark repellents, antitakeover issues, those are evaluated each and every time separately.

Another ProductCo executive gave a specific example of a shareholder value issue, again contrasting the fund's diligence with its laissez-faire approach to social issues:

> If the management says they want a particular compensation package and it's needed, the proxy voters are likely to go along with it. Now, we will look to see if we think they're pulling a grab of some sort. One thing we particularly don't like—because we've never done it in this corporation and we don't think it's right—is that after management grants themselves stock options, if the stock price goes down, then they decide to erase all of those options and regrant new ones at a lower price. That we would view as an egregious act, doing something that really shouldn't be done. We would probably vote against them. On a social issue, we won't pay much attention to how the thing is voted by the external manager.

In fact, however, challenges to management are rare. Regardless of whether a fund's proxies are voted internally or by its external managers, the working assumption is that they will be voted in favor of management. Most private funds have a policy that those who are voting proxies must raise a red flag whenever they intend to oppose management.

At ChemCo, for example, outside managers have total discretion in voting proxies, but they must notify the fund when they plan to vote against management:

> Voting against management is unusual. . . . You can assume that the outside managers vote with management unless they get back to you and say they voted against management. Right now there is

no policy on whether to vote with management or against management. The only obligation our outside managers have under their contracts with us is if you're going to vote against management, please let us know.

At TransCo, the procedure is more complicated. Once again, however, the critical point is that a pro-management vote is the presumptive course of action:

> If it's a poison pill or a takeover, and one manager says, "Hey, I want to sell out," we say, "OK, we hear you. Give us the reasons. Let's go talk to the other managers and see what their views are." . . . We go to the pension committee if we're going to vote against management. If we're going to vote with management, we will also notify the pension committee that this is the issue that's been raised, this is the way we're going to do it. So it's a process where we make the final determination any time a manager wants to do anything out of the ordinary.
>
> *How would "out of the ordinary" be defined? Voting against management?*
> For the most part, I think that's practical.

External money managers rarely propose to do anything out of the ordinary. Their perception is that attention to corporate governance is unrelated to their incomes. Although many have strong reservations about management practices, they have no incentive, financial or otherwise, to get ahead of their clients on governance issues.

Private funds are equally reluctant to challenge corporate managements in informal ways. For the most part, private funds have not attempted to negotiate with management on issues of mutual concern. The single exception among the funds we studied is IndustrialCo.[17] The chief pension executive at ProductCo contrasted his own fund's hands-off policy with IndustrialCo's approach, which he saw as an aspect of its value-investing philosophy:

> *Do you ever have an occasion to take an active role in the sense of offering a resolution or attempting to lobby management?*
> Well, that's not the way our internal asset management group works. That's not their investment style. We happen to know another major pension fund that does most of its investing in-

house and it follows a very different approach where they like to buy just a relatively few stocks that they believe in, that they've already had discussions and dialogue with the management about, and they follow those stocks closely, to constantly talk to the management. . . . If they felt the management was doing something wrong they'd go talk to them about it and ask them to change it.

IndustrialCo's own chief pension executive told the following story to illustrate how his fund's negotiation policy works. He emphasized that this was a rare event, and took pains to distance himself from the high-profile negotiations conducted by some of the public funds:

We have had a few instances of companies that we've known for a long time, and knew very well, where we owned a lot of stock, who called us and said, "We're thinking of putting a poison pill on our proxy. Would you support it?" Or "We're thinking of putting a fair-price amendment in our proxies. Would you support it? We're taking a poll of our big stockholders and we'd like to know what you think." And for a long time our standard reply was, "If you put it into the anti-greenmail clause, we'll support your fair-price amendment as long as we agree that the outer limits of what we are talking about on both of these are good. The anti-greenmail is good, the price range of the poison pill, that's fair. We're getting something out of it and we'll support it." It doesn't happen very often. One company wound up sitting in here, in my office with their lawyers, and talking over what the appropriate kind of constraints on both would be. It showed up in the proxy and it passed. That doesn't happen very often, but in that case it did. I mean that never made *The Wall Street Journal*. Nobody ever knew, nobody outside the company. We had the influence there.

In the aggregate, however, private pension funds provide strong support for the corporate status quo. They almost always vote their vast holdings in favor of management, and they are usually silent on potentially contentious issues. On the extraordinary occasions when they do speak up, it is with a discreetly muffled voice.

Private fund executives offer a variety of reasons for this policy of disengagement. First, they claim that they do not know enough about other companies' businesses to second-guess their managements. In the words of ChemCo's chief pension executive:

I think this company [ChemCo] feels they've got enough to do to run themselves. Not that we are not concerned with how other companies are doing and may have some ideas about how to do it. I question whether I could be so astute as to follow 200 to 250 companies that I have in the portfolio.

Second, they are fearful of disrupting the relationships that they and their sponsors have with the companies in which they invest. To quote ChemCo's chief executive again:

It's terrible to be doing business with people where you don't have a oneness of philosophy or to ruin a good relationship because you cannot see eye to eye on a certain issue.

An IndustrialCo executive made the same point, tying the importance of good relationships to his fund's long-term investing strategy:

Because of the longer-term continual nature of our investing philosophy, individual contacts are very important. Which is not to say that we can't disagree with management and even say so from time to time, but it's also very important to have a good relationship with the people of the company you're holding.

Third, many fund executives mentioned the possibility that conflicts of interest might arise if they took an active role in corporate governance. Suppose, for example, a critical supplier of the fund's sponsor proposes to enact a poison pill. Where does the pension executive's duty lie? Should he oppose the poison pill on economic principle, even though it might anger the supplier's management? The consensus view is that the best course is to maintain as low a profile as possible on governance issues.

None of the arguments in favor of disengagement is especially convincing. The first—ignorance of the details of other companies' businesses—seems irrelevant. How much does one need to know about making widgets to decide that strong independent directors are good and excessive executive compensation is bad? On the second point, why is it important to maintain good personal relations with companies in which the fund invests? An investor (particularly a fiduciary investor) should be interested in how corporate managers perform, not how pleasant it is to have lunch with them. And on the third point, the potential conflicts seem so stark as hardly to be conflicts at all. A

TransCo pension executive wondered aloud "if sometimes we don't look at our suppliers' situations and maybe that might influence us." But then he brought himself up short: "That would get us in jail, gentlemen."

We suspect that the strongest motivation for disengagement is a pension fund version of the Golden Rule: Do unto other companies as you would have their pension funds do unto your company. In other words, if you become a nuisance to the management of another company, you may find that company's fund bothering your sponsor's management—an outcome not calculated to please your sponsor's CEO. We heard of no specific instances of overt pressure along these lines. However, a number of independent money managers believe that this absence of evidence is significant. Their perception is that private pension executives are acutely aware of the Golden Rule, and very careful to follow it.[18]

There is some evidence that private fund executives are not entirely comfortable with their acquiescent role in governance. The problem as they see it is that their public sector counterparts have strong personal incentives to continue their well-publicized confrontations with corporate management. If the private funds remain on the sidelines, the public funds will have free rein to push the corporate governance debate in whatever directions they choose. Given their suspicions about the political motives of those in the public sector, most private fund executives believe that those directions will be counterproductive. ProductCo's chief pension executive talked about the dilemma that the private funds face:

> The private funds would probably prefer to continue the way they have been, but they may be forced by events to change, because I don't view it that we as private funds can stand aside and let Ned Regan and some California politician decide to pick somebody for Texaco's board and let Jay Goldin decide to agree with Exxon about putting an environmentalist on their board and so on and so on and so on. The private funds just stand aside and say, "We're going to let you all make those decisions with the company managements and we're going to do nothing." I don't think that can go on forever. So to the extent that the public funds are really serious about pressing for this dialogue and hands-on management, then I

think that the private funds are going to have to respond in some way. This is where we are with the ferment.

It seems unlikely, however, that the private funds will do anything more than just stand aside. The disincentives to action are simply too great. The Golden Rule is a real if rarely acknowledged motive for inaction. Moreover, to challenge the public funds' control of the governance debate would mean confronting them in the media as well as in the boardrooms. To act publicly, though, is to act contrary to a fundamental value in private pension management (recall the IndustrialCo executive's comment about staying out of *The Wall Street Journal*). In all probability, private executives will continue to look wistfully at their public counterparts, to complain and criticize, but to do nothing.

THE FUTURE

Pension funds show limited promise of being able to close the governance gap. Every indication is that the private funds will continue their present policy of staying out of sight and out of mind. There are no incentives for corporate pension executives to become active participants in the governance debate. On the contrary, challenging management control and in the process drawing attention to oneself and one's fund are not calculated to advance an executive's career. The likelihood, therefore, is that private funds will remain in the background, paying enough attention to proxies to meet their legal obligations, but almost always acquiescing in management's wishes. There is no reason to believe that private funds will emerge as strong advocates of shareholder supervision of management.

The future role of public funds is more difficult to predict. Public fund executives have many incentives to participate in the governance debate. By taking a strong stand on shareholder value issues, they may be able to preempt the demands of politicians who want to use the funds as instruments of social policy, a trend that fund executives decry. As political figures themselves, the fund executives view the attendant publicity as a benefit. Most of the publicity is positive, in any event, since it is hard to go wrong attacking overpaid and underperforming corporate managers. The bitter criticism from corporate CEOs and private fund executives only enhances the appeal.

The primary disincentive to activism is that this notoriety can prove to be too much of a good thing. As public pension funds become richer and more powerful, they can arouse the predatory instincts of governors and legislators. Politicians who previously had not paid much attention may begin to see the funds' assets as a public resource, and to resent the political good will that their corporate populism has generated. The result can be what has recently occurred in California, where the governor has attempted to gain control of the CALPERS board of trustees. The stated purpose of this move is to get the board to approve use of the fund's surplus funding to balance the state's budget—on a one-time-only basis, of course. It is hard not to suspect that the high profile of CALPERS CEO Dale Hanson is an equally tempting target.

The public funds have begun to tone down their rhetoric, and to move from confrontation with management to negotiation. According to the funds' executives, this shift in strategy is a measure of the success they have had in getting management to pay attention to them. But it may also be motivated by a fear of hostile political takeovers, on the California model. Whatever the cause, the effect will be to transform the public funds from outside agitators to inside players in the world of corporate governance. This transformation may make them more effective in promoting their shareholder value agenda. As their own executives acknowledge, it may also lead to their being co-opted. We suspect, regrettably, that the temptations of the boardroom will prove too much, and the public funds will settle into a new role as willing players on management's team. If they do, it is difficult to see who else will step forward to take on the job of corporate watchdog.

NOTES

1. According to a recent survey by Jay Lorsch and Elizabeth Mac-Iver, 63 percent of the outside directors of the 1,000 largest American companies are themselves chief executives of other corpora-

tions. Jay Lorsch and Elizabeth MacIver, *Pawns or Potentates: The Reality of America's Corporate Boards* (Boston: Harvard Business School Press, 1989).

2. The economic argument against antitakeover provisions begins with the presumption that a company is likely to become a takeover target only if its total stock market value drops below the sell-off value of its assets. At this point, it makes economic sense for a raider to offer a premium above the depressed stock price in order to acquire the company's assets. Since hostile takeovers typically result in the dismissal of incumbent managers, they are seen as a form of free-market punishment for management's failure to maintain share value. For a discussion of the relationship between takeovers and management accountability, see John C. Coffee, Jr., Louis Lowenstein, and Susan Rose-Ackerman, eds., *Knights, Raiders, and Targets* (New York: Oxford University Press, 1988). Of particular interest is chapter 1, a panel discussion featuring the legendary investor Warren Buffett.

3. See Bernard S. Black, "Shareholder Passivity Reexamined," *Michigan Law Review* 89 (1990), pp. 520, 566–68.

4. For an analysis of these barriers, see Black, "Shareholder Passivity," pp. 530–65.

5. These exceptions include the successful effort of the California Public Employees Retirement System to nominate a member of the Texaco board, and the letters written by CALPERS and the New York State Retirement System inquiring about the process by which General Motors would choose Roger Smith's successor. We discuss these instances later in the chapter.

6. In their current form, these rules prohibit a shareholder from contacting more than 10 others for the purpose of soliciting proxy votes unless a series of complex filing and disclosure requirements are met. Many observers believe that this provision has had a chilling effect on efforts by large institutional shareholders to work cooperatively to oppose management. The SEC is now in the process of reviewing the proxy rules, and has issued revised draft rules which, if adopted, would make such cooperation easier. A number of large public pension funds have been leaders in the fight to liberalize the antisolicitation rules.

7. See Black, "Shareholder Passivity," pp. 536–42.

8. The reference is to a category of state corporate law provisions that protect companies from hostile takeovers. Delaware has long tried to create a legal climate friendly to corporations, and has succeeded in becoming the favored state of incorporation for Ameri-

can companies. It is, in effect, the Cayman Islands of the United States. As a result, other states often follow Delaware's lead on questions of corporate law.

9. Many administrative agencies, including the Department of Labor and the Internal Revenue Service, issue opinion letters in response to specific questions. These letters are published and are treated by others subject to the agency's jurisdiction as authoritative statements of how the agency will deal with similar questions in the future. The *Avon* letter is reproduced in the *BNA Pension Reporter* 15 (1988), p. 391, and excerpted in John H. Langbein and Bruce A. Wolk, *Pension and Employee Benefit Law* (Westbury, N.Y.: Foundation Press, 1990), p. 562.

10. Many in the pension community believe that unqualified delegation of proxy voting to an outside manager absolves the fund of any legal liability in connection with the proxies. This view is not universally held, however.

11. Although the *Avon* ruling technically did not apply to public funds, they, too, took it seriously. Most public fund executives believe that the common law of trusts sets standards at least as exacting as those of ERISA. *Avon* was thus taken as a strong reminder to continue the development of rigorous procedures for voting proxies.

12. See "Taking Charge," *Business Week*, July 3, 1989, p. 66.

13. Regan and Hanson were accused of acting in concert, a charge that they vigorously denied. Regan gave his version of the episode in an article entitled "Why We 'Interfered' with GM" in *The New York Times*, February 11, 1990, p. F1, col. 1.

14. James A. White, "GM Bows to California Pension Fund by Adopting Bylaw on Board's Makeup," *The Wall Street Journal*, January 31, 1991, p. A6, col. 2.

15. Some observers question this assumption. They claim that with careful orchestration it is possible to sell out even a very large position without having any impact on the market.

16. Some public executives are also concerned about the motives of a few of their colleagues. State C's chief executive commented:

> I think our activism in corporate governance can be a force for good. It can also be a force for evil, and I think it ultimately is going to boil down to who controls the current and the direction and that's one of the reasons, quite honestly, that I've been very, very outspoken for more independence of the public funds away from the political process.

17. Executives at several private funds also told us that they expected that their outside managers consulted with corporate management from time to time. We were not told of any specific instances of such consultation, however, and the managers themselves indicated that it was rare.
18. The money managers themselves adhere to the Golden Rule, of course, lest they do anything to upset their clients.

CHAPTER 9

PENSION FUNDS AND THE GLOBAL ECONOMY

> An American investment firm recently led a group of U.S. pension executives on a fact-finding tour to the Soviet Union. The investment firm was seeking to channel pension money into the newly privatized Soviet satellite-launching industry. The pension executives were wined and dined by Soviet politicians and aerospace scientists. The highlight of the trip was a tour of the formerly top-secret Proton rocket facility. Speaking anonymously, several of the pension executives gushed with enthusiasm for the historic venture in which they were being asked to invest.

—Item from a network news broadcast on November 22, 1991

This story serves as a reminder that national borders (and even the former East–West divide) are increasingly irrelevant in the business and financial worlds. Like it or not, every major company and every substantial investor is participating in a global economy and must evaluate every significant transaction from a global perspective. The story also suggests that pension funds are important and sophisticated players in the global investment market. As we shall see in this chapter, however, while their importance is indisputable, their competence to function in the international arena is open to serious question.

Pension funds comprise the largest category of investors in the world's largest economy. They are thus in a unique position to affect, as well as be affected by, the global economy. As major investors in corporations, both American and foreign, that do business worldwide, the funds' investment performance is heavily influenced by the health of global markets. The funds' status as owners of these same corporations gives them the potential to influence strategic decisions that will have international economic implications.

Consider a company like General Motors. At the end of 1989, almost 11 percent of its stock was held by the 20 largest pension funds, and more than 40 percent by institutional investors generally (see Tables 2–7 and 2–9 in Chapter 2). Given the state of the domestic economy, GM's economic prospects—and, consequently, the value of these funds' investments—may depend heavily on the corporation's ability to expand its export markets. GM also faces ongoing decisions about who will manufacture and assemble its products and where they will do it. The decisions it makes will have an impact not only on its own balance sheet but on job markets in the United States and abroad,

---

BOX 9–1
Stock Ownership in the United States, the United Kingdom, Germany, and Japan

- Despite a sizable reduction in the proportion of equity held by individuals in the United States (falling from 72.2 percent in 1970 to 50.2 percent in 1988), in 1988 the United States still had the highest percentage of individual ownership of the four countries.

- Germany had the lowest individual percentage ownership in 1988, with only 16 percent of common stock held by individuals. Individual ownership was 28 percent in the United Kingdom and 22.4 percent in Japan.

- Of the four countries, financial institutional ownership is highest in the United Kingdom, at 52.8 percent of outstanding common shares. Japan is next with 51.2 percent, followed by the United States at 30.4 percent and Germany at 15.0 percent of common stock.

- In 1988, foreigners held four times as much common stock (21.0 percent) in Germany as they did in the United States (5.4 percent). Japan has the lowest foreign ownership, with only 4 percent of outstanding common stock. Foreigners own 6.5 percent of United Kingdom common stocks.

on the international trade balance, on the rate and pattern of growth in the affected countries, and, conceivably, on the international flow of technology. As some of GM's largest shareholders, these pension funds can claim a right to be informed on how management will make these decisions. (And they are likely to assert that right: Two of GM's pension fund shareholders, the New York and California state funds, sparked controversy in 1989 by their demands for information about the choice of Roger Smith's successor.)

Given the extent to which they are tied into the global economic network, large pension funds might be expected to have developed considerable expertise in international business and finance. One might expect that this expertise would be evident both in the funds' dealings with U.S.-based multinational corporations and in their exploitation of foreign investment opportunities. The reality is quite different: Because of the funds' inability to deal with the cultural complexities of international investing, their efforts are late in coming and often shortsighted and superficial.

Most large pension funds now do a limited amount of international investing, on the theory that it presents a diversification opportunity that cannot prudently be ignored. But few of them have developed any in-house international expertise. Instead, most allocate small portions of their portfolios to external managers and take a hands-off approach.

The nine funds we studied illustrate this pattern. Seven of the nine engage in international investing, defined as investing in securities of foreign issuers that are not available on domestic markets. None of the seven did any international investing prior to 1980, and most of them began in the mid- to late 80s. They allocate 5–15 percent of their portfolios to international investment, with most of the funds clustered at the low end of that range.

In this chapter we address four major questions: Why do these funds invest internationally? How do they do it? How do they deal with questions of international corporate governance? What role will pension funds play in shaping the global financial environment in the future?

WHY DO PENSION FUNDS INVEST INTERNATIONALLY?

The pension fund executives we interviewed understand the phenomenon of globalization. They grasp the interdependence of product and financial markets and acknowledge that investors can no longer ignore events beyond their own borders. More specifically, they are aware that in recent years some foreign economies have done better than America's. These realizations have led them to consider international investment as another possibility to be evaluated in their ongoing pursuit of diversification. The chief pension executive at TransCo summarized these factors as follows:

> It was our belief that international markets offered better returns, that our economy was maturing and returns were going to mature, and that we could get a much better environment there, number one. Number two, I think there was a recognition on our part that things were globalizing real quickly and that if you were going to invest in the best value automobile company, you shouldn't restrict yourself to the three in the United States, that you needed to look in other areas of the world. And that was equally true whether you were looking at beer companies or drug companies.

For some, the motivation for international investing appears not to go beyond the general desire to leave no stone unturned in the diversification process. According to ChemCo's chief pension executive, the decision that was made in 1984 was, "Let's expose ourselves to some additional investment opportunity overseas." One of State C's trustees was more explicit about the diversification rationale:

> I not only think that we ought to be into international investments. I think we would be violating our fiduciary duty to our beneficiaries, in terms of risk, return, proper investment, diversification, and asset allocation, if we did not take advantage of the international field.

At two of the funds, unique factors reinforced this general desire for international exposure. At TransCo, the fund began to invest internationally at a time when the sponsoring company's operations were entirely domestic. The company subsequently began to do business abroad, and this expansion has influenced the fund's outlook, as its chief executive explained:

> We started earlier with, "Hey, this is a mystique." Our ability to travel is unrestricted, so we get over there. We meet with those managers more on their turf than ours and visit a lot of those countries a lot more regularly, business or pleasure [than some funds]. We attend a lot of the conferences. So, we're probably a lot more comfortable with the process. In connection with that, the company has become more international over the years. So, I think we've gotten the comfort, as we've gone along, of the globalization of the business as well as the investment process.

At MaterialCo, the sponsor's corporate treasurer explained that the company looked on international investing "as a diversification move." He told us that the chief pension executive had "strong feelings over the years" about international investing because he had worked for many years in Latin America. As a result, the corporate treasurer continued, even though international investments are "there just for diversification" and comprise only 5 percent of the total portfolio, they receive a great deal of attention: "We feel it's an important sector, and manage it as such."

Only one of the funds went beyond the general principle of diversification in explaining the objectives of its international investment program. Executives at ProductCo identified two such objectives: exploiting currency fluctuations and taking advantage of differences in the economic cycles in the United States, Europe, and Japan. ProductCo's willingness to undertake market-timing strategies in the international arena reflects its highly active multistyle approach to investing generally.

An in-house financial analyst at ProductCo who specializes in the international markets (none of the other funds we studied has a comparable specialist on its staff) gave an example of how the fund achieved its two international investment objectives during the 1987 U.S. stock market crash. First, as the value of the dollar and U.S. interest rates both fell, ProductCo realized substantial gains on its foreign bonds. Second, because the Japanese stock market bounced back before the American market, the crash's impact on ProductCo's equity portfolio was reduced:

> The stock market crashed here in October 1987. We had a significant amount of money in nondollar bonds. The nondollar bonds in the fourth quarter alone went up something like 25 percent, because interest rates were reduced and the dollar went down sharply. That is diversification. We are the largest investors in [an international mutual fund]. That fund has been a tremendous diversification, because when all the other markets were going down, that thing has continued to go up. We have realized annual returns, annualized returns of 40 percent in the two years that we have been in that fund. Well, there is a tremendous diversification aspect to that fund, but this is a diversification and an opportunity to enhance your portfolio return. At the end of December of 1987, the Japanese market came back in the fourth quarter. And the diversification of the international investments helped out the U.S. investments of the pension fund.

Executives at two of the funds that do invest internationally reported some internal resistance to the idea. At TransCo, some union representatives objected to investing the assets of the defined contribution plan in foreign markets, characterizing it as "just a boondoggle for the pension committee to go to London." The union's attitude has vacillated according to the year-to-year performance of the international investments in comparison to the domestic portfolio. At State C, some of the trustees have raised similar objections to the perquisites that often go along with an international portfolio—for example, a seminar at which the chief executive "happened to have the misfortune to go to Paris and spend a week in a chateau, worrying about international investing, having dinner with Helmut Schmidt and talking about the Common Market in 1992." These occasional complaints have not caused the fund to alter its commitment to international investing.

Two of the nine funds, MediaCorp and IndustrialCo, do not invest internationally. In both cases, not doing so is less a matter of a policy against such investments than an aspect of the overall approach to money management at each fund. Each of these funds adheres to a consistent investment philosophy, is satisfied with its performance, and may simply see no compelling reason to deviate from its established strategy. At Media-Corp, the portfolio is in the hands of two external managers who practice long-term value investing and who have had a long and close relationship with the fund and its sponsor. The Indus-trialCo fund implements a similar value investing approach internally. As we noted in Chapter 3, this strategy is the product of a lengthy evolutionary process and is widely respected in the pension community. The fund has not yet moved into international investments.

In addition to lacking any incentive to diversify into international markets, these two funds may also be influenced by the difficulty of applying their value investing approach abroad. The essence of this approach is to invest in a limited number of companies that managers study carefully and know intimately. Most other countries impose less demanding financial reporting requirements than the United States, which makes it difficult for American investors to gather adequate financial data on foreign countries, and there are logistical, linguistic, and cultural barriers to kicking the tires at foreign companies and making intuitive judgments about their managements. For these reasons, MediaCorp and IndustrialCo may feel that the potential benefits of international diversification would entail an unacceptable cost: the sacrifice of their value investing standards.

HOW DO PENSION FUNDS MANAGE THEIR INTERNATIONAL INVESTMENTS?

All the funds that invest internationally employ outside managers to handle their international portfolios. (This is true even of ProductCo, which has a full-time international specialist on its in-house staff.) With few exceptions, these managers are foreign-based (most often in Tokyo or London) or at least have a substantial foreign presence. The funds employ them because of their knowledge of the languages, economies, and business cultures of the countries in which they invest.

Barriers to In-House Management

The international specialist at ProductCo talked at length about the factors that mitigate against in-house management of an international portfolio. The basic problem is that each major financial market is to some extent unique, so that investment know-how is not readily transferable from one market to another. As he described it, "You are dealing with 18 local equity markets, and all of the factors that affect those local markets." The language barrier is one such factor, and it is particularly acute in dealing with Japan. One might assume that a large pension fund could simply hire multilingual staff members, but this is rarely done or even seriously considered. Even at ProductCo, which prides itself on having a sophisticated and successful international operation, the international specialist said only, "We do have an individual on the staff, it's my understanding, who could speak Japanese, but if we were to invest in-house internationally, then you would have to address that question." The funds end up adopting a familiar American outlook on foreigners and their languages: If they can't speak English, we can't be bothered with dealing with them.

Currency differences pose another problem. The prevailing view is that investing is difficult enough without adding the further complication of fluctuating exchange rates. Everyone with whom we discussed international investing thought that it would be impossible for the management of an American pension fund to master the subtleties of currency fluctuation on a country-by-country basis.

The most often cited and, ultimately, the most daunting barrier to direct management of international investments is what the ProductCo specialist described as the cultural aspect. He and many of his counterparts grouped a wide range of considerations under this, from the general sensibilities of different nationalities to the specific ways that business is done in particular foreign markets. While the realization that business cultures differ from country to country is an astute one, many of the fund executives' comments were remarkably superficial. Overall, the commentaries that we heard on foreign business cultures had the tone of vintage *National Geographic* articles.

The basic issue is that the unwritten rules for doing business vary from country to country. As one pension executive described it, "It's just all these nuances and little things that you can't compare." At the highest level of abstraction, this variation is attributed to differences in national character. The pension executives we interviewed appeared to have drawn their inferences about these differences from such anecdotal sources as personal travel experiences and occasional contacts with foreign financial experts. For example, in commenting on the continental aversion to LBOs, the ProductCo international specialist observed that "the Germans are a very conservative type of people, as are the Swiss." He noted that the French, by contrast, have shown more interest in leveraged acquisitions. He offered some similarly sweeping generalizations about Dutch business culture, citing as sources a business colleague and his own travel experience:

> The Netherlands appears to have the strongest focus on environmental issues, a tremendous focus, a tremendous concern. For example, one of the gentlemen who sits with me on the board of directors of an investment organization heads up a large pension fund in the Netherlands. He has asked an investment manager to look into setting up a portfolio which would just invest in the companies that are involved with the environment—cleaning up the environment, for example—because he thinks it's such an issue in the Netherlands. He thinks that it is going to be an issue globally, and that it might present investment opportunities for him. In addition to the Green Party, the thing I picked up in the Netherlands is that the environment is very strong.

Some comments on cultural differences were considerably more specific. One recurrent theme in the interviews was that investors in some countries, most notably Japan, do not seem to pursue what Westerners would view as rational economic objectives. In the words of TransCo's chief pension executive, it is "a lot more trying" to invest overseas because "some markets like Japan aren't necessarily value-driven markets."

On this issue, ProductCo's international specialist provided the most detailed and insightful commentary. He noted that by Western standards of measurement, Japanese investors appear to be throwing away enormous sums of money for the purely symbolic value of owning stock. However, when one compares domestic stock earnings with competing opportunities on the Japanese market—as Japanese investors do—then the behavior of ProductCo with regard to international investments does not seem so irrational after all:

> The Japanese stock market has a P/E of 60. I'll give you a good example. Their telephone company, NTT, went public in 1987. People bought that stock when it was selling for a P/E multiple of 300, and they paid $20,000 a share at one point for a piece of paper that they framed and hung up on their wall. . . . A portfolio manager in the United States wouldn't, I don't think, buy a stock that is selling for a P/E of 300 or 100, or 75, or 50. And yet, the Japanese will do that.
>
> *Are they doing something nonrational or non-economic, or something?*
>
> It depends on whose eyes you are looking through. If you are looking through Western eyes, you might say that it is not terribly rational to put your money into a stock that is going to take you 300 years to get back what you put in. But if you look at it through their eyes, what you see is entirely different. They take the relationship between the bond yield and the earnings yield on the stock, and look at that historically, and say, "The differential is three." It is in the historic range, and so the market is fairly valued even though it is selling on a P/E of 60.

Another specific problem that can bedevil American investors is the structure of foreign markets. The German market, for example, is said to be "not very liquid and dominated by the banks." In such an environment, according to a leading independent money manager, large companies "don't feel any real responsibility for providing much in the way of information." Because public holdings are limited, he continued, corporate management's attitude toward even large institutional investors is "trust us and don't bother us." Pension executives believe that the Japanese market is dominated by an even more tightly knit group of insiders: giant corporations, banks, and insurance companies that cross-hold each other's stock. To outsiders unable to get access to American-style financial reporting data, the

European and Japanese markets are what one executive called "this great big casino."

International markets thus present the pension fiduciary with a difficult dilemma. On the one hand, the booming economies of Asia and Western Europe may be an investment opportunity that is too good to pass up. On the other, the inability of American pension executives to deal with the many complexities of foreign investment (or, at least in the case of language, their unwillingness to do so) make this an opportunity that is fraught with risk. From both the financial and legal perspectives, there is a substantial probability of going wrong whichever way they turn.

The Solution: Outside Managers

Pension funds uniformly believe that the best way to resolve this dilemma is to hire outside managers with international experience. The most desirable managers meet three criteria: They are physically present in the important foreign markets, they are run by nationals of the countries in which they are present, and they know how to deal with Westerners.

We heard arguments on both sides of the question of whether managers must be physically present in the countries where they invest. Some American pension executives suggested that modern communications made local presence a moot point. One even noted that there might be some benefit in being removed from the market because "you just don't get caught up in the emotion."

The prevailing view, however, is that the local know-how and local contacts that an on-site foreign manager can contribute are indispensable. Because official financial reporting is inadequate in most countries, it is essential to have the access to informal sources of information that only local people can provide. Local people speak the local language, follow the local financial press, and can do the sort of intelligence gathering that an American investor would do at lunch or on the golf course. One of our sources also pointed out that it is important to have managers who do business in the relevant local time zone.

Hiring a purely local investment concern in a foreign country can be almost as difficult as doing the investing directly. For this reason, many American pension funds use large, multinational management firms that have offices in London, Tokyo, Frankfurt, and other foreign financial centers. They insist, however, that the foreign offices actually be managed (as opposed to merely staffed) by nationals of the countries in which they are situated. The chief pension executive at ProductCo made this point by describing a visit he made to the fund's Japanese manager, apparently for the purpose of verifying that the people running the office were really Japanese:

> Their office in Tokyo is very different from many others in that when we went there it didn't even have a sign on the door identifying it with this international investment operation. And all of the people in the office were Japanese nationals. We went there and visited with them, and talked to them, and so on. They claim that they are staffed by Japanese nationals, and they do all of their business with Japanese. We could see clearly that that was the case by having been there and visited them. When we looked around some other operations in Tokyo, it became clear that the key decision makers were British or Americans.

The ideal foreign manager employs not just any local people, but local people who specialize in dealing with Americans. Earlier in this chapter, we noted the widespread concern that Japanese and, to a lesser extent, European investors pursue strategies that seem irrational to Americans. Pension funds prefer dealing with foreign managers who understand American investment objectives. Such managers offer both knowledge of the local investing culture and sensitivity to their clients' cultural concerns.

ProductCo's international specialist dealt with this issue in talking about the fund's Japanese manager. He pointed out that although it is run by Japanese, it handles only Western accounts, and manages them from a Western perspective:

> The managers are Western in their approach, because they focus on the P/Es. . . . They are significantly underweighted in the Japanese market today, which is something to say for Japa-

nese management. You wouldn't expect a Japanese manager, normally, to be significantly underweighted in his own market. That was not something that you expect. So, they are managing it to some degree like a Western portfolio.

Is that the way they do it all the time, or do you think that to some extent they are playing to you in doing this for your benefit with your account?

The question is, do they do it for all of their non-Japanese accounts? They certainly do it. This manager, to my knowledge, only manages non-Japanese accounts, and all of the accounts are managed with the same investment objectives and with the same guidelines.

Not surprisingly, American pension executives find it difficult to evaluate the performance of their foreign managers. They agree that foreign managers should be given longer to prove themselves than their domestic counterparts (a seven- to eight-year period was suggested), but find it difficult to establish benchmarks. For example, should the performance of a Japanese equity manager be compared to the performance of the fund's entire portfolio, or its equity portion, or perhaps some Japanese equity index, or even to the performance of Japanese equity managers who use similar strategies?

In Chapters 3 and 4 we discussed the difficulties that funds have in choosing benchmarks for evaluating their domestic managers. In the case of foreign managers, these inherent difficulties are compounded by all the cultural complexities that caused them to hire the foreign managers in the first place. In evaluating managers, as long as foreign and domestic returns are generally comparable, funds seem to focus on "comfort level"—whether the manager seems to be both attuned to the local environment and properly sensitive to the fund's needs. The result of this focus on intangibles is that foreign managers, once hired, are almost never terminated.[1]

An important question is whether American pension funds receive adequate value for the money they place with international managers. Among the people we talked to, no one is quite sure. Most funds report that aside from the occasional outstanding currency play or market-timing decision (for example, ProductCo's success in taking advantage of the recovery of the Japanese market after the U.S. crash of October 1987), their foreign and domestic portfolios have produced similar rates of return. Since they find it so difficult to set financial benchmarks for evaluating foreign investments, the best they can say is that they are losing nothing (except some additional administrative costs) and gaining the protection of one more form of diversification.

WHAT ROLE DO AMERICAN PENSION FUNDS PLAY IN INTERNATIONAL CORPORATE GOVERNANCE?

The short answer to this question is almost none. The pension executives we interviewed believe that foreign corporate governance is fundamentally undemocratic, with few significant issues ever put before the public shareholders. Even when a fund does view a particular issue as important, it may find insuperable procedural obstacles to voting its shares. As a result, American pension funds that invest in foreign companies find themselves to be simply along for the ride.

In sharp contrast to their activity in the domestic arena, the funds we studied make virtually no effort to investigate or vote their foreign proxies, or to try to influence corporate management through informal channels. Three reasons are advanced for this lack of interest. First, some executives believe that foreign proxy issues are irrelevant simply because they are foreign. The chief financial officer at MaterialCo explained it in these terms:

> I don't want to vote shares in Japanese companies, if you could vote shares in Japanese companies. I don't want to get involved with that. It's not the U.S. corporate governance issue.

Others offered a second reason: the lack of issues to vote on. In general, according to a TransCo executive, "Proxies don't have the same vote or meaning in other countries that they do here." In both Japan and Western Europe, proxies lack meaning because of the relative insignificance of public ownership. In the words of ProductCo's international specialist, "There is a tremendous amount of cross-holding—when I buy your stock I'll put it in my bag, and you put my stock in your vault—and it just sits there." The important communication on corporate governance issues takes place in off-the-record conversations among the bankers and corporate executives who control most of the stock in the largest corporations.[2] As a result, all that is left for public shareholders (including American pension funds) to vote on are such nonissues as the ratification of auditors.

Simple procedures pose a third set of barriers to the funds' participation in foreign corporate governance. ProductCo's international specialist enumerated some of these barriers:

> When you get to Japan, the proxies are in Japanese. Someone will have to see that those proxies are translated into English and sent to the UK, and then sent back to Tokyo, and then voted on. That's one problem you've got. Then you've got the problem with time; there usually is not enough time for something like that to be completed.[3] You've got local requirements, like in Japan. I think that the local requirement is that you physically have to be present at the annual meeting to vote the proxies, and the annual meetings are held for all of the companies on the same date.[4]

One reaction to these barriers might be that they are simple logistical problems that could be solved by a modest infusion of effort and money. An organization with the resources of a large pension fund could presumably hire local people to keep track of annual meeting dates, obtain and translate proxies, and attend the meetings to vote the fund's shares. If pension funds wanted to vote foreign proxies, it is hard to believe that American brokerage houses, hard pressed on so many other fronts, would not compete to sell the necessary services.[5]

The problem is lack of incentive. With so few important issues on the ballot, fund executives see no reason to overcome the logistical barriers themselves or to pay someone else to do it. They also do not believe that American fiduciary law compels them to undertake what would ultimately be a futile effort, an attitude that contrasts strongly with their understanding of the legal requirements pertaining to domestic proxies.

Most of the pension executives we interviewed believe that this state of affairs will change. Some expect to see American-style proxy issues put before European and Japanese public shareholders in the next 10 to 20 years. At a minimum, everyone with whom we discussed the subject expects foreign corporations to become more democratic and open.

European and Asian corporations will move toward the American style of corporate governance either because they decide that it is in their interest to do so or because the law forces them to. One might well ask what advantages foreign corporate managers or lawmakers could see in adopting the American model. As ProductCo's international specialist described it:

> I think that they look at America and say, "That's a country with a lot of economic problems, and they can't get their house in order. And someday, they will have to do it." But I don't think that they want to emulate the United States in that fashion. No. I don't think so.

It is difficult to dispute his assertion that Europeans and Asians have no present incentive to emulate American business behavior. It is not clear, however, why "someday, they will have to do it." Unless and until the relative economic fortunes are reversed, what would cause foreign businesses to follow our lead in corporate governance or any other area of business or finance?[6] It seems unlikely that there will be any pressure to do so from our largest investors, the pension funds. They have decided that the potential benefits of participating in foreign corporate governance are far outweighed by the costs, and are on the sidelines, apparently indefinitely.

HOW WILL AMERICAN PENSION FUNDS INFLUENCE THE GLOBAL ECONOMY?

Foreign influences on the U.S. economy have become pervasive. Foreign investors finance our national debt, control some of our largest corporations, and own some of our most visible properties. Pension funds feel these influences both directly and indirectly: directly, as they expand their international investments, and indirectly, as American corporations and markets are increasingly integrated into a worldwide economy.

BOX 9–2
Pension Funds Worldwide

- Three of the top 10 foreign pension plans (ranked by total assets) in 1990 were Japanese. The United Kingdom and the Netherlands each accounted for 2 of the top 10 foreign funds, including the largest fund in the world, a Dutch fund. Sixteen of the largest 25 pension funds in the world were American.

- Total Japanese pension fund assets reached $240 billion in 1991 and are expected to almost triple over the next decade. Recent changes in laws governing pension fund management, including increased allowances for foreign exposure and management, are expected to contribute to this growth.

- In 1990, the 300 largest pension funds in the world had assets in excess of $2.4 trillion, with the largest 25 funds' assets in excess of $937 billion. Many predict that foreign pension funds' conservative approaches to asset allocation will give way to greater equity and international exposure in the coming years, partly in response to such factors as aging populations and governments' inability to finance pension obligations.

- Along with increased international exposure, foreign funds are expected to continue diversification of their portfolios, deemphasizing U.S. investments and increasing their exposure in Europe and Japan.

Top 10 Foreign Pension Plans, 1990

Rank	Fund	Country	Total Assets (U.S. dollars in billions)
1	Algemeen Burgerlijk	The Netherlands	$ 93,710
2	Allmaana Pension	Sweden	70,990
3	Pension Welfare Service	Japan	67,919
4	Public School Teachers	Japan	44,000
5	National Government Employees	Japan	34,114
6	British Coal	United Kingdom	25,090
7	Central Provident Fund	Singapore	23,500
8	PGGM	The Netherlands	22,176
9	British Telecom	United Kingdom	20,858
10	Ontario Teachers	Canada	17,242
Total			$419,599

Source: *Pensions and Investments.*

The major U.S. pension funds might be expected to be a source of reciprocal American influence on foreign economic interests. They are, after all, the largest source of independent, nongovernmental investment capital in the world. They should also have access to unlimited international expertise. Many are affiliated with multinational corporations, and all appear to have the resources to bring in whatever additional help they might require. Finally, the active role that many of them are taking on the domestic corporate governance front suggests a principled interest in economic policy issues.

Contrary to this expectation, what we heard was a tentative, almost naive approach to the increasingly global economy. Most funds say that they have gone into international investing simply to diversify. Few of the people we interviewed claimed any specific, country-by-country knowledge; those that did made sweeping generalizations about national character and business culture. As a result, specific investment decisions have largely been delegated to external managers. Because of the same cross-cultural complexities that cause the funds to rely on these middlemen, they find it difficult to evaluate how good a job they are doing. They also see little prospect for affecting the governance of the foreign corporations in which they invest. The final, remarkable outcome is that these multibillion-dollar investors are almost helpless in the international arena, and perceive themselves as likely to remain so.

Ironically, several of the people we interviewed described foreign investors as unsophisticated by American standards. For example, an outside money manager who handles domestic equities for one of the nine funds commented that Europeans "are generally not very sophisticated investors," perhaps because "it may be tougher to find that [American] kind of talent overseas." Yet those unsophisticated Europeans are on the verge of creating the world's most powerful economic entity, while America's investing elite generalizes about Swiss conservatism, Dutch environmental consciousness, and Japanese inscrutability. This kind of comment confuses mastery of esoteric investment products with financial sophistication. It suggests that traditional American arrogance will reinforce fear of the unknown, ensuring that U.S. pension funds will continue to play a passive role in the global economy for the foreseeable future.

NOTES

1. ProductCo's international specialist reported, for example, that only one foreign manager had been terminated in the eight years he had been on the job, and that one after a seven-year evaluation.
2. ProductCo's international specialist also observed that small- to medium-sized foreign companies are typically family-owned and not open to American investors.
3. Another executive pointed out that the international managers often did not get the proxies until after the voting was over.
4. As was the case with many issues in foreign investing, the people we interviewed expressed only a superficial knowledge of these procedural problems. The ProductCo international specialist concluded his remarks on the subject by acknowledging, "I think that may be the case. I'm not sure, but you've got these local practices, OK?"
5. We were told of one large American bank that is looking into providing international stock custodian services to American pension funds.
6. The current scandals on the Japanese stock market may provide an interesting test case. One might expect Japanese investors to be so offended by the disclosures of insider manipulation that they would demand American-style openness. A more likely outcome, however, is that after some suitably public contrition by the wrongdoers the scandals will be forgotten, dismissed as a minor cost of maintaining an efficient economy.

CHAPTER 10

THE CULTURE OF CAPITAL

Numbers dominate the discussion of economic and business issues. Ask an economist a question and statistics will turn up before the end of the first sentence of the answer. Business schools, which emphasize practical problem-solving skills rather than abstract theory, put more and more emphasis on the techniques of quantitative analysis. Even the law, with its centuries-old tradition of qualitative, case-by-case analysis, is increasingly influenced by quantitative economic thinking.

This trend is, up to a point, necessary, and often salutary. Economists are supposed to identify trends, analyze problems, and propose solutions, and it is obviously desirable that they do so with as much precision as possible. Those who will manage businesses need to understand the marketplace on many levels and will surely require the descriptive and predictive power that only numbers can provide. And since so much of the law deals with the regulation of economic behavior, it can only benefit as well from the same kinds of insights.

This focus on the quantitative is not without cost, however. Statistics are most meaningful when they aggregate large numbers of cases. The statement that one institutional investor dedicates 30 percent of its portfolio to equities is of limited value; to say that, on average, 10,000 institutional investors do the same thing is to identify an important trend. In the rush to aggregate, however, quantitative analysts inevitably forgo many opportunities to investigate potentially significant kinds of questions. Why, for example, do individual institutional investors choose to invest in equities? Are all of those who do so motivated by the same factors? How do particular institutions go about making the decision? What might cause them to reverse themselves?

Even though economists and other quantitative analysts generally disclaim any interest in the answers to such questions, the answers are often important to those who make use of their analyses. For example, economic policymakers in Washington may look at the relevant numbers and decide that the country's supply of patient, long-term investment capital is inadequate. In response, they will propose a legislative package of incentives and disincentives designed to induce investors to be more patient. But how can they know what the appropriate carrots and sticks are? To take another example, many lawyers, legislators, and regulators are concerned about institutional investors' lack of interest in corporate governance. The response has been to propose a variety of incentives, both financial and regulatory, to prompt greater participation. But how do they know that the incentives will have the desired effect?

The answer in both instances is that those who deal with the quantitative big picture are often relegated to making assumptions about how individuals behave. At least since Adam Smith postulated his invisible hand, it has been a basic tenet of economics that when confronted with choices people will try to maximize gain. This general principle is regularly translated into more specific assumptions in a variety of contexts. For example, those who study the stock market assume that investors base their buy and sell decisions on financial considerations. Similarly, many corporate law theorists believe that institutional investors weigh the economic costs and benefits in deciding whether to participate in corporate governance.

To many of those who make them, such assumptions are beyond question. To us as anthropologists, they are anything but. Our reaction is driven initially by the realization that each of the systems that economists and business analysts study— the economy as a whole, the stock market, institutional investment—is in reality the sum of the behavior of a great many people. In other areas of human endeavor, the motivations for behavior are complex; it is almost unheard of to find a large group of people all pursuing the same objective at the same time. Instead, individuals are continually influenced by concerns about such diverse issues as survival, power, prestige, responsibility, and personal relations.

Anthropology's fundamental insight is that within a social group the individual responses to these basic human concerns are neither automatic nor random: rather, they are shaped by the shared beliefs and practices that comprise culture. The roots of the anthropological method are far removed from Wall Street, both in time and place. Throughout most of the history of the discipline (which goes back at least to the mid-1800s), its practitioners have focused almost exclusively on small, pre-industrial societies—Pacific islanders, Amazon tribes, African pastoralists. But in recent years, anthropologists have also turned their attention to large, pluralistic societies and have analyzed their constituent institutions from a cultural perspective. They have found that entities like courts, hospitals, and businesses have identifiable cultures that strongly influence their members' behavior.

Our primary objective in undertaking this study was to determine whether a cultural approach could also illuminate the workings of the organizations that dominate institutional investment. Simply put, we wanted to discover what the people in these organizations do and why they do it—to learn to see the world through their eyes. In the course of this process of discovery, we hoped to give some life to the numbers and, most important, to examine the assumptions that underlie most quantitative analyses.

Among the many things that we have learned from the cultural study of institutional investment, three strike us as particularly significant: first, investment decisions are often motivated by cultural factors; second, institutions are, for cultural as well as economic reasons, unlikely to be the solution to the country's corporate governance problems; and third, institutions seem ill-prepared to participate in the emerging global business culture.

INVESTMENT CULTURE

The evidence we have gathered at nine of the country's largest pension funds suggests that institutional investment decisions are fundamentally indistinguishable from the everyday kinds of decisions made in the most ordinary of social contexts. The trappings of rigorous financial analysis are all around: Pension executives' desks are cluttered with reports, strategic options are dissected by committee after committee, outside money managers hawk their services with charts and graphs. But these are not the things that the executives choose to talk about when they analyze how and why they make their decisions. Instead, they gravitate toward such themes as responsibility and blame, the influence of the past, both real and mythic, and an overriding concern with managing personal relationships.

Even at nine institutions, we saw an enormous variety of management structures, from a one-person shop to a bureaucracy that the Pentagon would envy. In some instances, the people within the structure think that it is working well; in others, they have significant doubts, or simply cannot tell. In every instance, the structure now in place owes its origin in substantial part to cultural factors. Recall the IndustrialCo creation myth, the effort at ProductCo to make important people comfortable with the decision-making process, and State A's apprehension about the press. And in none of the nine cases has the present structure been validated by a careful study of alternatives. Like other kinds of practices with deep cultural roots (religion, for example), the management structures are accepted uncritically and are very resistant to change.

The most pervasive cultural theme that we encountered was the need to manage responsibility and blame. Those institutions with the most active investment styles tend to have elaborate committee structures for making strategic decisions. These structures make it all but impossible to assign individual credit or blame for particular decisions. By several accounts, the use of outside managers is another effective device for displacing responsibility and avoiding blame. The managers themselves are keenly aware of this perception and try to take advantage of it in marketing their services. Similarly, public-sector supporters of indexing were enthusiastic about how successfully it relieves them of responsibility for portfolio performance.

We were also continually reminded of the significance of history as a determinant of culture. People who manage pension funds rarely study their organization's history, but it influences them strongly, and sometimes binds them. Within an organization, the belief that a practice has been around a long time makes it hard to argue that it needs to be changed. If the practice is also associated with important figures in the organization's history or with its core values, then it is unlikely that people will even think about whether it needs to be changed. Over and over again, we found that these principles are no less powerful just because the practices in question have huge financial consequences.

Finally, and perhaps most surprisingly, we discovered that people in the institutional investment world pay an extraordinary amount of attention to maintaining and nurturing personal relationships. What we found was far from the stereotype of Wall Street as impersonal, coldly analytical, and uncompromisingly dedicated to the bottom line. Instead, we heard regularly about how pension executives select outside managers on the basis of "gut feeling" and "comfort level." Once the hiring is done, they rely on similarly subjective evaluation criteria, often retaining managers with whom they have good relations even in the face of consistently poor performance. The managers know this, of course: They report that the keys to continued employment are avoiding absolutely disastrous results and paying proper attention to the sensibilities of the people who hired them. This concern for relations also shows up in internal management procedures, with some funds acknowledging that the need to keep important people happy has led to less than ideal decision-making processes.

We do not mean to suggest that there is anything wrong with giving attention to the personal side of business relations. On the contrary, American business is rightly criticized by, among others, the Japanese for ignoring the obvious connection between productivity and personal well-being. Our point is that in the institutional investment world the balance may have tipped too far. Pension fund executives, hiding behind a thin veneer of financial rigor, admit to parceling out lucrative management contracts on the basis of intuition. We leave it to others to judge the bottom line; we argue simply that everyone with an interest in institutional investment (and that includes just about everyone) needs to understand how the system works.

CULTURE AND CORPORATE GOVERNANCE

Many influential people in law and business see institutional investors, and particularly pension funds, as the last best hope for closing the corporate governance gap. It could hardly be otherwise, given the dearth of alternative candidates. As we reach the fourth stage in Robert Clark's model of the evolution of capitalism, the gap between ownership and management seems almost unbridgeable. The patient, knowledgeable, interested citizen-investors of the idealized past are long gone. In their place are a variety of institutional arrangements that have divorced legal from beneficial stock ownership. The most important of these, the pension funds, have carried this process of attenuation a step further. They have created a class of beneficial owners who do not even participate in the basic decisions about whether and how to invest, let alone in the subtle choices concerning the governance of the companies in which they are invested.

As a result of these developments, it is widely argued that those who run the largest pension funds must assume a leadership role. Advocates contend that these executives are the only players in the current market with the requisite combination of financial resources, expertise, and long-term interest. Skeptics question their motivation, however. They point out that governance activism is expensive and yields little in the way of an immediately measurable return. Moreover, governance activism by one fund tempts others to become "free riders." There are also major legal barriers to activism—for example, the requirement that pension trustees act solely in the interests of the beneficiaries, and the restrictive proxy solicitation rules that inhibit collective action. The advocates' comeback is that the issue of motivation can be managed by appropriate tinkering with the existing incentives and disincentives. They argue that the legal prohibitions against concerted shareholder action can be eliminated, and that this in turn will make activism more attractive from an economic perspective.

Our response is that this entire debate ignores a significant reality: that there are cultural constraints on pension funds' participation in corporate governance. On the private side, those who would be active on governance issues confront an all-powerful Golden Rule: *Do unto other corporations as you would have their pension funds do unto your sponsoring corporation.* We heard little evidence of direct meddling by corporate executives in the affairs of their pension funds, but subtler forms of influence were apparent everywhere. Pension fund executives and the external money managers who work for them know who ultimately hires and fires them. They are reluctant to be detected taking an antimanagement position or doing anything else that would call into question their loyalties in the ongoing shareholder-management tug-of-war. On a more specific level, they are particularly wary of offending the managements of companies that are important to their sponsors, such as lenders, suppliers, and distributors. All of these considerations counsel anonymity in corporate governance, a position that is difficult for any activist to maintain for very long.

The cultural pressures in the public sector are more complex. Several factors mitigate in favor of shareholder activism. First, given the prevalence of indexing in large public funds, many fund executives see participation in governance as the only acceptable way to discharge their fiduciary duty. In addition, the public fund arena is highly politicized, and publicity is usually perceived as a good thing in the political world.

There are countervailing considerations, however. While publicity is generally highly valued in the public sector, it is not an unmitigated benefit in public pension fund management. If the public funds have a Golden Rule, it may be: *Out of sight, out of the legislature's mind.* Until recently, as long as there have been no scandals, state legislatures have generally left public pension funds alone. Now, however, as some of the larger public funds have become highly visible in the corporate governance debate, it may not be coincidental that governors and legislatures are casting an increasingly covetous glance at their wealth. In California, for example, chief pension executive Dale Hanson has emerged as a vocal advocate for institutional shareholders' rights, and Governor Pete Wilson made a partially successful raid on the pension assets to balance the state budget.

Many observers believe that a cause-and-effect relationship is at work. As state pension executives become media stars, they attract the attention of legislators. When the legislators look more closely, they find a pleasant surprise: an enormous pool of money, often more than is required to meet full funding requirements. The temptations are obvious. The legislators' acquisitive instincts are probably reinforced by a natural hostility toward an emerging and potentially competing power center.

The increasing and largely unwelcome attention that the public funds are receiving from their legislatures appears to be creating a disincentive to shareholder activism. Some public fund executives told us that they are moving from a posture of confrontation to one of negotiation. Their explanation for the change is that the new strategy will be more effective in achieving their goals; critics charged that they are being co-opted by management. The real explanation may be that they are realizing the risks attendant to publicity, and are lowering their profiles accordingly. In any event, the mood at the large public funds is clearly one of retrenchment. It may be that the stridency that led, for example, to landmark compromises between the California state fund and some of America's largest corporations is a thing of the past.

INSTITUTIONAL INVESTORS IN THE GLOBAL MARKET

As pension funds and other institutions increasingly realize, no substantial investor can ignore the globalization of financial markets. Large pension funds originally saw international investing merely as a diversification option that could not prudently be ignored. Now, however, as they compare American growth rates to those in Germany and Japan and contemplate the meaning of the post-1992 Common Market, they view the international arena as a significant money-making opportunity.

One might reasonably expect that institutions like pension funds would be singularly well-equipped to meet the challenges of global investing. Their financial resources are enormous, they have vast experience with every sort of investment product, and they would appear to have unlimited access to whatever expertise they need.

The reality as we found it was strikingly different. American pension executives express understandings of foreign markets, foreign business cultures, and the world in general that are sometimes remarkably naive. Much of the commentary consisted of sweeping generalizations about the national character of other countries: We were told, for example, that the Dutch are environmentally conscious, the Japanese are inscrutable, and the Germans are obsessively conservative. Many people we interviewed also derided foreign investors and their practices as primitive and backward. This attitude evokes memories of pre–World War II American isolationism, and even of the colonialist ethic that advocated profiting from other countries without bothering to become engaged with their cultures.

As interesting as the attitude itself is the fact that the people espousing it did not see their understandings as inadequate in any way. They spoke as if they truly believed that foreign business cultures could be reduced to simple generalizations. When they talked about what has to be done in the future, they emphasized the need for foreign markets to catch up with American sophistication rather than the need for Americans to improve their understanding of the rest of the world. Although they may adopt the rhetoric of a global economic network, they divide the world into American and Other, and they see the Other through American eyes.

This limited and unambitious perspective on the non-American world derives ultimately from the cultural constraints under which institutional investors operate. Developing a thorough understanding of, say, Japanese investment opportunities would require in the first instance the recognition that investment is a cultural phenomenon. One would then have to go beyond glib generalizations and strive for a deeper appreciation of the ways in which the culture of Japanese business and finance differs from our own. Finally, that appreciation would have to be translated into concrete investment strategies.

All of this is unlikely to happen. The fundamental problem is that American institutional investors do not recognize the cultural nature of investing. They believe their own rhetoric about financial rigor, and assume that numbers will provide the key to unlock the secrets of the world economy.

Even if America's financial institutions got beyond this initial misconception and undertook the meaningful study of foreign business cultures (as the Japanese have done with us), there is little reason to believe that they would succeed. The culture of American business and finance has never valued ostensibly "abstract" knowledge. There is no model for seeking it and no place in the corporate structure for those who do, and little precedent for factoring soft data into hard financial decisions. The far more likely prospect is that the largest of this country's institutional investors will continue to dabble in international markets through intermediaries, but will yield the leadership role to those in other countries with a better appreciation for the significance and complexity of culture.

THE FUTURE OF CULTURAL RESEARCH

Our experience with pension funds has suggested several specific directions for future cultural research. Other types of institutional investors would be a logical extension of this study. Banks, mutual funds, and insurance companies undoubtedly have distinct cultures of their own. What are those cultures like, and how do they influence investment behavior?

The discovery of cultural influences on institutional investing raises the broader question of whether similar influences are at work on business management generally. There is a growing popular literature on business culture—a cult of culture, so to speak. But the systematic ethnographic study of business management practices remains to be done.

Corporate boards of directors hold particular promise for cultural study. As we spoke with members of corporate boards and listened as others talked about boards, we were intrigued by the prospects of investigating the cultures of these powerful organizations. Some research has been done on the backgrounds and motives of people who sit on corporate boards, and popular books like *Barbarians at the Gates* provide tantalizing anecdotes. There is still room, however, for detailed study of the specific ways in which cultural factors influence board behavior.

Future research should also focus the cultural method on a number of specific investment practices not explored in this book. We have examined the cultural determinants of such practices as indexing, reliance on outside managers, and international investment. But we know little about other, equally important issues. For example, major pension funds have long exhibited a strong preference for investing in large-capitalization companies. This bias is a source of concern to many observers, given widely cited statistics that smaller companies account for most of the wealth creation in the United States. It would be useful to discover how this bias came about, what perpetuates it, and what it might take to dislodge it. This issue is a specific instance of what for many is the ultimate question: How does culture affect investment performance? Does the cultural environment at a particular institution contribute to the bottom line?

In the first place, no one currently knows the answer to the bottom-line question. Investment performance is a closely guarded secret at private funds. Public funds publish a great deal about their investment activities, but it is hard to ferret out the results of particular investment strategies. Carolyn Brancato is in the early stages of a study of pension fund turnover and investment performance, but publishable results are at least two years away. Even when more is known about how well particular funds do, it will still be extremely difficult to delineate cause-and-effect relationships between elements of fund culture and investment gains and losses. Indeed, the danger of attributing complex outcomes to simple causes has been a principal theme of this book. Nonetheless, the question of bottom-line impact is one that must be kept in mind in setting the agenda for future cultural research.

More important, the bottom-line economic performance of pension funds is not the only question. In the long run, it may not even be the most important question. When we judge pension funds only in terms of their economic performance, we blind ourselves to other critical issues. Pension funds typically deny any responsibility for helping to solve such pressing social problems as failing education, declining economic competitiveness, and the lack of affordable housing. Citing their duty to the bottom line, pension executives plead enforced neutrality on such issues. Their professed neutrality is an illusion, however. Because of their vast wealth, every decision that large pension funds make has social consequences, whether intended or not. When they make an overt decision to address a social issue— investing in below-market mortgages, for example—the consequences are clear. But decisions that appear to be politically neutral and driven solely by the bottom line (e.g., moving capital from one industry to another) may have a far more significant social impact. If pension executives believe that they can disengage themselves from their social context, they practice self-deception. If we accept their argument, so do we.

We would never claim that cultural studies alone can provide a complete picture of the economic world. We do claim, however, and claim strongly, that any picture that fails to include a cultural perspective is necessarily incomplete. Business and finance are human enterprises, and human beings always behave in cultural ways. Anyone who aspires to a real understanding of these enterprises must therefore come to terms with the culture of capital.

INDEX

Also Available from IRWIN *Professional Publishing*

CLASSICS
An Investor's Anthology
CLASSICS II
Another Investor's Anthology
Edited by Charles D. Ellis and James R. Vertin
The definitive writing on investment practice and theory from the industry's leading thinkers. You'll find answers to all of your investment challenges from professionals that include Babson; Buffet; Graham; Price, Jr.; Samuelson; and many others. (759 and 480 pages respectively)
ISBN: Classics   1-55623-098-2
             Classics II   1-55623-358-2

INVESTMENT POLICY
How to Win the Loser's Game
Charles D. Ellis
Increase your financial gain with a fresh approach to professional investment. Ellis gives you a new strategy for investment management that involves active client participation and focuses on long-term success. (200 pages)
ISBN: 0-87094-713-3

RECENT DEVELOPMENTS IN FINANCE
Edited by Anthony Saunders
New York University Salomon Center Series
For those who manage portfolios, corporate funds, or deposits, this book shows how today's events will affect how you do business tomorrow. Includes evidence to support why the design of securities markets should not focus exclusively on bid-ask spreads and more. (224 pages)
ISBN: 1-55623-706-5

MANAGING YOUR INVESTMENT MANAGER
Third Edition
Arthur Williams III
The most definitive guide on how to structure investment funds. Written from a sponsor's point of view, this completely revised resource describes methodologies for measuring performance and risk, pointing out each one's limitations.
ISBN: 1-55623-515-1